Historical Sociolinguistics

LONGMAN LINGUISTICS LIBRARY

General editors

GEOFFREY HORROCKS, *University of Cambridge*

DAVID DENISON, *University of Manchester*

For a complete list of books in the series, see page v.

Historical Sociolinguistics: Language Change in Tudor and Stuart England

Terttu Nevalainen
Helena Raumolin-Brunberg

An imprint of **Pearson Education**

London · New York · Toronto · Sydney · Tokyo · Singapore · Hong Kong · Cape Town
Madrid · Paris · Amsterdam · Munich · Milan

PEARSON EDUCATION LIMITED

Head Office:
Edinburgh Gate
Harlow CM20 2JE
Tel: +44 (0)1279 623623
Fax: +44 (0)1279 431059

London Office:
128 Long Acre
London WC2E 9AN
Tel: +44 (0)20 7447 2000
Fax: +44 (0)20 7447 2170
Website: www.pearsoneduc.com

First edition published in Great Britain in 2003

© Pearson Education Limited 2003

The right of Terttu Nevalainen and Helena Raumolin-Brunberg
to be identified as Authors of this Work has been asserted by them
in accordance with the Copyright, Designs and Patents Act 1988.

ISBN 0 582 31994 3

British Library Cataloguing in Publication Data
A CIP catalogue record for this book can be obtained from the British Library

Library of Congress Cataloging in Publication Data
A CIP catalog record for this book can be obtained from the Library of Congress

10   9   8   7   6   5   4   3   2   1

Set in 10/12.5pt Palatino by Graphicraft Limited, Hong Kong
Printed and bound in Malaysia

The Publishers' policy is to use paper manufactured from sustainable forests.

LONGMAN LINGUISTICS LIBRARY

Contents

Contents

Preface

> All changes diffuse socially, and it is therefore argued that we need to take into account social factors in addition to intra-linguistic factors in order to come closer to explanations. (J. Milroy 1998: 41)

This book has taken a long time to write. Even more time has gone into the empirical research it discusses, not to mention compiling the *Corpus of Early English Correspondence* (CEEC) and its databases, which have enabled the research in the first place. But 10 years is a relatively short period compared with the centuries through which we have travelled in the course of our work.

In modern sociolinguistics the present has traditionally been used to explain the past, but in recent years the past has also established its relevance to the present. This is manifest, for instance, in the discussion of the roots of African American Vernacular English (AAVE). At the same time, history has come to be appreciated in its own right as the key to our understanding of sociolinguistic variation and language change within a broader, real-time context. It is to this discussion that we hope to make a contribution in the following chapters.

This book is the result of our joint efforts, starting from setting up the project to sharing the research and writing processes. Some division of labour was, however, deemed necessary: Helena became responsible for much of the data retrieval and most of the frequency analyses, wrote Chapters 3, 4, 5 and 7, and compiled Appendixes I and II; Terttu carried out some data retrieval and frequency analyses, the significance tests and VARBRUL analyses, and wrote Chapters 1, 2, 6, 8, 9 and 10. Needless to say, the contents of the book reflect our shared views of the issues addressed, based on countless hours of discussions.

Our project, Sociolinguistics and Language History, was launched back in 1993, when we got our first two-year funding from the Academy of Finland. The completion of the CEEC in 1998 was made possible by the funding received from the University of Helsinki, and the research and writing for this book were completed during the last couple of years, partly with the financial support given by the Academy of Finland to the Research Unit for Variation and Change in English at the Department of English of the University of Helsinki. We are grateful to the Academy and our *Alma Mater* for this vital support.

This funding made it possible to gather a group of junior scholars to become our travelling companions to Tudor and Stuart England. The CEEC would never have been completed without the sustained efforts of Jukka Keränen, Minna Nevala, Arja Nurmi and Minna Palander-Collin. We also owe them a great intellectual debt, and would like to thank them for their input into the team's original research, part of which can be seen in the bibliography of this volume. A special note of thanks goes to Arja for allowing us to include her work on periphrastic DO in ours, and to her and Minna Palander-Collin for permission to reprint in Appendix III the list they compiled of the source texts used in the CEEC.

We would like to thank all our Helsinki colleagues at the Research Unit for Variation and Change in English, particularly Matti Rissanen, the father of the 'Helsinki School', for believing in team efforts. We are also grateful to the many colleagues further afield who have taken an interest in historical sociolinguistics in the course of years, including James and Lesley Milroy, Ingrid Tieken-Boon van Ostade, and Peter Trudgill, just to name a few. To David Denison we owe the idea of writing a book based on our work and, when the manuscript finally materialized, our thanks go to Mark Shackleton for helping us make it more readable.

Our gratitude also to all our hundreds of native speaker informants, who were never there in person, but whose presence was not only felt on the pages of the printed collections of their personal correspondence, but was literally made tangible when we consulted the hand-written letters in the Manuscripts Reading Room of the British Library, the Public Record Office and the Sheffield Archives.

Last but by no means least, we would like to thank our families – Reijo Aulanko, and Börje and Janne Brunberg – for their invaluable contribution: for simply being there every day for the last ten years.

Terttu Nevalainen
Helena Raumolin-Brunberg
Helsinki, 24 May 2002

List of Tables

List of Figures

Publisher's Acknowledgements

We are grateful to the following for permission to reproduce copyright material:

Table 2.1 adapted from *Grundlagen der Soziolinguistik*, Max Niemeyer Verlag GmbH (Dittmar, N. 1997); Table 3.2 after Table in *The World We Have Lost – Further Explored, 3rd Edition*, Routledge (Laslett, P. 1983); Table 3.3 adapted from *Popular Cultures in England 1550–1750*, © Addison Wesley Longman Ltd 1998, reprinted by permission of Pearson Education Ltd (Raey, B. 1998); Figure 4.1 from *Principles of Linguistic Change. Volume 1: Internal Factors*, Blackwell Publishers (Labov, W. 1994); Figure 4.2 from *Language Change: Progress or Decay?, 3rd Edition*, Cambridge University Press (Aitchison, J. 2001); Figure 5.1 adapted from *Language and Society, 2nd Edition*, Cambridge University Press (Downes, W. 1998); Figure 10.1 adapted from *Linguistic Variation and Change: on the Historical Sociolinguistics of English*, Blackwell Publishers (Milroy, J. 1992).

In some instances we have been unable to trace the owners of copyright material, and we would appreciate any information that would enable us to do so.

Chapter 1

Introduction: Issues in Historical Sociolinguistics

> Not all variability and heterogeneity in language structure involves change; but all change involves variability and heterogeneity. (Weinreich, Labov & Herzog 1968: 188)

It is an everyday observation that young people do not speak like their parents, let alone their grandparents. Where we come from, what we do for a living and the company we keep may also be related to the way we speak. Northerners usually differ from southerners, TV announcers and lawyers rarely sound like dockers or farmers, nor do people use quite the same language when speaking in public and chatting to their friends. All these aspects of linguistic variability are of interest to sociolinguists as they set out to study how language can vary in patterned ways when it is used by individuals and groups of people in various social situations for different communicative purposes. In due course, this variation may lead to **language change**. It is the processes of language change that constitute the subject matter of this book.

Language variation and change have intrigued sociolinguists from the very beginning. Back in 1968, when sociolinguistics was a relative newcomer as an academic discipline, Uriel Weinreich, William Labov and Marvin Herzog drew up an agenda for the study of language change in its social context. The process consists, they suggested, of the **actuation** of a change in a language at a given time, its **transition** from one state or form to another, its **embedding** in the linguistic and social structures where it emerges, and its social **evaluation** by speakers. We now know a great deal about the transition, embedding and evaluation of language changes, but the first issue, actuation, appears to defy empirical investigation. Although it is possible to come up with a number of **constraints** on the kinds of change that could take place in a language – no language could lose all its consonants and survive with only vowels, for instance – it is hard to predict whether the changes that are possible will ever take place, and impossible to tell exactly when and where they might take place.

Although historical dictionaries furnish their entries with dates of first attestations, tracing back the actual origins of a linguistic innovation is not

easy. A new word may indeed sometimes be attributed to a known individual, but even then there is no guarantee that it had not been coined
earlier by somebody else whose innovation had simply gone unrecorded.
Following the distinction made by James Milroy (1992) between **speaker
innovation** and **linguistic change**, we will argue that it is only when an
innovation has been adopted by more than one speaker that we can talk
about change in the linguistic system. As Milroy (1992: 169) put it: 'it is
speakers, and not *languages*, that innovate'. By introducing the term **historical sociolinguistics** in the title of this book we wish to stress that issues to
do with language use, and language users in particular, are also relevant to
the historical linguist. Because no language evolves in a social vacuum, the
speakers of earlier English should not be ignored when their language is
looked at through the telescope of historical linguistics.[1]

Suzanne Romaine's *Socio-historical Linguistics* (1982a) was the first systematic attempt to analyse historical data using sociolinguistic models.
Romaine studied relative markers in Middle Scots in a twenty-year period
between 1530 and 1550. Her study included both linguistic and stylistic
variation, which she based on such categories as official, nonofficial and
epistolary prose and verse. In the last three decades the notion of **genre** has
dominated historical studies of language variation. Their focus has been on
the linguistic description and textual embedding of language changes, and
they have demonstrated, for instance, that such speechlike genres as drama
and personal letters are more likely to foster linguistic innovations than
typical written genres, such as legal and other official documents.

In this book we will use the evidence provided by personal letters and
focus on a range of external factors including the writers' age, social status,
gender, domicile and relationship with their correspondents. We are interested in a number of morphological and syntactic changes that have shaped
the English language over the last six hundred years. Our material goes
back to the Late Middle and Early Modern English periods, ranging from
1410 to 1681, with the main focus on the Tudor and Stuart times. They
furnish the historical sociolinguist with the earliest data that can be relied
on in analysing language use in its various social contexts. However, before
going into the details of our approach, a few words will be said about some
alternative approaches that might be, and have been, used to assess the role
of social factors in variation and change in earlier English.

1.1. Sociolinguistic Backprojection?

One of the methodological options open to modern sociolinguists is that
they may explore their own speech communities. This was done, among
others, by Peter Trudgill in his Norwich study (1974). He benefited from
having native-speaker knowledge of the social factors that influenced the

way his subjects spoke, and from being able to switch to the local accent himself. The situation is different when some considerable length of time separates those to be studied from those who study them. Investigating the past stages of a language, historical sociolinguists cannot safely rely on their modern intuitions about the range of linguistic variation available and acceptable to the people they investigate. Consider examples (1.1) and (1.2). In 1534, a year before his execution, Sir Thomas More wrote the following words to his daughter Margaret Roper in the Tower of London, where he was being held prisoner:

> (1.1) And thus haue I mine owne good daughter disclosed vnto you, the very secrete botome of my minde, referring the order therof onely to the goodnes of God, and that so fully, that I assure you Margaret on my faith, I neuer haue prayde God to bringe me hence nor deliuer me fro death, but referring all thing whole vnto his only pleasure, as to hym that seeth better what is best for me than my selfe dooth. Nor neuer longed I since I came hether to set my fote in mine owne howse, for any desire of or pleasure of my howse, but gladlie wolde I sometime somewhat talke with my frendes, and specially my wyfe and you that pertein to my charge. (Thomas More, 1534; MORE, 543)[2]

In our second example, Sabine Johnson, a London wool-merchant's wife writes to her husband John in 1545, to inform him about the harvest and other household matters. Her letter was sent from the Johnsons' country home Glapthorn in Northamptonshire to the port town of Calais, part of England at the time, where John often went on business.

> (1.2) Whan Willyam Lawrens doyth com, I well send Haryson, hoye doyth mistrust hym to be crafty, wherefore I well not trust hym noy farther than Haryson doyth geve me counsell. All thynges shal be provyded for harvest, with the which the Parson well nout be content, for I thynke if anybodye wold by thay . . . he wold sell it, for he haith sold the tythe melke allredye, and hath made awaye vj or vij tythe calveis. (Sabine Johnson, 1545; JOHNSON, 289)

Looking at (1.1), a modern reader will be struck by a number of unfamiliar features in the language of this famous humanist who served as King Henry VIII's first secretary and Lord Chancellor, and had studied at the University of Oxford and in the Inns of Court in London. However, what makes More's English appear strange in the twenty-first century is not necessarily his vocabulary – with the possible exception of *fro* 'from' (cf. *to and fro*), the words in (1.1) are familiar to a modern reader. Part of the strangeness is caused by his spelling, which, despite being fairly regular, differs from the modern standard. More systematically writes, for instance, <u>

instead of <v> word-medially (*haue, neuer*), and restricts <v> to word-initial position (*vnto*). It should, however, be added that the passage has been rendered easier to read by Elizabeth Rogers, the editor of More's writings, who modernized his capitalization and punctuation for the benefit of modern readers.

The editor of the Johnson correspondence, Barbara Winchester, similarly modernized Sabine Johnson's punctuation and use of capitals. Sabine Johnson had not received any formal schooling, and Winchester assumes that she had only learned to write as a young adult. To a modern reader her spelling looks less regular than More's, to the extent that some familiar words might not be immediately recognizable (e.g. *doyth* 'doeth', *well* 'will', *hoye* 'who', *noy* 'no', *nout* 'not', *by* 'buy' and *haith* 'hath'). *Thay* in *if anybodye wold by thay* combines the definite article *the* and *hay*, which has lost its initial /h/. *Tythe melke* ('tithe milk') and *tythe calveis* ('calves') refer to tithes on livestock to be paid to the parish.

Perhaps the main reason for the mixed feelings present-day readers may have about More's language is his grammar. More inverts his word-order after adverbials like *thus* and *gladly* (*thus haue I; gladlie wolde I*). He uses *mine* instead of *my* before *own* (*mine owne good daughter; mine owne howse*). He avoids the possessive form *its* of the personal pronoun *it* and resorts to a periphrasis with *thereof* (*the order therof*). His indefinite pronoun for 'everything' is *all thing*. He systematically attaches the suffix -(*e*)*th*, and not -(*e*)*s*, to verbs to signal the third-person singular present indicative (*that seeth; my selfe dooth*). Finally, More surprises his modern readers by using multiple negation (*nor neuer longed I*) and omitting the auxiliary *do* in a negative clause – something a middle-aged Englishman with university education would not be expected to do today, not even in his private correspondence.

In Sabine Johnson's passage we find some of the same features as in More's: she, too, uses multiple negation (*not trust hym noy farther*) and the suffix -*th* in the third-person singular present indicative (*doyth, haith*). Where More fails to use the auxiliary *do* in a negative sentence, Sabine Johnson would appear to overuse it in affirmative contexts, in (1.2) as many as three times in the first sentence. Her variant for the indefinite pronoun 'everything' is *all things*, and besides the relative pronoun *who* she also uses *the which*.

One conclusion we might draw on the basis of these data is that the English language of an educated man in the early sixteenth century must have been very different from what it is today. A number of the features used by More would be considered simply ungrammatical if judged by the norms of Present-day Standard English. They include most of his word-order inversions and non-use of the auxiliary *do* in negative clauses with no other auxiliary. As they do not look like performance errors on More's part, their grammatical status cannot have been the same as today. Moreover, features such as multiple negation were evidently not branded and socially stigmatized in the early sixteenth century the way they are today. On the stylistic side, More's context of writing – a father writing to his favourite daughter – would suggest to a modern reader that the third-person suffix -(e)th could not have been regarded as archaic at the time, and that there need not be a poetic tinge in More's systematic use of the long possessive form *mine* before *owne*.

Had we not looked at More first, we might perhaps have put Sabine Johnson's use of multiple negation down to her lack of education. This modern interpretation would have been supported by the evidence of [h] -loss in *thay* ('the hay'). However, there would have been counterevidence as well. If Sabine Johnson was uneducated, how to interpret her use of the third-person -(e)th? It could hardly have been read as a sign of literary or archaic usage, unless we thought of it as a dialectal feature. Similarly, the literary-sounding compound relative pronoun *the which* would have been incongruous with our initial line of reasoning and assumptions as to what to expect of the language of an uneducated person. Present-day social evaluations clearly do not make much sense with historical data.

We may now begin to bridge the temporal gap between the present day and the early sixteenth century by presenting some general questions. They include the following:

1. When and where did such forms as -(e)th, shared by Sir Thomas More and Sabine Johnson, get replaced by those used today?
2. How did these new usages gain popularity and spread in the language community?
3. Who were the people who promoted them, and what was their social status?
4. How did the evaluation of these usages, old and new, change over time? How did, for instance, a feature so widely spread in English around the world today as multiple negation become stigmatized?

These questions largely correspond to those raised by Weinreich, Labov and Herzog (1968). The first two are concerned with the transition and diffusion of changes in the community, the third with their embedding in society, and the fourth with their social evaluation. While in agreement in theory, historical and present-day studies usually approach the time factor differently at the empirical level. A historical sociolinguist will normally begin by charting the time course of the process studied, and then proceed to describe its social embedding in the course of time. This is rarely what happens in present-day studies. They typically analyse linguistic variation as it is displayed by different generations at one point in time, the present. Any differences in their distributions of linguistic features may, but need not, be interpreted as changes in progress, frequently with the younger generations leading the process.

As these present-day patterns are synchronic, or 'apparent-time', phenomena – and not diachronic and 'real-time' – their social evaluation in the speech community is expected to be constant. Speech communities may even frequently be defined by referring to shared speaker evaluations of linguistic features (see Labov 1972; Romaine 1982b). When it comes to standard languages, these shared views extend to the entire community of speakers of a given language. So multiple negation is one of the most heavily stigmatized features throughout the English-speaking world. But as we have seen, social evaluations cannot be expected to remain constant across time, and modern consensus views are not useful in explaining the social evaluation of past forms of a language. Historical answers to our embedding and evaluation questions need to be looked for elsewhere.

1.2. Contemporary Perceptions of Usage

It is obvious that present-day intuitions will not serve as secure guidelines for interpreting historical data in social terms. Historical sociolinguists may therefore look for contemporary comments on earlier usage to place their interpretations on a firmer footing. These accounts are invaluable in that they provide first-hand information on how linguistic variation was perceived by contemporaries. Comments on Tudor English come from a mixed variety of sources ranging from prefaces to early printed books by William Caxton, and handbooks on classical rhetoric by Thomas Wilson (1553) and George Puttenham (1589), to treatises by sixteenth-century spelling reformers led by John Hart (1569). In the seventeenth century, comments on language variation and use begin to appear in monolingual dictionaries and grammars, and in works of eminent literary figures like John Dryden and Jonathan Swift. The market is finally flooded with normative grammars in the eighteenth century.[3]

First-hand though they may be, contemporary comments also have their problems as sources of sociolinguistic evidence. The information they provide is patchy at best: the earlier the period, the thinner the coverage. The well-known passage in Puttenham (1586) on 'the best English' and regional variation hardly fills one whole page, and Gil's (1619: 15–18) equally famous description of regional variation no more than four. As many areas of variation are merely mentioned in passing or anecdotally, no far-reaching generalizations can be based on them. One such issue is gender variation in language use. In *The Gouernour* (1531), Sir Thomas Elyot has this general comment to make on women's speech forms as an influence on the pronunciation of noblemen and gentlemen's children:

> (1.3) the nourises and other women aboute hym . . . that they speke none englisshe but that which is cleane, polite, perfectly and articulately pronounced, omittinge no lettre or sillable, as folisshe women often times do of a wantonnesse, wherby diuers noble

> men and gentilmennes chyldren (as I do at this daye knowe), haue attained corrupte and foule pronuntiation. (Thomas Elyot, 1531, *The Boke Named the Gouernour*, fol. 19*v*.)

The reader is left wondering whether a similar corrupting influence could have been detected if men had been the caretakers of noblemen's children in their infancy. In that case Elyot would only be pointing to a general difference between fast-speech and slow-speech forms. A very different case emerges if we assume gender variation to be at issue. Women's fast-speech forms could then be thought of as phonologically advanced in the speech community, and Elyot's 'foolish women' could be connected with the *Mopsae*, whose fashionable pronunciation Alexander Gil condemns in *Logonomia Anglica* (1619: 16). Another plausible interpretation may, however, be found in social status differences. As wet-nurses in particular came from the lower social orders, Elyot's reference might be indicative of social rank distinctions in sixteenth-century pronunciation. Whatever the basis for his remark might have been, the comment should not be read out of context: Sir Thomas Elyot, a gentleman with classical education and a close friend of Sir Thomas More, included it in his treatise on the education required of the future 'governors' of the state.[4]

More ample documentation on language issues in this period may be found in some linguistic controversies. Apart from a spelling reform, the thrust of the linguistic debates in the sixteenth century was directed at new vocabulary, and the arguments for and against borrowing gave rise to the Inkhorn Controversy (Barber 1976: 56–70). Large-scale debates like this are usually rare and restricted topicwise, but instructive in that they draw attention to the larger context of published comments. The Inkhorn Controversy squarely falls in with what is sometimes called a 'complaint tradition'. In the sixteenth century, it revolved around the concern that educated men like Elyot, More and Wilson had about the adequacy of the vernacular: could English fulfil all the functions of a national language? A debate like this could indeed only arise among educated circles, not among the illiterate majority of the population. But it was of consequence to the entire language community and reflected the instability of social evaluations of linguistic features. A large part of the English wordstock would look very different today had those in favour of native means of enriching the vernacular won the day, and not those in favour of foreign borrowing.[5]

Contemporary views need not be divergent or unstable in order to pose problems of interpretation for later observers. Even the prescriptive grammars published in the eighteenth century, one of the richest sources of social comment on the English language, may not always be easy to interpret. As Görlach (1999: 515) remarks, not only do the attitudinal labels attached to proscribed items overlap (e.g. *coarse, low, vulgar*), but they may not have an unambiguous address. It often remains unclear whether a given comment is directed at a linguistic feature (i.e. spelling, pronunciation, grammar) or at the way it is used (style, social context). Moreover, as the frequency of citations from Shakespeare and the 1611 King James Bible in the grammars suggests, not all eighteenth-century prescriptivists were concerned with contemporary usage alone.[6]

Another kind of source of metalinguistic comment is provided by dramatic dialogue from the Middle English period onwards. While the fifteenth-century mystery plays were still written in local dialects, printed plays from the sixteenth century onwards were typically nonlocalizable. However, comedies, in particular, also displayed a wide range of social and regional stereotypes. The stage dialect used to depict them drew on certain stock features diagnostic of varieties such as Kentish or the West Country. There is therefore no guarantee, over and beyond a number of stereotypical features, that the dramatist could present anything like a true picture of a *Zummerzet* speaker, or a speaker of any other local variety of Early Modern English. By definition, stereotypes represent features that are consciously evaluated by the language community. When a linguistic feature has not reached this level of public awareness, which is frequently the case with a change in progress, one should not expect to find such subtle social information on its use in drama or fiction – or indeed in any other contemporary evaluations of language use.[7]

1.3. Sociohistorical Reconstruction

Apart from empirical data, historical sociolinguists need conceptual tools for describing and analysing them. The method that has been developed to explore earlier forms of English involves reconstructing past stages of both language and society. The approach is interdisciplinary, drawing on historical linguistics and sociolinguistics, as well as social history. In the following we will briefly introduce various aspects of this method, and discuss the requirements of validity that can be set for them.

As in research in general, some basic tenets will be taken as given. The fact that we assumed that multiple negation was *not* stigmatized in the early sixteenth century is based on the assumption that as an educated humanist Thomas More, who is also found using multiple negation in his official correspondence, would not resort to negatively valued language when confiding in his daughter. Our assumption is founded on the basic sociolinguistic principle that language use is socially embedded and that social evaluations like stigmatization can be recovered by sociolinguistic analysis. We will therefore not contest the empirical foundations of the model proposed by Weinreich and his associates. It will be connected to a more general notion of **uniformitarianism** in historical linguistics, which will be discussed in Chapter 2.

These foundations could, however, hardly be studied on the basis of one man's usage in one particular situation only. A sufficient amount of **baseline data** is needed from other contemporary writers of the same age and social status, compared with people coming from different social circumstances. Only then can we arrive at more valid generalizations of the sociolinguistic relevance of the issues we are studying. As the social historian Amy Louise Erickson (1993: 17) has noted in another context, generalizations based on groups of people in any particular period of time are needed to 'map the terrain'. The need is similarly recorded in literary scholarship by writers like Lynne Magnusson (1999: 3–4), who wish to anchor Shakespeare and other literary figures more firmly in the linguistic practices of their time. We shall call this need to have a systematic and broad enough database in historical sociolinguistics the requirement of **empirical validity**.

In order to practise their trade, all historical linguists naturally need to develop a degree of 'surrogate competence' – a term used by Nyman (1982: 13) – in the language(s) they study. Extensive reading of historical texts will help them to achieve this competence. But no matter how good one's command of a past language might be, it is not possible to arrive at valid sociolinguistic generalizations of the way the language was actually used without systematic empirical study. Empirical study is of course also needed today, even when the researcher has the advantage of being a native speaker of the community s/he is investigating (cf. Trudgill 1974).

Empirical validity is clearly an issue that will have to be evaluated both in general terms and for each historical period separately. Linguists simply do not have the same textual resources for Old English as they have for later periods like Early Modern English. Up until the twentieth century, historical sociolinguists will have to make do without authentic spoken materials. Our decision to base our research on personal letters was partly informed by our work in compiling the Early Modern British English section of the multigenre *Helsinki Corpus of English Texts* in the 1980s (Nevalainen & Raumolin-Brunberg 1989, 1993). The corpus has proved extremely useful in historical studies focusing on genre variation, the way in which English varies in different kinds of writing, but it is not comprehensive enough to meet the needs of more detailed sociolinguistic research. In order to be able to capture processes of change that diffused from below the level of social awareness, as well as more conscious ones, we needed more ample data from individual speakers of Late Middle and Early Modern English.[8]

The empirical work discussed in this book is based on the *Corpus of Early English Correspondence* (CEEC: 1410–1681). It is an electronic collection of personal letters compiled by our research team in the 1990s specifically for historical sociolinguistic research. Consisting of 6,000 letters and nearly 800 writers, the corpus makes it possible for us to study how a number of grammatical changes were diffused through the literate sections of the population in England between the early fifteenth and late seventeenth centuries.

A basic limitation with all written data, and the CEEC is here no exception, is that the researcher will not have access to all sections of the language community, and will therefore not be able to draw on its full range of language users. In the Late Middle and Early Modern English periods problems arise from the English population's low average degree of full literacy, i.e. the inability to write. The requirements of empirical validity are naturally easier to meet for the seventeenth century than for the fifteenth. However, as will be seen in Chapter 3, the CEEC remains socially quite balanced throughout the period it covers, which enhances its validity in diachronic studies.

Although the goals of our research are naturally period-specific, to describe Late Middle and Early Modern English, this is not our sole aim. Both methodological issues and modern sociolinguistic generalizations are relevant to our topic. It is precisely testing the historical applicability of these generalizations that raises the level of abstraction in the historical enterprise. There are a number of methodological issues to be settled, beginning with how exactly to chart time courses of historical changes, before the scope can be broadened to cover such social factors as the speaker's age, social status and mobility, gender, occupation, education and domicile. All these speaker variables have been found to correlate with language variation and change today. Adding them to the research agenda improves the **social validity** of the sociolinguistic study of the earlier periods of English. These and other factors need to be explored in order to capture the dimensions of social embedding of language changes in earlier times. Such cumulative information will not only enhance the social validity of English historical sociolinguistics but, in the long run, of sociolinguistics at large. How the issue of social validity is perceived and investigated in present-day sociolinguistics will be discussed in more detail in Chapter 2.

Reconstructing how language changes diffuse socially is one of the major tasks, if not *the* major task, of historical sociolinguists. This is an area where the "historical" in 'historical sociolinguistics' is connected not only with historical linguistics but also with social history. The fact that sociolinguists subscribe to the basic principle of social embedding of linguistic changes does not automatically mean that they would know what the relevant distinctions were 500 years ago. Indeed we might expect major differences in social conditions between industrial and preindustrial societies. As reconstructing the social world of the past is the proper task of social history, historical sociolinguists should be able to rely on social historians when exploring, for example, the connection between social status and language change in Tudor and Stuart England. A good starting point is provided by social historians' consensus model of the early modern social order discussed in Chapter 7. Building their reconstructions of the past on social, economic and cultural history, historical sociolinguists hope their work will meet the requirement of **historical validity**.[9] We shall return to this topic in Chapter 3.

In later chapters we will also see that some of the generalizations based on present-day findings may either be irrelevant in the periods we study, or that they cannot be investigated with the data that have come down to us. In both cases we are faced with the limits of extending the sociolinguistic enterprise into history. Only the first one is theoretically interesting, however, in that it suggests that some modern 'facts' only extend so far back in time to earlier societies. A good candidate for a historically weak generalization is the **Sex/Prestige** pattern that is often presented as a sociolinguistic universal in the English-speaking world (Hudson 1996: 195). It is a common sociolinguistic observation that nonstandard features are avoided by women, including women who speak varieties where these features occur; a case in point is multiple negation. As we shall see in Chapter 6, this was not the case in the sixteenth and seventeenth centuries. In order to interpret this finding, reference will need to be made to at least two other factors: social stratification and educational opportunities in early modern England.

It is only when the three requirements of validity, empirical, social and historical, are met that historical sociolinguistics can make reliable generalizations on the social embedding of **real-time language change**. The discipline has made a good start but has obviously not reached that stage yet. As the work progresses, as many sociolinguistic 'universals' will be put to the historical test as possible. This is also what we will be doing in the empirical part of this volume, basing our research questions on consensus views that have been arrived at in sociolinguistic research with present-day data, the kinds of basic 'facts' listed by Hudson (1996: 202). In this book we shall concentrate on macro-level social factors, in order to be able to add to the baseline data. They include such speaker variables as age, gender, and social and regional mobility, which will all be discussed in the empirical part of this book. Although some variables can only be reconstructed in terms of broad trends, most of them have also proved to be historically quite robust.[10]

1.4. Research Topics

One of the advantages of having a large corpus that provides a reasonable coverage of a particular period is that the **time courses** of many linguistic changes can be traced over periods as short as 20 years or even less. As empirical research in the field is not yet very extensive, even a factor so central to the historical approach as **real time** has often been explored in terms of traditional periodization of two to three hundred years. Shorter subperiods, minimally of 70 years, are implemented in studies based on electronic corpora such as the *Helsinki Corpus* (Rissanen *et al.* 1993). In contrast to what we assumed at the beginning of our project in the mid-1990s, a number of processes of change that go back to the Early Modern English period have not been systematically documented. So even their basic transmission question has not been adequately addressed before. In Chapter 4 we will consider the time courses of all the changes discussed in this volume. For ease of comparison, they will be scaled to periods of 40 years in Chapter 4, but 20-year periods will also be referred to in later chapters.

Another advantage that a systematic electronic corpus will provide is that a number of parallel changes can be traced over time and with the same people. We can therefore compare real-time and **apparent-time** approaches and go as far as individual life cycles. This duality of method enables the historical sociolinguist to investigate questions to do with communal as opposed to generational language changes. Are people, in other words, capable of acquiring new linguistic features as the features diffuse across time and space, i.e. communally, or are linguistic features only acquired once by each generation (Labov 1994: 43–112)? This issue will be the topic of Chapter 5. We will also address the related question whether people are generally more likely to have categorical than variable grammars of those features that are undergoing change. If a change progresses communally, variable grammars are a plausible alternative.

As noted above, one the most robust findings in sociolinguistics today is **gender** differentiation in language variation and change. The topic has largely been excluded from the agenda of traditional historical linguists and philologists, partly for lack of suitable materials. What we have is anecdotal references to women deviating from the expected male norms, including their 'corrupt and foul pronunciation' mentioned in 1.2. Sometimes women are also referred to as the guardians of the standard language (Chambers 1995: 124–125). Personal correspondence therefore offers the historical sociolinguist a unique opportunity to analyse gender differences in processes of real-time language change. One of the modern generalizations to be tested in Chapter 6 is the suggestion that women are generally the leaders of linguistic change.

In traditional historical linguistics and philology, the role of **social status** in language variation and change has also rarely merited more than a cursory treatment. Or if it has, as in works like Wyld's *A History of Colloquial English* (1936), the authors usually take it for granted that the language of upper- and lower-ranking people was evaluated socially in the same predictable way across time. The lack of systematic, empirical study is understandable if we consider how young sociolinguistics and social history are as academic disciplines, going back only to the second half of the twentieth century. As social status differences were probably even more deeply entrenched in medieval and early modern realities than they are in western civilizations today, testing their relevance cannot be excluded from the agenda of historical sociolinguists in general, and the study of language change in particular. The period from the fifteenth to the seventeenth century is also unique in that it represents the time before normative grammar.

We may therefore explore social status and language change before the norms and social evaluations of Standard English were laid down in writing and began to be imposed from above.

Modern sociolinguists have sometimes been criticized for overly rigid social categorization. The brunt of the criticism is levelled at the fact that speakers' socio-economic status is reduced to a single scale, and that factors such as occupation, education and income may not all be equally relevant to linguistic variation (Hudson 1996: 184–190). Determining the relevance of these factors to language change remains an empirical matter but there are others such as **social mobility** that can pose even greater problems in a synchronic setting. It is no easier to study the relevance of social status in a diachronic context, but at least individual mobility can be observed and social movers identified. Their linguistic behaviour is one of the issues that we shall pay particular attention to when studying the role played by social status in language change in Chapter 7.

The Early Modern English period has traditionally been studied from the perspective of the standard language. This narrowed focus of interest may partly be explained by the fact that, as the compilers of *A Linguistic Atlas of Late Mediaeval English* (*LALME*) observe, most texts are not localizable on the basis of spelling from 1500 onwards (McIntosh *et al.* 1986: 3). Unfortunately, the nonlocalizability of spelling has also had repercussions on other areas of Early Modern English studies. It has blinded much of the past scholarship to any **regional variation** in writing in this period, suggesting that what is being described is the history of one relatively homogeneous variety of the language. This is problematic for various reasons. First, there are hardly any attempts to codify a standard grammar before the eighteenth century. Before that, supralocal usages did develop, but they did not result from conscious monitoring or language planning. As illustrated by Biber *et al.* (1999) and Cheshire (1999), even today casual conversations are likely to contain a number of grammatical features that are not acceptable in formal writing; many areas of language use are much more difficult to standardize than spelling.

More fundamentally, why should we expect language change to be geared towards standardization at any given time? Dialect-levelling with no standard influence continues to take place in today's Europe, where national languages have standard varieties (Auer 1998). As the changes in English that we study spread throughout the country in the early modern period, it is logical to assume that these processes of **supralocalization**, too, had their regional origins. This hypothesis will be tested in Chapter 8. The letter corpus consists of material from various parts of the country, which makes it not only possible but also a challenge to trace the regional diffusion of the linguistic processes in progress.

As pointed out above, genre and text type have occupied a central role in historical variation studies in the past. Thanks to this research, we know a great deal about where personal letters come on the continuum of genres. Although often viewed as one genre, letters nevertheless contain variation due to factors other than the writer-specific variables of age, gender, social status, and domicile. We will therefore introduce the notion of **register** to the discussion of real-time language change in Chapter 9. Within our framework, register differences will be defined as the relation between writer and addressee, the idea being that writers accommodate linguistically to their addressees. Having analysed a whole range of social factors independently in the previous chapters, it is now time to raise the question of their relative significance in the course of linguistic change. We are interested in exploring how the three variables of region, gender and register pattern as a change progresses across time. The results will be compared with the general predictions presented by Bell (1984, 2001) within his **audience design** framework for sociolinguistic variation.

In the concluding chapter, our findings will be placed within a broader sociolinguistic framework. Drawing on the data gathered on the social embedding of linguistic features in the sixteenth century, we will also be better able to place in their sociolinguistic contexts our two main witnesses in this chapter, Sabine Johnson and Thomas More. Their more rounded linguistic profiles will emerge in the course of our discussion in the following chapters.

Notes

1. *Historical sociolinguistics* now appears to be the established term. It is found, for instance, in the titles of the article collections edited by Jahr (1999) and Mattheier (1999). It already occurred in Romaine (1988), Milroy (1992), and Machan and Scott (1992). Romaine's (1982a) term, *socio-historical linguistics*, appears in the titles of Tieken-Boon van Ostade (1987) and Kielkiewicz-Janowiak (1992). In Nevalainen and Raumolin-Brunberg (1996), we also referred to the field by the conjunction of *sociolinguistics* and *language history*.

2. All quotations from the *Corpus of Early English Correspondence* have a text identifier consisting of the writer's name followed by the year of writing, a short title of the collection the letter comes from and a page reference to it. See Appendix III.

3. Early modern evidence of, and attitudes to, the vernacular are reviewed e.g. by Jones (1953), Barber (1976) and Görlach (1999). The difficulty of interpreting the contemporary phonetic descriptions is discussed by Lass (1999: 58), who finds them 'a rich but problematic source'. Early modern comments on women's language are discussed by Okulska (1999).

4. Elyot may also be just evoking a classical *topos*. The passage comes from a context where learning Latin is being discussed, and earlier in the same chapter Elyot quotes Quintilian on the topic. In his *Institutio Oratoria* (1,1,4–5) Quintilian advocates care when employing nurses: children may learn from their nurses undesirable speech habits which they will have to grow out of later on. We would like to thank Dr Antti Arjava for this reference.

5. Foreign borrowing in Early Modern English is discussed in Nevalainen (1999a). For a discussion of the complaint tradition, see Milroy and Milroy (1985a: 29–53). They trace it through the history of English in three stages: (1) creating a

standard language ideology, (2) keeping the ideology alive, and (3) warding off any abuses of the standard in public and formal language.

6. The role of normative grammar in the evolution of English is addressed both by sociolinguists (e.g. Milroy & Milroy 1985a) and by chroniclers of the normative tradition (Sundby *et al.* 1991; see also McIntosh 1998 and Tieken-Boon van Ostade 2000a).

7. Drama also has its diachronic limitations. The first prose plays only appeared in the latter half of the sixteenth century, and verse continued to be used as a major stylistic resource until much later. Many other drama conventions were similarly subject to variation; the social ranks depicted in comedy typically varied from the middling ranks in citizen comedies around 1600 to the upper echelons of society in Restoration comedies in the late seventeenth century (for further discussion on the use of early drama in corpus work, see Nevalainen 1991: 106–109).

8. Recent corpus-based research supports our initial decision. A number of studies have shown that personal letters pattern more like conversation and drama than other written genres such as fiction, essays, medical and legal prose, both today and in earlier periods of English. These results were reached independently for the nineteenth century by Arnaud (1998), for the period from 1650 to the 1990s by Biber (1995: 280–300), and for the fifteenth and sixteenth centuries by González-Álvarez and Pérez Guerra (1999).

9. Whether historical sociology might not be a more suitable partner discipline is another question – in the same way as sociology is often viewed as the 'teacher' discipline of its 'pupil', sociolinguistics. Some social historians feel that historical sociology has not reached sufficient methodological sophistication for operationalizing their findings for empirical research purposes (Wilson 1993: 41). The whole question of partner disciplines is a complicated one and cannot be given a satisfactory answer here. Suffice it to say that social history provides working models for many of the social factors that interest historical sociolinguists.

10. This decided emphasis on external factors in language change might earn this book a title like *A Historical Sociology of English*. Our starting point is indeed the opposite of Romaine's, for instance, who starts with a detailed linguistic analysis of her data. We, however, fully agree with her when she writes that 'the so-called boundary between the sociology of language and sociolinguistics does not matter very much, since one needs two sets of data, social and linguistic, to describe covariation' (Romaine 1982a: 139, note). Relations between the different disciplines dealing with language and society are discussed in Chapter 2.

Chapter 2

Sociolinguistic Paradigms and Language Change

> . . . our knowledge of the social forces that motivate linguistic change has become increasingly sophisticated, so that to ignore them is to run the risk of reinforcing the view that language is impervious to society and that society could be constituted without language. (Romaine 1992: 257)

The relations between language and society are highly complex, and can be approached from different angles. Some approaches have grown into disciplines of their own, informed by different theoretical views of both language and society. Those who stress their shared properties place them all under the umbrella term of **sociolinguistics** (Crystal 1991: 319–320). But a line can also be drawn between sociolinguistics and the **sociology of language**. Although both disciplines study the relationships between language and society, the sociology of language may be said to do so in order to understand society, whereas the goal of sociolinguistics is to understand language (Chambers 1995: 10–11).

The core area of sociolinguistics in this narrower sense is the study of linguistic variation and its social significance. It often concentrates on three major social correlates of linguistic variation: class, gender and age, but several others may also be included, such as region, neighbourhood and ethnicity. This paradigm has been given various labels depending on the angle from which it is viewed. Concentration on urban varieties has earned it the name **social** or **urban dialectology**, to distinguish it from rural dialectology. As it focuses on linguistic variation, the approach has also come to be known as **variation(ist) theory**, and because it employs quantitative methods, it is called the **quantitative paradigm**. Finally, it is also labelled **correlational sociolinguistics**, because it aims to account for linguistic variation in terms of social factors. But by whatever name the approach is known, one of the research topics that it takes on board is the relationship between linguistic variability and **language change**.

It is obvious that a number of issues that interest historical linguists fall within the domain of the sociology of language. This is particularly true the further back in time we go and the sparser our textual sources become. Although there might not be much material to throw light on matters such as social gender differences in Old English, it is quite possible to find out about bi- and multilingualism, code-switching and language policies in Anglo-Saxon England.[1]

But as we move on to the Late Middle and Early Modern English periods, our chances to reconstruct the social dynamics of the language are greatly improved. It becomes increasingly possible to investigate the role of speakers in language change from the correlational perspective, as will be shown in the empirical part of this book. Ampler textual resources also make it possible to investigate various aspects of **communicative interaction** in earlier periods of English. Some of these aspects will be referred to in the subsequent chapters.

2.1. Sociolinguistic Paradigms

Not all disciplines combining the study of language and society explore linguistic variability in order to understand language change. Returning to the research traditions that have been established within sociolinguistics, a comparison of three major approaches may clarify their foci and lines of inquiry. Adapted from Dittmar (1997: 99–100), Table 2.1. gives a synoptic view of the sociology of language, social dialectology, and interactional sociolinguistics. They are often associated, among others, with names such as Joshua Fishman, William Labov and John Gumperz, respectively. The distinctions made in Table 2.1. do not provide in-depth accounts of these approaches but are instead intended to illustrate the range of research agendas they cover between themselves.

In social dialectology, the object of study is the 'orderly heterogeneity' of linguistic variation, while the sociology of language focuses on languages and language varieties at the macro level with the aim of accounting for their status and use in speech communities. Interactional sociolinguistics, finally, works at the micro level and is concerned with the verbal and non-verbal organization of discourse interaction. Seeing their different objects of study, it is natural that the three paradigms should also largely employ different methods to achieve them, **quantitative** in the case of social dialectology and the sociology of language, and **qualitative** in the case of interactional sociolinguistics. What they aim to find out is also different. Interactional sociolinguistics is concerned with communicative competence and discourse construction, while social dialectology is the only one of the three approaches to model processes of language change.

Comparing and contrasting sociolinguistic paradigms reveals their research programmes. They were developed for different purposes and can be expected to present divergent views of their objects of study. This divergence has also resulted in a major dualism pulling these paradigms apart, that is, the opposition between 'correlational' and 'constructivist' approaches.

Table 2.1. Three paradigms in sociolinguistics (adapted from Dittmar 1997: 99–100)

Paradigm/ Dimension	Sociology of language	Social dialectology	Interactional sociolinguistics
Object of study	• status and function of languages and language varieties in speech communities	• variation in grammar and phonology • linguistic variation in discourse • speaker attitudes	• interactive construction and organization of discourse
Mode of inquiry	• domain-specific use of languages and varieties of language	• correlating linguistic and sociological categories	• organization of discourse as social interaction
Fieldwork	• questionnaire • interview	• sociolinguistic interview • participant observation	• documentation of linguistic and non-linguistic interaction in different contexts
Describing	• the norms and patterns of language use in domain-specific conditions	• the linguistic system in relation to external factors	• co-operative rules for organization of discourse
Explaining	• differences of and changes in status and function of languages and language varieties	• social dynamics of language varieties in speech communities • **language change**	• communicative competence; verbal and nonverbal input in goal-oriented interaction

Basically, what is at issue in the controversy is the **social theory** underlying each tradition. After addressing the two approaches and their implications for our work in the next section, we will move on to some fundamental theoretical issues that are of major concern to the topic of this book: the limits of the historical sociolinguistic enterprise.

2.2. Descriptions and Explanations

As suggested above, the several sociolinguistic paradigms do not always lead a peaceful co-existence. Instead of being seen as complementary, they are often pitted against one another. As the correlational approach, in particular, has been criticized by social constructivists, some tension has been felt between social dialectology and interactional sociolinguistics. In what follows we will discuss some of the criticism that has been levelled at traditional social dialectology. Much of it has been directed at what is seen as the weak explanatory power of the approach, on the one hand, and at its potentially static view of social constructs, on the other.[2]

When patterns of linguistic variation are correlated with social and demographic factors such as age, gender and social class, the argument goes, we are merely **describing** sociolinguistic patterns, and not really **explaining** them within a wider sociological framework. It is the general quest for a theory in sociolinguistics that is at issue here (see further 2.3.). The other topic raised by critics of the correlational paradigm is precisely how it relates the linguistic with the social. If social categories are posited as primary, and language is presumed merely to reflect them, we run the risk of pigeonholing all linguistic variation in a predetermined way. By contrast, constructivist approaches generally operate on the micro level without any prior extra-linguistic categorization, assuming that meanings are constructed by the interlocutors and emerge in the course of discourse interaction. In this view, the speaker's freedom to produce linguistic variation is maximized.

Let us begin with the criticism that social dialectology produces 'mere' descriptions. As noted by generative grammarians a few decades ago, one would have thought that adequate descriptions constituted the cornerstone of all disciplines.[3] Seeing that historical sociolinguistics is still at its fact-finding stage, we set for our work the basic requirement of empirical validity. The validity of social categorization is, of course, another matter, and should be approached critically in both modern and historical studies. However, if the robustness of results is anything to go by, the correlational paradigm has not fared so badly: the work carried out over the last 40 years in different speech communities has produced results consistent enough to re-emerge in a large number of studies. For this reason some of them have been proposed as possible candidates for sociolinguistic universals (Hudson 1996: 202). *Mutatis mutandis*, these descriptive generalizations will provide good test cases for the historical sociolinguist, and inevitably form part of historical sociolinguistic theory.

As noted above, proponents of interactional paradigms often start from the assumption that, as meanings are constructed in the course of discourse interaction, no direct connection ought to be made between the speaker's social background and his or her linguistic performance in the way proposed by the correlational approach. Taken to its logical extreme, the social constructivist approach argues that the social world is not only enacted but also constructed through language. In our field of interest, language change, the argument could well be applied to certain indexical uses of language. Social role and status distinctions, for instance, may be created and maintained by the use of address forms. We do not, however, agree that the argument could be universally tenable when it comes to the choice of accents and dialects. Individuals do not command the full range of regional and social dialects of their mother tongue and therefore cannot construct them at will. As noted by Cameron (1997: 62), speakers may not be sociolinguistic automata, but neither are they free social agents linguistically.[4]

Apart from their spoken **vernaculars** acquired in early childhood, people have what Fishman (1997: 28) calls **verbal repertoires** which are constrained by their backgrounds. Access to the various regional, social and professional repertoires can only be ensured by sufficient exposure to them. Traditionally, social dialectology has mostly been interested in the speaker's vernacular both as 'the language used by ordinary people in their everyday affairs' and 'the style in which the minimum of attention is given to the monitoring of speech' (Labov 1972: 69, 208). But in order to gauge the range of variation displayed by individuals and social groups under different communicative circumstances, systematic attention has also been paid by social dialectologists to stylistic variation (for details, see Chapter 9).

Many sociolinguists steer a middle course in the controversy, and share Coupland's (2001: 14) conclusion that 'decategorializing' may be as pernicious a way to skew readings of data as 'overcategorializing'. Our position is similarly a mediating one: the correlational and constructivist perspectives constitute complementary methodologies. However, we also endorse the views of those sociolinguists who emphasize that, in order to be able to make valid generalizations, purely qualitative investigations of language use need to be combined with quantitative approaches (Bell 2001; Schilling-Estes 2002).

The variable linguistic behaviour of individual speakers is also appreciated within the quantitative paradigm. Rather than pigeonholing speakers in a predetermined way, their deviation from established norms and active role in shaping their mother tongue can be revealed using this methodology. With the relevant baseline data available, the role of the individual in language change has also been foregrounded in recent work in social dialectology. So Labov (2001) not only describes the ways in which the various social groups participate in ongoing linguistic changes in Philadelphia, but also identifies the individuals who lead the changes. He gives detailed portraits of such individual leaders, who are shown to be women of the upper working class with a high density of interaction within their own neighbourhoods, but also with a large number of weak ties outside of them.

As pointed out in Chapter 1, the need for quantitative baseline data has similarly been recognized by social historians and literary scholars. To those historical sociolinguists who study language change, the issue is of particular relevance for two reasons. Firstly, there are few systematic historical investigations of language changes in their social contexts to date. This means that in many cases we have no knowledge of such basic issues as the time courses of the changes that took place in English over a given period of time, and cannot therefore relate a qualitative case study to the overall line of development of a given feature. Secondly, without baseline information it is not possible to tell whether in a qualitative study we are dealing with laggers or leaders in linguistic change. As shown in detail in Chapter 5, speakers of Late Middle and Early Modern English are no different from Present-day English speakers in that they vary in the degree to which they participate in ongoing linguistic changes.

2.3. Theoretical Pluralism

As we have seen, constructionists and correlationists take diametrically opposite views on how the linguistic is to be related with the social. The views stem from different theoretical orientations. We might therefore wish to inquire into the status of theory in sociolinguistics generally in order to see where to situate historical sociolinguistic theory. Three basic alternative views are considered by Coupland (1998, 2001), who thinks that sociolinguistic theory could be conceived as (1) a linguistic theory, (2) an accumulation of socially relevant mini-theories, or (3) a social theory. If general linguistic theory is 'a theory about language without human beings', as it appears to be after thirty years of sociolinguistics, Coupland (1998: 112) rules out the first alternative: the theoretical impact of sociolinguistics must be made elsewhere. A number of sociolinguists would agree on the second alternative. There are many sociolinguistic subtheories, such as the **accommodation**, **social-network** and **acts-of-identity** theories of linguistic choices and the **face (politeness)** theory of interaction (Hudson 1996: 228). Seeing the diversity of social processes investigated by sociolinguists, it is perhaps no wonder that a unified sociolinguistic theory does not exist.

As to the third option, sociolinguistics as social theory, Coupland sets up three social-theoretic perspectives that are relevant to language and have been drawn on by sociolinguistic paradigms: theories of social structure and social behaviour by the correlational paradigm, and theories of social praxis and rational action by interactional approaches. Coupland (1998: 115) concludes that the problem is therefore not the lack of social theory but its recognition:

> The general point is again that sociolinguistic traditions, diverse and even mutually exclusive as they may appear, have rather well established forebears in theoretical social science. A more open recognition of this fact might promote clearer reflection on sociolinguistic theory as a set of alternative perspectives within a largely established field.

If Coupland is right, the question is not really about lack of theory and social validity as such, but about theoretical diversity that is not very well articulated by the different sociolinguistic paradigms.[5]

2.4. Theory in Historical Sociolinguistics

The quest for sociolinguistic theory does not become simpler when we cross over to the realm of history and into a less well-established field of empirical research. The question first comes to mind whether historical sociolinguistics needs a social theory, or theories, of its own. We would argue that the answer crucially depends on the level of abstraction of the discussion. In principle, historical sociolinguistics – just like historical linguistics in general – may be justified by the **uniformitarian** principle referred to in section 1.3. Historical linguists should not expect that human languages in the past were in any fundamental way different from those spoken today, or as Lass (1997: 25) put it: 'there are no miracles'. Labov (1972: 275) expands on the extralinguistic side of the principle by stating that:

> If there are relatively constant, day-to-day effects of social interaction upon grammar and phonology, the uniformitarian principle asserts that these influences continue to operate today the same way that they have in the past. (Labov 1972: 275)

Suzanne Romaine, the pioneer in historical sociolinguistics, promotes the uniformitarian principle to an axiom of sociolinguistic reconstruction:

> The linguistic forces which operate today and are observable around us are not unlike those which have operated in the past. This principle is of course basic to purely linguistic reconstruction as well, but sociolinguistically speaking, it means that there is no reason for believing that language did not vary in the same patterned ways in the past as it has been observed to do today. (Romaine 1988: 1454)

Romaine's 'same patterned ways' is not to deny that the past must have been different from the present, but makes the more abstract point that human languages have always been used in speech communities and, consequently, have been socially conditioned throughout their histories. In theoretical terms this implies, for instance, that if socially motivated mini-theories, Coupland's category (2), above, work for the present, they are worth bearing in mind when studying the past as well.

Over the last ten years, historical sociolinguistic studies have been informed by both the **politeness** theory of interaction (Brown & Levinson 1987) and the **social-network** theory (L. Milroy 1987).[6] But if we are interested in language change, the issue of baseline evidence re-emerges especially with the network approach. The problem is shared by historical and modern sociolinguists alike (Labov 2001: 327). Another limitation to extending this approach to language history is posed by missing evidence. Lesley Milroy (2000: 220) notes the historical sociolinguist's difficulty in obtaining the ethnographic information needed, first, to determine which network ties are meaningful to particular communities and, secondly, to assess an individual's degree of connectedness to a local community. The larger and more diffuse the community, the more difficult the problem of tracing patterns of interaction becomes.

Moving on to Coupland's third category, sociolinguistics as social theory, we must state at the outset that any uniformitarian social model could only be sketched in the broadest of terms. One possible candidate for such a model will be considered below. It was originally constructed by the sociologist Erik Allardt in the 1980s for purposes of comparing the standard of living and quality of life in Scandinavian countries. Allardt proposes that human welfare and living conditions should be evaluated in terms of need-satisfaction rather than simply in terms of resources. He starts from the assumption that there are both material and non-material basic human needs that have to be considered when designing indicator systems to assess the actual level of living conditions in a society. This basic-needs approach focuses 'on conditions without which human beings are unable to survive, to avoid misery, to relate to other people, and to avoid alienation' (Allardt 1989: 3).

Allardt uses the catchwords **Having**, **Loving** and **Being** for these necessary conditions of human existence and development. **Having** refers to those material conditions which are necessary for human survival and avoidance of misery, and it covers, for instance, the needs for nutrition, water, shelter and protection against diseases. It can be measured in terms of economic resources, housing and working conditions, employment, health, and level of education. **Loving** stands for the basic human needs to relate to other people and to form social identities; it can be assessed in terms of attachment to family and kin, patterns of friendship, contacts in the local community, in associations and organizations, and relationships at work. **Being**, finally, refers to the human need to integrate into society and live in harmony with nature. The indicators of Being can measure, for instance, the extent to which an individual can participate in decisions and activities influencing his or her life, take part in political activities, and have opportunities for leisure (Allardt 1989: 3–7).

It is obvious that a general framework like Allardt's can only serve as a broad frame of reference in cross-societal comparisons. As with the Nordic welfare research, specific indicators for measuring similarities and differences will have to be developed each time the model is applied to new settings. Allardt (1989: 4) makes the point explicitly by noting that the indicators he proposes for Scandinavian countries would not apply, for instance, to what were considered Third-World countries at the time the study was published. We will use the framework in Chapter 6, where gender in late medieval and early modern Britain is discussed in general terms. The model will also be referred to in Chapter 7, which considers social structures in the Tudor and Stuart periods. A general basis for compsrison is useful in that it helps the historical sociolinguist keep the larger picture in mind when analysing changing social conditions.

Focusing on actual, concrete differences between the present and the past, Labov (1994: 11) coins the term **historical paradox** to stress the point that we know the past was different from the present, but do not know how different. Subscribing to any strong version of this paradox would, however, amount to denouncing entire disciplines such as social and economic history. An alternative course of action is to minimize the effects of the paradox by consulting social history and related disciplines, whose business it is to know about the social conditions of past societies. This is where we return to the topic of social reconstruction.

While modern sociolinguists have proposed some sociolinguistic universals, such as the role of gender in language change – in the vast majority of the changes discussed by Labov (2001: 501) women were a full generation ahead of men – for the historical sociolinguist the issue remains an empirical one. The historical paradox might be reformulated by saying that there are no absolute, ready-made sets of social constructs that would automatically correspond to linguistic variation in the past. In other words, there is no one way of relating the linguistic to the social in history so as to guarantee a meaningful sociolinguistic generalization. It is the historical sociolinguist's task to find the relevant patterns of co-variation. In this respect historical sociolinguistics is no different from its modern counterpart.

By way of illustration, let us consider the reconstruction of **social class** in history. Social class has emerged as one of the significant speaker variables in the work of modern western social dialectologists. As shown by Chambers (1995: 41–48), these studies have indexed class membership in various ways. But even those who are not fully convinced of the social relevance of class distinctions in Britain today, would argue that their impact must have been felt much more 50 years ago (Coupland 2001: 13). Similarly, social historians agree that social status differences were of significance in early modern England. It probably does not matter in principle that the models used by social historians to discuss Tudor and Stuart England do not refer to social status differences in terms of social class, a concept which does not readily apply to preindustrial societies, but in terms of **estates** or **social ranks** instead. But what does matter is the alternative conceptualizations proposed ranging from basic two- and three-tiered models to finely graduated ones with a maximum of more than 20 different social ranks (Burke 1992a: 61–67; Cannadine 1998).

In our pilot studies we experimented with a ten-rank system that could be reconstructed with the correspondence material (Nevalainen & Raumolin-Brunberg 1996a, 1998; Nevalainen 1996b). With more data available for the present work, we can now conclude that, while the finer distinctions can prove relevant for some processes of change, meaningful generalizations can also be arrived at with less delicate frameworks (see Chapter 7).

Notes

1. See Toon (1983), Thomason and Kaufman (1988), and Machan (2000).
2. For these arguments, see e.g. Romaine (1984), Cameron (1997), and Eckert (2000), and for sociolinguistic metatheory in general, Figueroa (1994) and the essays in Coupland *et al.* (2001). Some general questions of explanation are also addressed by Downes (1998), Ch. 11.
3. Cf. the notion of **descriptive adequacy** in Chomsky (1965).
4. For discussion on social realism and sociolinguistics, see e.g. Carter and Sealey (2000) and Fairclough (2000).
5. This does not mean that all aspects of even structuralist social theory have been addressed by sociolinguists. Some recent discussions of social structure and mobility, and the interface between social class and gender in Britain, for instance, are yet to make their way into sociolinguistic research (cf. Butler & Savage 1995).
6. For applications of the politeness theory to the correspondence corpus, see Nevalainen and Raumolin-Brunberg (1995) and Nevala (1998, 2001), all dealing with forms of address. The social network approach has been implemented in several studies by Tieken-Boon van Ostade (e.g. 1996, 2000b). The special issue of the *European Journal of English Studies* 4/3 (2000) is devoted to social network analysis and the history of English. We will refer to differences in social network structures as an explanatory framework in Chapter 10 (see also Nevalainen 2000b; Nevalainen & Raumolin-Brunberg 2000a).

Chapter 3

Primary Data: Background and Informants

> Historical linguistics can then be thought of as the art of making the best use of bad data. (William Labov 1994: 11)

> Thus, technical linguistic explanations of change should be linked to the best possible understanding of the economic, social and political forces which may have influenced it, but should also be aware of the agendas which underlie the writing of the history that they draw upon. (Derek Keene 2000: 93)

3.1. Data in Historical Sociolinguistics

3.1.1. The 'Bad-Data' Problem

It is true that researchers of the earlier varieties of a language cannot gather their data in the same way as a person studying present-day languages. The standard sociolinguistic methods, such as **interview** and **elicitation**, are automatically excluded. Recordings of **spoken language** are available only from the last century onwards. What serves as primary data necessarily represents **written language** and, as Labov says (1982: 20), 'the fragments of the literary record that remain are the result of historical accidents beyond the control of the investigator'.

In our experience, however, there is no need in historical linguistics to overstress what Labov calls 'bad data'. True, historical data can be characterized as 'bad' in many ways, but we would rather place the emphasis on making the best use of the data available (Nevalainen 1999b). This requires systematicity in data collection, extensive background reading and good philological work, in other words, tasks that are demanding and time-consuming but by no means unrealizable.

Labov's additional comment (1994: 11) '[w]e usually know very little about the social position of the writers, and not much more about the social structure of the community' seems to us rather inaccurate if not misleading, at least as far as the history of English is concerned. Extensive studies of how people lived in the past have been carried out by historians, from general investigations to research on particular areas and communities as well as families and individuals. Integrating information gathered by historians into linguistic research has been one of the challenges of this study.[1] We would not argue, however, that it is always possible to assess an individual writer's social position or the conditions of his or her community.

Rather than complaining about the quality of the information we have, we need to regret the shortage of material concerning particular sections of society. Owing to widespread illiteracy in the past, it is not possible to gain access to the language of the lowest social strata and most women, not at least in an autograph form. The level of **full literacy**, comprising both reading and writing skills, varies a great deal between different historical periods but, on the whole, most of the material that has come down to us has been produced by upper- and middle-ranking male informants.

The whole field of historical linguistics has been revolutionized by the emergence of computer-assisted data processing techniques. Besides huge computerized corpora on present-day languages, there are also corpora on historical varieties. The first such corpus on the history of English, the *Helsinki Corpus of English Texts*, carefully compiled by a project team at the University of Helsinki in the 1980s, has paved the way for a number of new, second-generation corpora (e.g. Hickey *et al.* 1997; Meurman-Solin 2001). The trend has been from textually balanced multi-purpose corpora towards larger single-genre corpora, such as the one on correspondence used in this study. Computer technology has proved to be a great help in making the best use of the data available in historical sociolinguistics.

3.1.2. The Advantages of Historical Data

The comments on bad data easily lead to an impression that historical texts would be inferior to present-day material in every respect. This is not necessarily the case. The first advantage is the time depth itself, which makes it possible to carry out research in **real time**. It is difficult to underestimate the superiority of real-time analyses of language change to hypotheses based on **apparent time**, i.e. differences in usage by successive generations of speakers. We shall return to the issue of apparent time in Chapter 5.

Another advantage is the genuine nature of communication that all historical data represent, though naturally within the limits of the prevailing generic conventions. The very methods of producing material for present-day sociolinguistic research, allowing researchers to control their data, i.e. interviews and elicitation, also produce problems. The participation of the researcher in interaction may affect the linguistic choices people make.

From the earliest phases onwards, sociolinguists have been aware of the **Observer's Paradox**, stated by Labov (1972: 209) as follows: 'the aim of linguistic research in the community must be to find out how people talk when they are not being systematically observed; yet we can only obtain these data by systematic observation'. Various methods have been invented to bypass this problem, ranging from changes in the subject matter (danger-of-death situations) to long-term participant observation (Labov 1972: 209–216). The main concern has been people's propensity to use less colloquial variants in the company of strangers. This may, of course, lead to a situation in which the collected data do not contain the widest range of styles, and casual speech in particular can be underrepresented.

It is not only the limited stylistic variation that may be worrying in interview situations. According to the basic tenet of **accommodation theory**, in linguistic interaction the interlocutors often try to reduce their dissimilarities through speech convergence. This is yet another way in which the linguistic data can be influenced by the interviewer (see e.g. Trudgill 1986). In the case of historical material, however, a researcher could not affect the actual form of the data in any way, and therefore they can be said to represent genuine communication.[2]

3.2. Generic and Temporal Concerns

3.2.1. Textual Variation and Historical Sociolinguistics

Unlike present-day sociolinguists who analyse one genre, spoken conversation, possibly supplemented by reading assignments, historical sociolinguists need to collect their data from the written texts that have come down to us.[3] These texts represent different genres, which are known to have changed over time. In all diachronic research textual continuity needs attention, and a great deal of research has been done in this area (e.g. Moessner ed. 2001; Diller & Görlach ed. 2001). It is worth mentioning that most of the 14 changes that are under scrutiny in this book have been studied previously within the framework of textual variation.[4]

The variationist approach is based on the observation that genres differ in many ways, for instance, in their conventions, level of formality and type of setting. One of the aims of historical sociolinguistics has been to find texts that mirror the informal spoken language of past times as closely as possible. This is not to say that we would question the validity of historical data in their own right (e.g. Romaine 1988: 1454), but our objective is motivated by the assumption that most linguistic changes take place in informal spoken language and spread later to the more formal varieties, representing in Labovian terms (Labov 1994: 78) **change from below** as opposed to **change from above**.

It has become a commonplace among textual historians not to accept a rigid division between the two modes of expression, written and spoken, but to work with a continuum of strategies, **'oral'** and **'literate'** constituting the end points. Some spoken genres, such as sermons, have been shown to resort to literate strategies, while some written genres, for example, personal letters, are found to be close to the oral end of the continuum. As expected, most linguistic innovations studied in the variation framework have first appeared in the oral genres.

This line of thought was elaborated by Biber (1988), who, with a factor analysis of the co-occurrence of specific linguistic features, showed that spoken and written genres could be placed in different textual dimensions.[5] So, for instance, in Biber's Dimension 1, 'Involved versus Informational Production' (1988: 128), personal letters occupy the same position as interviews towards the involved end of the scale and, similarly, professional letters and broadcasts the same place around the middle of the continuum. The dimension approach has also been applied to historical data (Biber & Finegan 1989, 1992, 1997; Biber 2001), resulting in interesting observations on the evolution of various genres from the seventeenth century onwards.

The present study differs from the mainstream variationist framework in the sense that, instead of focusing on **textual variation** in history, the language of **individual informants** is taken up for analysis. This makes our approach similar to present-day sociolinguistics. What also resembles contemporary sociolinguistics is the choice of only one genre, in our case personal correspondence, as the object of study. This choice provides commensurability of data, as far as that is possible, for a period spanning 270 years.

Furthermore, the suitability of personal correspondence for sociolinguistic analysis becomes obvious if one believes, as we do, that Biber's characterization of personal correspondence as one of the most oral written genres not only holds for Present-day English but also for past varieties. From the social point of view, personal correspondence stands out as first-class primary data. Thanks to the editors of letter collections and social and cultural historians, it is possible to identify individual letter writers, trace their social backgrounds, personal histories and relationships to the recipients of letters, in other words, the information without which sociolinguistc analyses and interpretations could not be made.

3.2.2. Periodization

This study covers the period from c. 1410 to 1681. The beginning is dictated by the earliest availability of personal letters in English. The reason for placing the end date in 1681 is not as obvious.[6] One point of interest was to see if the political tumults in the middle of the seventeenth century had any effect on language, and sufficient time had to be provided for their possible consequences to appear in written language.

The decision about the end point also had to do with research economy. At the start of our 'Sociolinguistics and Language History' project in 1993, we were aware that our resources would not be sufficient for the compilation of a corpus covering more than approximately two and a half centuries. Today we can argue that the temporal depth of c. 270 years, giving us access to the language of about ten generations of informants, is long enough for making interesting real-time observations on language change. Our period crosses the traditional borderline between Late Middle and Early Modern English, providing an opportunity for testing the validity of this temporal boundary.

The temporal focus is necessarily different between present-day and historical studies. In present-day studies linguistic data are considered contemporaneous only if they have been produced within a year or two. The general availability of linguistic material from the past calls for a less rigorous time scale. We originally divided our data into 20-year periods, which were taken to represent contemporaneous language. It turned out, however, that in many cases it was better to double this time in order to acquire reliable results on overall developments and correlations with external factors.

3.3. Tudor and Stuart England

This section, containing material that has been acquired from research on social, economic and cultural history, serves as the background for the **reconstruction of the social context** of language use in Tudor and Stuart England. We believe that historical sociolinguistics can only be successful if its analyses draw on the social conditions that prevailed during the lifetimes of the informants. It may be necessary to repeat that this is not in contradiction with uniformitarianism, discussed in Chapter 2, which is assumed to work on an abstract level, comprising the very basic human needs in the physical, psychological and social domains.

Transferring sociolinguistic concepts and classifications from present-day studies to historical research is not without its problems. In this sense our work is no different from general historical research wishing to take advantage of frameworks developed in modern social sciences. Peter Burke's *History & Social Theory* (1992a) offers an inspiring discussion of the modifications needed in the central concepts and problems when what he calls social theory is combined with history. His concepts include sex and gender, family and kinship, class, status, social mobility, power, centre and periphery and his problems deal with issues such as function, structure and culture. Wilson (1993), in turn, is an interesting survey on the development of social history, emphasizing the need to redress the relationship between historical disciplines and social sciences, including historical sociology.

3.3.1. Overall Developments and Major Changes

Table 3.1. (pp. 34–35) is a compact description of Renaissance England (see Raumolin-Brunberg 1996c: 21–23; for sources, see also Nevalainen & Raumolin-Brunberg 1989). The condensed format necessarily means simplification, but we believe that the general picture nevertheless holds. The temporal division into two[7] makes it possible to grasp the most conspicuous changes. As the table shows, the most enduring patterns can be found in family life and kinship relations, while other areas did not remain unaltered.

In terms of change, two developments rise above everything else: the **Reformation** in the sixteenth century and the **Revolution** in the seventeenth, straddling most fields of life. As a religious issue, the Reformation pertains to culture, and among cultural historians the character and length of the process have been objects of scholarly debate (Marshall ed. 1997; Kaartinen 1999). It is certain that religious beliefs and rituals did not change overnight, and there was regional variation in the spreading of Protestantism, London, Suffolk, Essex and Kent leading the process, with considerable Catholic enclaves in the north and west (Dickens 1997).

But the Reformation did not only affect religious beliefs and practices. Its effect on the educational system was marked, as most schools had been run by Catholic religious institutions. Also, Protestantism spoke for individuals' personal access to God's word and, consequently, lay literacy was encouraged after the Reformation (Ingram 1995: 103). Furthermore, the dissolution of the monasteries led to dramatic changes in landownership. According to Clay (1984 I: 144), in the middle of the fifteenth century the Church and the Crown together owned 25–35 per cent of the cultivated land in England. By the late seventeenth century this share had dropped to 5–10 per cent. A policy of sales was adopted by the Crown in the 1540s, and several million acres were transferred from institutional to private proprietorship, mostly to members of the nobility, gentry and well-to-do middle-ranking families.

To most contemporaries, the disruptions of the middle of the seventeenth century, the Civil War, Regicide and Interregnum, seemed to turn the world upside down (Walter 1991). Although the English Revolution in 1649 did not result in any lasting changes in the social system or social distribution of wealth and power, the two decades of upheaval must have left a lasting effect on the minds and lives of those who experienced all the rapid turns in the course of events.

The political, economic and religious issues concerning the English Revolution inevitably remain beyond the present discussion, but we would like to pay attention to one specific topic, the impact of the Civil War on geographical mobility and increasing encounters between people from different backgrounds. According to Morrill (1991: 9),

> This was after all a country in which it was extremely rare (perhaps only at a handful of county elections every few years) for more than

1,000 people to gather in one place at the same time. Yet there was now a war which saw armies of more than 10,000 criss-cross all but a few counties in each campaigning season, and in which the number of battle-dead after at least ten engagements exceeded the size of the crowds at all but the most populous of those county hustings.

It was not only armies of men that moved about; large numbers of civilians had to flee the battles. Most parts of the country suffered from physical damage caused by military activity, and people had to find new places, either temporary or permanent, to live.[8]

It is obvious that this was a time when many close-knit **social networks** broke down. Given the importance of loose ties in social networks for the diffusion of language change (e.g. Milroy 1992), we see acceleration of ongoing linguistic changes after the middle of the seventeenth century, suggesting that language change is connected with social change (Raumolin-Brunberg 1998; for the role of wars in the diffusion of linguistic changes, see Labov 2001: 227–228).

After this overall view of society, a number of issues of importance for the empirical part of the book will be taken up for detailed discussion. Age and gender, factors relevant for Chapters 5 and 6, are not dealt with in separate sections, but raised at appropriate points in the text. In general, however, particulars on the operationalization, classification and interpretation of the social factors will be postponed to the respective chapters.

3.3.2. Social Structure

To give a brief outline of the social order that prevailed in England for over 250 years is not an easy task. It is not only change over time that makes this effort hard. Historians offer several approaches, ranging from models based on social consensus to those on conflict, and it is not easy to make a choice (e.g. Burke 1992a: 1–21).[9] Another basic question involves the perspective. Shall we aim at an objective 'outsider's' survey or try to capture a more subjective contemporary self-identification? The latter, more difficult to grasp though it is, might better correlate with people's linguistic behaviour. Furthermore, as Barry notes, irrespective of the method, the reconstruction of past societies varies according to social layer.

> As each specific measure of social differentiation has proved unreliable, historians have come to view social identity as an amalgam of factors – strongest when a number of different measures work together, but often less clearcut. The complete correlation of such indicators as occupation, wealth, birth, life-style and political power is only found at the very top and bottom of society. (Barry 1994: 17)

This section introduces a hierarchical model of social orders, which more or less represents the consensus analysis, supplemented by a tripartite division and a conflict-oriented bipolar view of society. In line with what seems to be the majority view among social historians, instead of the controversial issue of **class** in a preindustrial society, we have chosen to use contemporary concepts, such as **rank, estate, order, degree** and **sort** (Wrightson 1991; Burke 1992b; Cannadine 1998).

Section 4 in Table 3.1., our starting point, presents the medieval view of society as consisting of three estates: clergy, i.e. those who prayed, nobility, i.e. those who fought, and labourers, i.e. those who worked. This division was understood as a divine intention, and it was both static and anti-egalitarian (e.g. Keen 1990: 1–3).

The tripartite estates view gradually gave way to a more complex social structure. According to Wrightson (1991: 32–34), Tudor and early Stuart writers recognized a multiplicity of estates instead of three. Social divisions were not only seen in functional but also in hierarchical terms, in a similar manner to our scheme in Table 3.2. (p. 36).

As Barry's quotation above points out, the top and the bottom of the scale are rather clear, while an analysis of the middle section is less straight-forward. The nobility and upper reaches of the gentry proper formed the absolute elite, comprising only a couple of per cent of the population. The upper clergy, the archbishops and bishops, have been placed among the nobility on the basis of their influential position, signalled, for instance, by the title 'Lord'. At the other end, there is no difficulty in placing labourers, cottagers and paupers at the lowest rungs of the social ladder.

Although the main dividing line was usually drawn between the gentry and non-gentry, this was not a rigid division. Besides a specific lifestyle, gentility involved land ownership and no need to work for a living, but the borderline could be crossed by people from the middle ranks. The middle section consisted of independent trading households, including people in legal and medical professions, merchants and craftsmen. Upward **social mobility** was also possible for wealthy yeomen, who were usually substantial free-holders (Stone 1966; Barry 1994).

One of the signs of upward mobility was the self-identification as gentleman that occurred among middle-ranking people. With time, the titles of the lower gentry, Master and Mistress, spread among the professionals and wealthy merchants. This is what happened in the Johnson family we met in Chapter 1. Example (3.1) is Sabine's hesitating reaction to her husband John's jokingly addressing her as 'Mistris Sabyne'.[10]

> (3.1) In moest loving wise, welbeloved husbond (master I shold saye, because yet doyth becom me baetter to call you master than you to call me mystres), your letter of 15 of this present I have receyved this day. (Sabine Johnson 1545; JOHNSON 515)

Besides intragenerational social mobility, i.e. people themselves advancing socially during their lifetimes, intergenerational mobility was at least as

Table 3.1. Social and economic conditions in England 1410–1680

Before 1558	After 1558
1. Demography	
Gradual recovery after the catastrophic loss of population in the Black Death (1348–1349):	Rapid growth of population, with a decline after 1650:
1500 over 2 million 1540 2.77 million 1556 3.16 million	1575 3.41 million 1600 4.11 million 1650 5.23 million 1680 4.93 million
Internal migration common though regionally varied.	Apart from internal migration, substantial emigration to America and Ireland.
The vast majority of the population lives in the countryside. Urbanization on the increase, but the fortunes of provincial towns vary.	Continued urbanization. The growth of London remarkable.
Mortality crises common: dearth, endemic and epidemic disease.	Continued mortality crises (disease, less dearth at the end of the period).
2. Political life	
Weak monarchy in the 15th century. Powerful great magnates. Central government strengthened during the first Tudors, with a diminishing influence of the great lords. Occasional uprisings curbed with a firm hand.	Relative stability under Elizabeth and James I. Political influence of the clergy diminishes with the Reformation. Increase in the influence of the merchant community on English politics.
Hundred Years' War 1337–1453 Wars of the Roses 1455–1487	A series of disruptions: Civil War 1642–1646, Execution of Charles I 1649, Interregnum 1646–1660, Restoration of the Stuarts 1660.
3. Economy	
Agricultural society: peasant farming.	Agricultural society: emergence of commercial farming with improved productivity.
Diversification of economic activity. Cloth replaces wool as main export commodity.	Continued diversification within the established industries. Introduction and increase in consumer goods production.
After a stable price level, inflation sets in in the 16th century.	High inflation continuing until the 1660s favours the upper ranks and adversely affects wage earners: polarization of society. General economic progress means welfare for all except the poor.
Scarcity of labour. High wage level with relatively good standard of living in the 15th century.	
Dissolution of the monasteries leads to far-reaching changes in land-ownership.	

Table 3.1. (cont'd)

Before 1558	After 1558
Preponderantly regional economies striving for self-sufficiency.	Integrated national economy emerging. Improved communication networks.
England a peripheral country in international trade.	Central position in international trade. London's role crucial.

4. Social order

Medieval feudal system with three estates (clergy, warriors, labourers) gradually gives way to a more complex social hierarchy.	Society highly stratified, with the main difference being between the gentry and the non-gentry. Landownership the basis for the position of the gentry.
Beside traditional military service, administration becomes a path to social advancement.	Upward social mobility via the professions, marriage or acquisition of land; paths open especially before the 1640s. Inflation of honours and multiplication of the gentry during the early Stuarts. Consolidation of the middle ranks.

5. Family and kinship
Nuclear family with paternal authority.

Different marriage patterns in different social groups: the upper ranks marry younger and their marriages are often arranged, the lower ranks marry later and have a freer choice.

Marriages preferred between people of equal status.	More intermarriage between the gentry and professional families.

Upper ranks have larger families.

The importance of kinship ties outside the nuclear family varies: kinship often used as a basis for economic and other assistance, patronage, etc. Kinship ties break social boundaries.

6. Culture

Catholic Church, with Reformation at the end of the period.	Church of England well established; Catholic threat and Puritan opposition.
From court culture to a widening cultural market.	'Popular' culture established.
Clergy lose their monopoly on literacy, but illiteracy a characteristic of the common people. An oral society.	Illiteracy becomes a special characteristic of the poor. A semi-literate society.
Introduction of the printing press in England in 1476.	Increase in educational opportunity at all levels, enjoyed by higher ranks and upper levels of the middling sort.
Schools mainly under church authority.	Interest in higher education decreases from 1650 onwards.
English used in several genres of writing; the role of Latin significant.	English accepted as the national language suitable for most purposes.
	Widening world view and heightened role of national identity.

Table 3.2. Rank and status in Tudor and Stuart England

Estate		Grade	Title*
GENTRY	Nobility	Royalty Duke *Archbishop* Marquess Earl Viscount Baron *Bishop*	Lord, Lady
	Gentry proper	Baronet 1611– Knight Esquire Gentleman	Sir, Dame Mr, Mrs
	Professions	Army Officer (Captain, etc.), Government Official (Secretary of State, etc.), Lawyer, Medical Doctor (Doctor), Merchant, Clergyman, Teacher, etc.	
NON-GENTRY		Yeoman Merchant Husbandman Craftsman Tradesman Artificer Labourer Cottager Pauper	Goodman, Goodwife (Name of Craft: Carpenter, etc.)

(*occupational titles given in brackets)
After Laslett (1983).

common. The offspring of wealthy middle-ranking families could advance socially by acquiring land and adopting a gentleman's lifestyle, or, as was often the case, by making a good marriage. On the other hand, downward social mobility was also common. Estates could be lost for economic reasons. The usual method of inheritance, primogeniture, according to which the eldest son received the estate and the title, often compelled the younger sons of gentry families to find their fortunes elsewhere, especially in the professions and trades (Heal & Holmes 1994: 257; Brooks 1994a).

The social structure in towns differed from the countryside. There wealthy merchants and craftsmen, freemen of a town, formed the topmost layer of society (Rigby & Ewan 2000: 300–301). Many professionals also lived in towns. Below the urban elite were lesser traders, craftsmen, journeymen and servants. Gentlemen also had their town houses.

The social position of women was mainly derivative: unmarried women were categorized according to their fathers' social position and the married ones followed their husbands. Some women could engage themselves in economic activity, e.g. widows occasionally had the opportunity of continuing their husbands' trade. Social mobility also existed among women, mostly taking place through marriage.

As mentioned above, the fine-grained hierarchical model is only one way of describing the social structure of early modern England. Society could also be seen as consisting of only two groups. The division into the gentry and non-gentry represents this view. Wrightson (1991, 1994) has documented this bipolar view in contemporary social comments from the latter part of the sixteenth century onwards. Contemporary comments only refer to two groups, the 'poorer sort', 'common sort', 'simpler sort' as opposed to the 'better sort', 'richer sort', etc. This language, no doubt, contained seeds for actual or potential conflict. It was only after the 1620s that the terms 'middle' or 'middling sort' were introduced, apparently reflecting a novel view of social divisions.

Returning to the question of how men and women identified themselves in social terms, we should probably not overestimate their understanding of abstract social structures (see Nevalainen 1994). Neither should we forget that the models introduced in the contemporary comments usually represent an elite view, possibly written for the purpose of justifying the existing social inequality (Burke 1992a: 45, 62). It is probable that people developed multiple identities, defining their own positions in terms of different models at the same time (Rosser 1997: 8). There is no reason to forget that a common way of looking at the world in the past as well as today is to divide people into 'us' and 'them' (Cannadine 1998: 20).

Owing to profound social, economic and political changes, new evaluations and social alignments were called for in early modern England, while older models of social order still persisted in modified forms. The incoming language of 'sorts' could

> lump together the distinguishable estates and degrees of inherited social theory into broad groupings which anticipated the social classes of the nineteenth century. It could imply alternative conceptions of the fundamental nature of social differentiation, express conflicts of interests, and edge perceptive contemporaries along the path towards a thoroughgoing reappraisal of the structures of society, the basis of social inequality, and the dynamics of social process. (Wrightson 1994: 50–51)

In Chapter 7 we make use of both the hierarchical model and the tripartite approach in a modified form. Linguistically sensitive **upwardly mobile** middle-ranking people, whom we call **social aspirers**, will play a significant role in our analysis. In singling them out, we can have the benefit of hindsight at its best: on the basis of personal histories it is known to us who advanced socially and who did not (see also Nevala 1998; Nurmi 1999a: 99–109).

3.3.3. Migration and Regional Differences

It is not only social mobility that needs to be observed in historical sociolinguistics. Patterns of **geographical mobility** provide tools for explaining processes of diffusion, in particular **dialect contact** and type of **social network**.

Migration has its natural links with demographic developments. The dramatic decline in population caused by the Black Death in the fourteenth century gave people opportunities to travel the country in search of better livelihood (Thompson 1983: 9–16). According to Stone (1966), the sixteenth and seventeenth centuries witnessed two major currents of migration: from the countryside to London and other large towns, and from densely populated farming regions to the more sparsely inhabited pastoral districts that had ample common land and possibly rural industries. Although urbanization was on the increase in Renaissance England, only a small minority of the population lived in towns (perhaps 10–15 per cent, depending on the way of counting).

Certain points of the life cycle, such as marriage and old age, were especially sensitive for migration (King 1997). People of both sexes changed their domiciles, women most often in connection with marriage. In addition to this more permanent kind of population resettlement, there was also temporary migration, since young people often moved about for education, apprenticeship and service before setting up a permanent home (Wrightson 1982: 42).

As Chapter 8 will focus on the regional variation in language use by exploring the differences between London, the Court, East Anglia and the North, these areas need a closer look.[11] In the following discussion most attention is paid to London because of its significance for the diffusion of linguistic changes.

By London we mean the City, the suburbs outside the walls and Southwark. The Court comprises the members of the royal family, courtiers and other high-ranking government officials, many of whom lived in the West End and Westminster. So, for instance, the merchant John Johnson, Sabine's[12] husband, is included among Londoners, whereas, despite being a native of London, Sir Thomas More as the King's Secretary and Lord Chancellor pertains to the Court. All informants living north of Lincolnshire are counted as Northerners, and East Anglia covers both Norfolk and Suffolk.[13]

London's growth in the late sixteenth and seventeenth centuries was phenomenal, not only in a national but also an international perspective. What contemporaries apparently felt is expressed by King James I: 'Soon London will be all England' (cited in Wrigley 1967: 44). The number of inhabitants[14] in the late Middle Ages was about 50,000, growing to c. 200,000 in 1600 and to 500,000 by 1700. This means that, in 1700, 10 per cent of the population of England lived in London, while in 1500 it had only been 2 per cent. By 1700, London had surpassed all West European cities in size.

In brief, London's massive growth depended on wealth and power concentrated in one place. According to Keene (2000: 97), in the early fourteenth century London contained about 2 per cent of the taxed wealth of England, rising to 12 per cent by the 1520s, while in the 1660s it produced about half of the ordinary revenue available to government. On the other hand, from the late thirteenth century onwards London was the centre for national administration and law. It is the centralization of both political and economic life in one city which was also the country's main port that made London's development unique in comparison with other European capitals (Beier & Finlay 1986: 11–14; Barron 2000).

London's growth clearly depended on a steady flow of migrants, since recurrent endemic and epidemic diseases meant that London's mortality rate exceeded its birth rate. It has been estimated that in the late sixteenth and in the seventeenth centuries London absorbed the total population surplus of England (Wrigley & Schofield 1981: 168–169). Sixteenth and seventeenth century court records suggest that only 15 per cent of Londoners were born there (Coleman & Salt 1992: 27).

Although it was natural to move to London in search of advancement in life, many people did not stay in the capital for long. It seems plausible that one English adult in eight in 1550–1650 and one in six in 1650–1750 had some experience of life in London (Wrigley 1967: 49). This is apparently true of all social strata. Service and schooling brought people of lower and middle ranks to London, but visits to London were also part of country gentlemen's life.[15] They came to London to see to various legal and administrative matters or to attend the Parliamentary sessions. Later on it became customary to bring along family members to participate in the capital's social events (Finlay & Shearer 1986: 46).

Actual patterns of migration can be reconstructed to some extent. The origin of London apprentices is relatively well documented for some guilds and periods. Wareing (1980: 243) shows that the share of those who came from the north was very high in the late Middle Ages (61 per cent in 1485–1500), gradually decreasing towards the end of the early modern era (11 per cent in 1654–1674) at the same time as the proportion of the Midlands increased from 10 per cent to 45 per cent. The role of the east was rather marginal, declining from 8 per cent in 1486–1500 to 3 per cent in 1654–1674. Rappaport (1989: 79) describes the origin of 876 immigrants who acquired London citizenship in the early 1550s. Even here the proportion of the northern counties is the highest (about 30 per cent), the south-east also playing an important part (24 per cent). By contrast, Norfolk and Suffolk sent only a few boys for apprenticeship to London. Kitch (1986: 228–229) shows that the proportion of London apprentices travelling long distances decreased considerably after the Restoration, but London's migration field nevertheless remained nationwide.

Life in a densely populated city meant frequent day-to-day contacts with people in their different social roles (for a lively picture of Restoration London, see Picard 1997). Social mobility was easier in London, and innovations of all kinds were accepted and new consumption patterns established here before other parts of the country (Wrigley 1967: 50–51). Studies of early modern London's social topography (Power 1985, 1986) show that people of different social strata did not live isolated from each other. Power's studies, based partly on John Stow's *Survey of London*, testify to occupational clustering rather than wealth clustering, which developed later. How far one's regional origins affected residential patterns is not clear, but people from the same shires at least formed clubs and gathered together for feasts. Despite some segregating tendencies, there was, according to Power (1985: 11), 'a considerable intermingling of rich and poor, commerce and craft, skilled and unskilled in the same parishes and even in the same streets'.

Unlike London and the Court, the informants that offer material for the analysis of East Anglian and northern varieties of English were often born in their home regions. The northern area, covering the counties of Cumberland, Westmoreland, Northumberland, Durham, Yorkshire and Lancashire, had two major towns, York and Newcastle, and formed an archbishopric. The significance of York as an administrative centre had decreased after the fourteenth century with the growth of London's importance. As shown above, the number of apprentices sent from the north to London was high until the seventeenth century. Although the distance was long, one of the country's main thoroughfares led from London to Berwick, forming the basis for the earliest system of regular contacts by standing posts (Brayshay 1991: 376–377).

After close connections with the capital up to the fourteenth century (Keene 2000: 106–107), East Anglia developed into a rather self-sufficient area. It seems that young men preferred to seek apprenticeship in its main town Norwich, the second largest in the country, rather than London (see Patten 1976). Early modern East Anglia has been characterized as a coherent area, undisturbed by the direct influence of London (Kitch 1986: 229, 235).

It is most likely that the massive influx of migrants into London, as well as its fluid social structure, affected London English. Keeping apart the Court and London gives us the opportunity of comparing a more prestigious variety with the natural speech of the capital, probably a dialect mixture. We also expect to discover differences in the linguistic behaviour between northerners and East Anglians.

3.3.4. Education and Literacy

A further issue meriting closer scrutiny is education, and, associated with it, the extent of literacy. Literacy, especially its most elaborate form, the ability to write, is the external factor that most powerfully limits the material for this study. On a more general level, the role of writing in the cultural environment affected the interest that people had in the acquisition of literacy, and this is where a major change took place between the early fifteenth and late seventeenth centuries.

Education, like most components of lifestyle, was socially stratified. The way children were trained for adult life varied according to the social background and gender. In general, the education of boys could be academic, while only exceptionally was this the case with girls (Fletcher 1995: 298).[16]

Home was, of course, the most important place for teaching children the skills they needed in the future. With time, the role of school attendance increased, but home tuition persevered. Children of the lower social strata rarely went to school and, if they did, their families could hardly afford it for more than a year or two. An apprenticeship, lasting seven years, was the most common form of education among the middling ranks, although, as we have seen above, this was also the training that many younger sons of gentry families had to choose (Brooks 1994a: 54). England's two universities, Oxford and Cambridge, mostly recruited their undergraduates from the gentry, but prosperous commoners also had access to them. The Inns of Court offered legal education. The most prestigious educational combination, enjoyed by the sons of the wealthiest families, included university studies, legal training at the Inns of Court, and a Grand Tour of Europe (Heal & Holmes 1994: 272–275). Girls had no access to the institutions of higher education, but there were some schools for girls and apprenticeship was also available for them, although only rarely (Brooks 1994a: 54; Hufton 1997: 65).

The differences in the content of education created an important social division. The curriculum of the educational institutions for boys, the grammar schools and beyond, was essentially classical. This means that it was predominantly boys from the upper and middling sections of society who came to command Latin, the most prestigious language of the time. Fletcher (1995: 302) goes as far as to claim that 'Latin became firmly installed as the male elite's secret language, a language of its own, a language that could be displayed as a mark of learning, of superiority, of class and gender difference . . .' The classical focus also minimized the time that was devoted to English (O'Day 1982: 106–131), and in this context women's educational disadvantage may not have been as marked as would seem at first sight (see section 6.2., below).

Furthermore, the educational system placed one prestigious variety of English, the language of law and administration, beyond the reach of the lower orders and women. As our empirical part will show, some linguistic changes seem to have originated among well-educated men. Seen against the social divisions of the educational system, we are unlikely to be far from the truth if we interpret them as changes from above in Labovian terms.

Table 3.3. Male signature literacy, c. 1580–1700, percentages

	East Anglia	North	London/Middlesex
Gentry	98	100	98
Professions	100	97	100
Yeomen	65	51	70
Trades/crafts	56	57	72
Husbandmen	21	25	21
Labourers	15	15	22

Adapted from Reay (1998: 40).

The level of literacy was also socially stratified. Most of the quantitative estimates of literacy have counted the proportion of the population who signed their names instead of inscribing a mark in different public documents. This method, created by David Cressy in his book on literacy and social order in 1980, is based on the fact that reading and writing were regarded as two separate skills and taught in succession, not simultaneously as today. Teaching a child to read took about a year, and only after this stage was writing taken up for training. Consequently, the acquisition of writing skills required school attendance for more than a year, and/or effective home tuition (Schofield 1968: 317; Barry 1995: 76).

The problems of interpreting the presence of signatures instead of marks in terms of general literacy have led to a recent coinage, 'signature literacy' (Barry 1995; Reay 1998). Counting signatures has been accepted as a reasonable way of giving statistical information, but the general picture should be complemented by qualitative interpretation. According to Reay (1998: 43), the method provides 'a confident *minimum* estimate of those able to read'.

Cressy (1980: 177) argues that this minimum estimate for the male population was about 10 per cent in 1500. Table 3.3. is a presentation of regional and social variation in men's ability to read for 1580–1700. It shows that the percentage of those with the ability to read reflects the social hierarchy discussed in section 3.3.2. The gentry and professions were almost fully literate throughout the country. London/Middlesex scored higher for yeomen, traders and craftsmen. The lowest ranks had the lowest level of reading skills, and regional variation seems quite small.

Literacy was more common in towns than in the countryside, and in particular the urban elite, merchants, grocers and haberdashers had literacy rates of around 90 per cent (Reay 1998: 41–42). Women's signature literature was as low as 1 per cent in 1500 (Cressy 1980: 177), and it grew more slowly than men's.

How much larger, then, was the population that had some ability to read, poor though it might have been? The wide circulation of popular literature, such as almanacs, jestbooks and religious tracts, suggests that this level substantially exceeded signature literacy (Spufford 1989; Barry 1995: 80).

As it is clear that the ability to sign one's name does not necessarily pre-suppose a more extensive writing skill, we may assume that the proportion of the population with writing skills was smaller than the percentages for signature literacy. The share of fully literate people must have been the largest among the professionals, especially lawyers and administrators. But with time, the upper-ranking men learnt how to write and, according to Heal and Holmes (1994: 253), by the mid-seventeenth century all gentlewomen, too, were able to write.

Our corpus, which will be described in detail in section 3.4., includes a number of letters written by people of relatively low social standing, showing that the ability to write did not unequivocally correlate with a person's social status. There were individuals who acquired this skill for various reasons, and they often helped their relatives and neighbours in matters where lit-eracy was needed.

3.4. The Corpus of Early English Correspondence (CEEC)

3.4.1. General Outline

Our primary data consist of personal letters which have been compiled to form a 2.7 million-word electronic corpus entitled *The Corpus of Early English Correspondence* (CEEC). This corpus is the result of the team work of the 'Sociolinguistics and Language History' project, launched by us in 1993 at the Department of English at the University of Helsinki (for details, see Nevalainen & Raumolin-Brunberg 1996b).[17] From the very beginning, our purpose was to design a corpus that would make it possible to test the applicability of sociolinguistic methods to historical data.

The CEEC offers an easy access to the language of people who lived in England between c. 1410 and 1681. It consists of **judgement samples** se-lected on the basis of extralinguistic criteria. Owing to the issues that were discussed above as the 'bad-data' problem, no attempt at random sampling has been made, but we believe that what we have achieved is a relatively balanced corpus (Leech 1993: 13).

The results of the studies that have used the CEEC so far, including the 14 morphosyntactic changes under scrutiny in this book, indicate that the requirements set at the beginning of our compilation work have mostly been fulfilled (Nevalainen & Raumolin-Brunberg 1996b: 39). Table 3.4. gives numerical information about the latest full version of the CEEC, the 1998 version, which has been used in this study.[18]

The properties of the CEEC can be summarized as follows. Firstly, as mentioned in section 3.2., personal letters are known to share a number of

Table 3.4. The Corpus of Early English Correspondence (CEEC)

Timespan	c. 1410–1681
Running words	c. 2.7 million
Letters	6039
Collections	96
Informants	778

linguistic features with the colloquial spoken idiom, thus forming a genre suitable for diachronic sociolinguistic research. Secondly, the timespan of about 270 years is sufficient to capture the time courses of several morphosyntactic changes in English. This does not mean, however, that all changes could be followed to their completion. On the contrary, some developments have turned out to be so slow that only part of their progression can be observed, but this, too, is a valuable research result.

Thirdly, the size of the corpus, 2.7 million running words representing over 6,000 letters selected from 96 collections, has proved large enough for the examination of grammatical phenomena of 'average' frequency. As Chapter 4 will show, there is a great deal of variation in the frequency of linguistic variables, but we believe that this study offers a reliable picture of the general development of the changes analysed. Fourthly, the number of informants, nearly 780 people, despite covering a long timespan, seems sufficient if it is compared with the numbers that occur in present-day sociolinguistic research. According to Labov (2001: 38), a reliable sample of a very large city can be achieved by less than a hundred speakers. Last but not least, details on the social backgrounds of all corpus informants have been traced and collected in a separate database in order to facilitate sociolinguistic analyses.

3.4.2. The Material

As a rule, the letters were selected and scanned from edited collections, but a small minority have been edited from original manuscripts by the members of the project team (Keränen 1998a; Nevala 2001).[19] Editions with modernized spelling were excluded from the CEEC proper, but some modernized letters have been included in the Supplement to improve the social representativeness for some periods. A list of the letter collections included in the CEEC proper and those of the Supplement used in this study are found in Appendix III.[20]

The project team has checked some problematic editions against the original manuscripts. We are convinced that the CEEC is a reliable tool for research on grammar, lexis and pragmatics but not necessarily for orthography and phonology, which should be studied from the most scrupulous editions and original manuscripts. The modernized collections in the Supplement are useful in morphosyntactic investigations.

The authenticity of the data was a further important issue in the corpus work. It is obvious that editions made from autograph letters which have actually been sent provide the best type of material. Drafts and copies written by identifiable people also clearly represent their language and hence form good data.

In addition to these self-evident cases, we had to decide about the inclusion of other types of material. With letters written by scribes we had no way of knowing whether they were dictated or written according to some general instructions. It was also relatively common to preserve copies of letters in letter books, written down by the writer or a secretary. Besides these contemporary sources, there are also editions of correspondence based on copies that were made decades after the writing of the original letters. All these cases had to be judged separately and, especially when the quality of the edition was good and there was a clear need to cover the period, rank or gender in question, collections of copies were included.[21]

3.4.3. The Informants: Social and Regional Coverage

What makes the CEEC different from other historical corpora is the fact that it has been designed to provide access to the language of individual informants, whose social backgrounds have been investigated as accurately as possible.[22] The best informants, 16 per cent of all, have yielded more than 5,000 running words each, ensuring the inclusion of a broad range of linguistic structures in the material produced by a single informant. Half of the CEEC informants contributed over 1,000 words. Since our main aim has been to reach as broad a social coverage as possible, smaller numbers have also been welcomed from lower ranks and women. Although their limited contributions do not allow individual linguistic analyses, pooled together they can produce powerful evidence of the social embedding of linguistic changes. The gender division of the data is given in Table 3.5.

Table 3.6. gives the social status of the informants. As expected on the basis of the figures for full literacy, the upper ranks are better represented than the lower. This is especially the case with women. However, our special efforts to find lower-ranking and female informants – even if only one letter per person – have paid off, at least to some extent: there is sufficient material for the sociolinguistic research on relatively high-frequency linguistic phenomena.

Table 3.5. Informants: gender[23]

	Men	Women		Total
Number of informants	610	168	26%	778
Running words	2.26 million	0.45 million	17%	2.71 million
Number of letters	4,973	1,066	18%	6,039

Table 3.6. Informants: social status (percentages)

	Men	Women	Total
Royalty	2	6	3
Nobility	12	23	15
Gentry	35	56	39
Clergy	16	6	14
Professionals	14	4	11
Merchants	10	2	8
Other non-gentry	11	3	10
Total	100	100	100

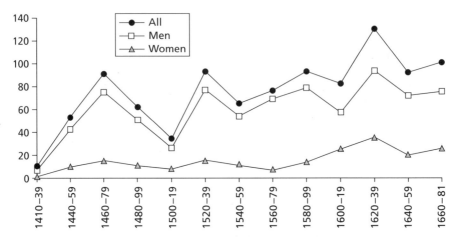

Figure 3.1. Number of informants per period: gender division. Absolute frequencies.

Tables 3.5. and 3.6. deal with the CEEC as a whole. For the study of the progression of changes, we also need to look at the temporal comparability of the data. Figures 3.1 and 3.2 depict the number of informants and words as well as the gender division of the data in absolute terms for successive 20-year periods.[24] The overall curves testify to the varying availability of letter data, in which the beginning of the sixteenth century forms an unfortunate drop.[25] Figures 3.3 and 3.4 give the proportion of female informants. The graphs show that the percentage of female informants does not vary a great deal, but their share of the actual data is quite small between 1520 and 1579. However, there are no radical differences between the periods, and the temporal division into 40-year periods, used in many discussions in the empirical part, helps to even out the fluctuations.

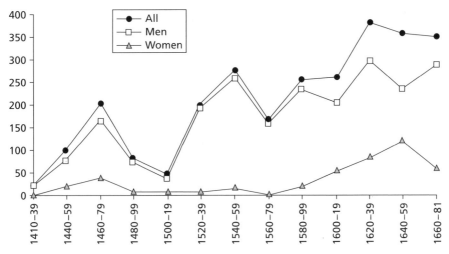

Figure 3.2. Number of words per period: gender division. Absolute frequencies.

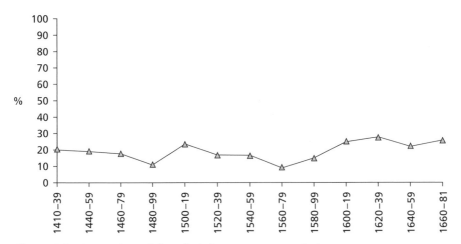

Figure 3.3. Proportion of female informants per period.

Figures 3.5 and 3.6 have been created to examine the social coverage of the CEEC. Figure 3.5 contains two curves illustrating the temporal development of the percentages of the highest (royalty plus nobility) and lowest social strata of the informants. Once again, we can see some fluctuations, but they rarely exceed 10 percentage points. In Figure 3.6 the curve for the highest ranks markedly falls and rises a couple of times, while the curve for the other non-gentry retains its regrettably low level. The high percentage of the first period depends on the inclusion of the royal Signet letters in the corpus, representing a time which does not provide much other material. The rise in 1580–99 goes back to the availability of large collections of

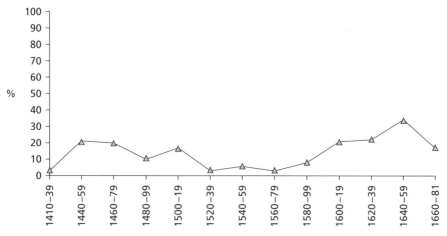

Figure 3.4. Number of words: proportion of data by female informants per period.

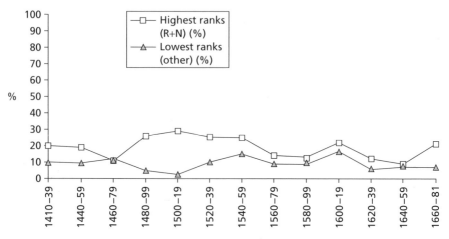

Figure 3.5. Proportion of informants representing the highest and lowest ranks per period.

authentic material by informants such as Queen Elizabeth I, Robert Dudley, Earl of Leicester, and William Cecil, Lord Burghley. Unfortunately, no such material can be acquired from the middle of the sixteenth century. Although variation is more noticeable here, collapsing categories and using 40-year temporal divisions are methods that help us draw realistic conclusions about the linguistic developments studied.

Table 3.7. on regional variation shows that approximately half of the CEEC informants came from the four areas to be analysed in Chapter 8. The grouping has been made on the basis of each individual's domicile at the time of correspondence. As far as the total figures are concerned, the distri-

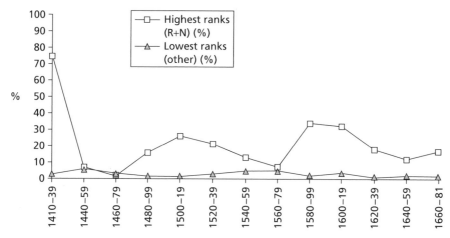

Figure 3.6. Number of words: proportion of data by the informants representing the highest and lowest ranks per period.

Table 3.7. Informants: regional division (percentages)

	Men	Women	Total
The Court	9	5	8
London	15	8	14
East Anglia	17	17	17
North	14	9	12
Other areas	45	61	49
Total	100	100	100

bution between the regions is quite even, although the figures for women are not as good as those for men. The good coverage of East Anglia depends on the two very large collections, the Paston letters from the fifteenth century and the Bacon letters from the sixteenth.

On the whole, we would like to argue that, while the CEEC may not in all respects represent the entire language community from the fifteenth to seventeenth centuries, it nevertheless provides quite a reliable sample of the informal language used by the language community, or at least by the literate writing community, of Tudor and Stuart England.

Notes

1. As mentioned in Chapter 1, much of the earlier research on sociohistorical linguistics has been based on textual variation alone. The rich sources of information offered by social and cultural historians have not been taken advantage of. For instance, the bibliographies of Romaine (1982a) and Milroy (1992) do not contain any works on social history. However, we are hardly exaggerating when

we claim that familiarity with relevant linguistic communities is one of the prerequisites for successful sociolinguistic analysis.

2. In her discussion of sociohistorical linguistics and the Observer's Paradox, Tieken-Boon van Ostade (2000c) offers a very different interpretation of the concept. She does not limit her attention to the role of the researcher observing people's linguistic behaviour but includes in the workings of the Observer's Paradox factors that prevent passages of the 'completely unmonitored' style – the term borrowed from Chambers (1995: 18) – being written down. The article contains interesting discussions, e.g. Fanny Burney's habit of taking notes about the language she heard around her, but it is difficult for us to see how, for instance, letter-writing conventions would be connected with the Observer's Paradox in the traditional sociolinguistic sense of the term. We would rather argue that every genre, including the spoken conversation which sociolinguists usually observe, has its own conventions, and therefore completely unmonitored speech is only a relative concept (see Chapter 9, below).

3. The information about informants' social backgrounds that is incorporated in modern multi-genre corpora such as the British National Corpus (BNC) makes it possible to study sociolinguistic variation in a broader variety of data than only spoken conversation.

4. The following variables have been studied in the variationist framework: MINE and THINE vs. MY and THY, possessive determiner ITS vs. OF IT and THEREOF, object and subject of the gerund, third-person singular suffix -TH vs. -S, periphrastic DO in affirmative statements, inversion after initial adverbs and negators, relative markers, and indefinite pronouns with singular human reference. The references are given in Chapter 4.

5. The dimensions in Biber (1988: 121–210) are as follows: (1) Involved versus Informational Production, (2) Narrative versus Non-Narrative Concerns, (3) Explicit versus Situation-Dependent Reference, (4) Overt Expression of Persuasion, (5) Abstract versus Non-Abstract Information, and (6) On-Line Informational Elaboration. They have been further refined in subsequent research.

6. To be accurate, a few private letters have been found from the first decade of the fifteenth century, viz. the letters of Lady Zouche (Payne & Barron, eds. 1997). Their late discovery by the project team placed them in the CEEC Supplement, and they are not used in this study. The odd-looking end year 1681 can be explained by the fact that we decided not to cut some interesting series of letters at 1680.

7. 1558 is the year of Elizabeth I's accession to the throne and is, of course, quite arbitrary from the linguistic point of view.

8. The literature gives the following numerical information about the Civil War. The New Model Army was 22,000 men strong in 1645. In four years of struggle, about 100,000 men were killed (Briggs 1985: 141). Approximately 150–200 country houses, 10,000 houses in cities and towns and 1,000 in villages were destroyed (Porter 1997: 66). For women's experiences of the period on both sides, see Hudson (ed. 1993).

9. Burke (1992a: 62–63) suggests that the rival models should be treated as complementary rather than contradictory ways of viewing society. According to him, the debate between two outstanding social theorists, Karl Marx and Max Weber, is 'complicated by the fact that the two men were trying to answer different questions about inequality. Marx was especially concerned with power and with conflict, while Weber was interested in values and life-styles. The class

model has become associated with a view of society as essentially conflictual, minimizing solidarities, while the model of orders has become associated with a view of society as essentially harmonious, minimizing conflict'.

10. The status inflation of the middle ranks, causing considerable problems for social classification in research, has been commented on in various studies (e.g. Brooks 1994a, 1994b). Sabine Johnson's husband John, a wealthy merchant operating in foreign trade, acquired an estate in Northamptonshire, and so fulfilled one of the gentry criteria, viz. landownerhip.

11. In previous studies, especially in Nevalainen & Raumolin-Brunberg (2000a) we only compared three different areas, London, East Anglia and the North. It seems, however, that the geographical area of London consisted of too heterogeneous a collection of informants to form one unit. The creation of a new category, the Court, to comprise the royal family and upper-ranking goverment officials, has given us the opportunity of comparing the language of two very different kinds of inhabitants of (greater) London.

12. Sabine herself lived in Glapthorne, Northamptonshire, on the estate the family had acquired, and is not included among Londoners (see note 10, above).

13. The choice of the four areas primarily depends on our interest to investigate linguistic variation in regional terms. However, the availability of the material in the end dictated the selection. The amount of data was also decisive in delimiting the northern area. As far as the west of the country is concerned, unfortunately there is not sufficient chronological continuity among the letter collections that we have been able to get hold of.

14. There are varying estimates concerning the number of inhabitants in London. The sources include: Beier & Finlay (1986: 3), Finlay & Shearer (1986: 39), Boulton (1987: 3), Rappaport (1989: 61), Dyer (1991: 33), Keene (2000: 97–98), and Barron (2000: 396–397).

15. So common were these visits that exceptions have been mentioned as curiosities. It was, for instance, said about one of our northern informants, Henry Clifford, Second Earl of Cumberland (d. 1570), that he withdrew from the public life after the death of his first wife so that he went to London only three times during the last 20 years of his life (Hoyle ed. 1992: 20).

16. The CEEC contains some letters written by women with classical learning, such as Margaret Roper (1505–1544; daughter of Sir Thomas More), Lady Anne Bacon (1528–1610), Queen Elizabeth I (1533–1603), and Viscountess Anne Conway (1631–1679).

17. The compilation process and principles of the CEEC have also been discussed in the following publications: Nevalainen & Raumolin-Brunberg (1994b); Raumolin-Brunberg (1997); Keränen (1998b); Laitinen (2002). In 2001 a project for tagging and parsing the CEEC was launched in cooperation between the Universities of Helsinki and York.

18. Earlier versions have been used in pilot studies. Some of the raw data in this book also go back to the earlier versions, the cases being duly documented in the text. A sampler version called the *Corpus of Early English Correspondence Sampler* (CEECS) has been released in the second ICAME CD-ROM containing the material that is no longer subject to copyright (Nurmi ed. 1998; Nurmi 1999c, see also Nurmi 2002).

19. Jukka Keränen has edited the letters of William Fawnte (1998a), and Minna Nevala a number of letters by East Anglian women (2001). Jukka Keränen, Terttu Nevalainen and Arja Nurmi have re-edited the Marshall letters from the

original manuscripts, and Terttu Nevalainen has edited the letters of Elizabeth, Queen of Bohemia, from State Papers 81. (For details, see Appendix III.)

20. We would like to thank Dr Arja Nurmi and Dr Minna Palander-Collin for letting us use the list of texts they compiled for their doctoral dissertations. The Supplement contains material from some modernized editions on the one hand and letters included after the completion of the 1998 version on the other.

21. In order to help researchers handle the varying authenticity of the corpus material, a code was attached to each letter. Most of the CEEC letters belong to categories A and C.

The authenticity codes are as follows:

A = autograph letter in a good original-spelling edition; writer's social background recoverable

B = autograph letter in a good original-spelling edition; part of the writer's background information missing

C = non-autograph letter (secretarial work or copy) in a good original-spelling edition; writer's social background recoverable

D = doubtful or uncertain authorship; problems with the edition, the writer's background information, or both.

22. The background information has been collected into a Sender Database, which contains the following parameters for each informant: name, title, year of birth and death, year of first and last letter, sex, rank, father's rank, place of birth, main domicile, education, religion, number of letters, number and kind of recipients, number of words, letter contents and quality, source collection, career and migration history (for coding details, see Nevalainen & Raumolin-Brunberg 1996b; Raumolin-Brunberg 1997).

23. Nine letters signed by the Privy Council have been included in the figures for men. They correspond to the small number of official letters signed by the Regents that have also been selected, mostly to serve as material for comparison.

24. The people whose writing 'career' crossed the 20-year-period boundaries have been counted separately for each period, which means that, given a long life as a letter writer, one person may have been counted three times. In analysing the social status of those whose position changed, we have assigned each person the status they had at the end of each 20-year period.

25. The small amount of edited correspondence representing the early part of the sixteenth century certainly depends on various factors, some of them probably accidental. However, the shortage of surviving correspondence may also have connections with the educational standards of the time (Heal & Holmes 1994: 258).

Chapter 4

Real Time

What historical studies can examine best are questions of how and when a linguistic change proceeded. (Devitt 1989: 15)

4.1. The S-Shaped Curve

It goes without saying that language change in **real time** can best be traced by using corpora that cover a long timespan. In a way, it is a paradox that we have learnt a great deal about language change from sociolinguists, who have not had access to historical data. The first chapters of Labov (1994) raise many issues concerning the character of historical linguistics and, nevertheless, the time depth in the real-time replications in that book hardly exceeds 20 years, a period which in our research is regarded as the basic unit of contemporaneous writing. Differences like this are indicative of the divergent perspectives between the sociolinguistic research into the present-day spoken idiom and the study of past language forms. The latter inevitably focuses on general trends and large-scale developments instead of minute details. However, this does not exclude micro-level observations on the linguistic behaviour of individuals who lived long ago.

An important sociolinguistic contribution to the description of the time course of language change is the **S-shaped curve**. This model, borrowed from studies of the diffusion of innovations among populations (e.g. Cooper 1982), has become a stock-in-trade for sociolinguists describing the spread of linguistic innovations. It refers to a pattern with a slow initial spread, a rapid middle stage, and a slower final phase (Figure 4.1). According to Labov (1994: 65–66), the motivation for this process lies in the frequency of contact between users of the new and the old forms and the subsequent adoption of the new form. At the beginning of the change, those who use the old form are rarely exposed to the innovation, and so only a small amount of transfer takes place. The rate of change is greatest at midpoint, when contact between the speakers is greatest. According to Labov (1994: 66), the nature of linguistic change explains the slow last phase. There is only a slight pressure to change, which leads to a slight shift at each speech contact. The rate of change falls, since the number of speech events where

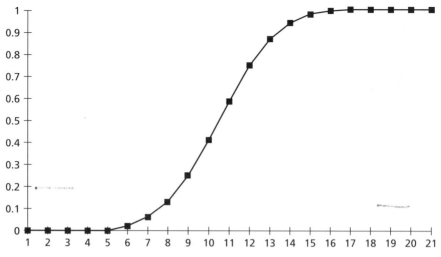

Figure 4.1. The S-shaped curve (Labov 1994: 65).

the shift can occur diminishes. We must not forget that there may be linguistic environments that resist a given change and hence slow down its operation in the final stages.

Figure 4.1 gives the abstract shape of the S-curve generated from the cumulative frequencies of the binomial distribution, and, as Labov (1994: 65) mentions, there are other functions which produce curves of this shape. We have found it sufficient for our purposes to use S-curves based on raw data without further mathematical elaboration.

The idea of the S-curve has been developed by Aitchison (1981: 100), who introduces a model of successive overlapping small S-curves, which form a cumulative S-shaped curve (Figure 4.2). Her model is especially suited to the description of changes that proceed from one linguistic environment to another in a regular manner. Owing to our focus on the nonlinguistic constraints, we mainly discuss the cumulative curves, but the existence of the overlapping S-curves can be assumed for most changes.[1]

Although there may be diverging opinions about the mechanism that lies behind the functioning of the S-shaped curve and especially its slow tailing off (e.g. Denison 2002), we find the concept a useful descriptive tool. It seems to us that, in addition to the frequency of contacts, **accommodation theory** and **audience design** might provide explanations for its operation (see Chapters 3, 9 and 10).[2]

Furthermore, we have found it useful to divide ongoing changes into five stages, covering different areas on the slope of the S-curve. In Labov's system (1994: 67, 79–83), these stages include incipient, new and vigorous, mid-range, nearly completed, and completed phases. We have applied the following classification in terms of the proportion of incoming forms:

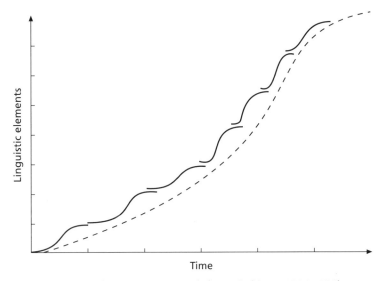

Figure 4.2. Overlapping S-curves (after Aitchison 1981: 100).

Incipient	below 15 per cent
New and vigorous	between 15 and 35 per cent
Mid-range	between 36 and 65 per cent
Nearing completion	between 66 and 85 per cent
Completed	over 85 per cent

Sociolinguists have introduced two ways of carrying out real-time studies (Labov 1994: 76–77). **Trend study** replicates an earlier study with the same population and the same methodology in sampling and analysis. It is, however, unlikely that the same individuals would be interviewed in both studies. In order to obtain reliable results on language change, the researcher should make sure that the community has remained unchanged between the two studies. **Panel study**, on the other hand, means that the same individuals whose language has been studied are located at a later date, and a new study is carried out.

Our model resembles trend study, since we use a socially representative corpus from successive periods. The condition that the community should remain unchanged is, however, inapplicable to historical linguistics. As pointed out in Chapter 3, societies inevitably change in the long run. The only way of tackling this question is through qualitative interpretation. Social change has to be analysed and assessed at the same time as language change is reported.

Some CEEC informants have provided letters from several decades with the consequence that their material has been divided between different subperiods. In this way these people's input complies with the idea of panel study, the same individuals contributing research data for successive periods.

4.2. Timing Linguistic Changes

The accurate timing of linguistic changes has not been a central issue in historical linguistics. There is still a great deal of truth in Chen and Wang's argument (1975: 256) that 'one of the most neglected aspects of historical linguistics, which professes to be a study of language evolving across time, is the time element itself' (see also Raumolin-Brunberg, forthcoming).

Timing linguistic changes is not necessarily such a straightforward matter as one would expect at first sight. It is clear that, if a change has reached Labov's fifth, completed stage, the new form has triumphed and language has changed. But it is not unusual that the old form lingers on in some linguistic environments, some dialects or a genre or two. For instance, the possessive determiner ITS[3] has not ousted its postnominal variants OF IT and THEREOF from the language, and the third-person singular suffix -TH is found in King James Bible, which is still in use today. Can we speak of language change, although these processes have not been completed? If we can, as we assume is the case with our examples, what then is the limit, how much linguistic and nonlinguistic variation is allowed? If we look at the question from the angle of the speech community, how large a percentage of speakers should have adopted the innovation or used it as their main variant before we can say that language change has taken place?

There is no one answer to these questions. In what follows we shall look at a number of processes of change as we see them in our data. In some cases we are tempted to speak about change when totally new elements are introduced, although it takes time until they become firmly established in the language. This is what happened, for instance, when ITS was introduced into the possessive paradigm around 1600 (Nevalainen & Raumolin-Brunberg 1994a). On the other hand, shifts in uses and frequencies of existing elements, such as the object form YOU replacing YE as subject, tend to make us feel that language change has taken place only when most people have changed their usage. One might even suggest that there are two points of change, namely when the variation leading to a shift begins and when the process comes to an end, or at least when the old form is understood to be archaic or only limited to a specific use or type of writing.

 Timing linguistic changes cannot be discussed without taking into account their multidimensional character. Besides linguistic and social embedding, textual aspects also need attention. At the same time as changes spread among people and across linguistic environments, they also find their way from one register or genre to another.

As pointed out in Chapter 3, by choosing personal letters as the material for this study, we have aimed at capturing linguistic innovations as quickly as possible after their emergence in colloquial spoken language. However, there was probably some time lag before spoken-language innovations found their way into writing, at least to any larger extent.[4] It seems plausible, however, that the CEEC dates changes of this type earlier than more formal and literary genres would do. Some changes discussed in this book most likely in Labovian terms came from above and followed a written-language model. Their introduction into personal letters presumably occurred later than their innovation in formal genres. Systematic research on the time courses of linguistic changes in different types of writing is needed for the corroboration of these assumptions.

4.3. Previous Studies

Despite the abundance of diachronic studies dealing with individual linguistic changes over time, it is not easy to find publications that concentrate on the temporal aspects of change, such as timing, rate of change and the S-curve. Temporal issues come up as 'natural' by-products, but they are seldom problematized. In many recent studies the temporal frame is furnished by the corpus used, often the *Helsinki Corpus of English Texts*.[5] Some studies of temporal issues have been, however, sources of inspiration in our work.

Devitt (1989) is an empirical study of the anglicization of Scottish English 1520–1659. She explores five linguistic changes in terms of both real and apparent time and concludes that the S-shaped curve has considerable descriptive power, although not all of her changes form an S-pattern. In addition to empirical results, Devitt's study contains valuable methodological discussions.

Kroch (1989) introduces a constant-rate hypothesis of language change. On the basis of crosslinguistic quantitative evidence, and in particular the development of the periphrastic auxiliary DO in Late Middle English in Ellegård's 1953 corpus, Kroch argues that change proceeds at the same rate in all linguistic contexts. His curves mostly follow the S-pattern. Kroch's hypothesis seems to challenge some widely accepted models of linguistic change, such as lexical diffusion. His argument focuses on the linguistic conditioning of language change, and he is fully aware that external factors may disrupt the pattern he introduces.

In his book on language change in an evolutionary framework, Croft (2000: 183–190) relates Kroch's constant-rate hypothesis to general sociolinguistic and invisible-hand models of linguistic change. Croft argues for a difference between the innovation and propagation of new elements and deals with the difficulties in identifying the beginning and end of a process of change. He also examines the S-curve in relation to neogrammarian change and lexical diffusion.

Ogura and Wang (1996) deal with the snowball effect in lexical diffusion, arguing for different rates of change for the diffusion from word to word, site to site and speaker to speaker. This study of the third-person singular suffix also claims that, with progressing diffusion, the successive S-curves become steeper. Although our view of the wave model is not in full agreement with Ogura and Wang's (see Chapter 8, below), we find their discussion highly insightful.

Lass (1997) contains a chapter on time and change. By means of a detailed presentation of the history of rhoticity in English, Lass (1997: 281–287) problematizes the standard notion of a change occurring at a particular point of time. He argues for two complementary descriptions, the macro and micro story, and emphasizes the role of the historian in the interpretation of existing primary data and the timing of linguistic changes.

Denison (1999, 2002) provides thought-provoking articles on the character of the S-curve. On the one hand, he experiments with the idea of looking at the traditional periods of the history of English, i.e. Old, Middle and Modern, in terms of the S-curve. On the other, he questions the theoretical basis of the whole concept. Significantly, Denison's discussion connects linguistic and pragmatic aspects of language change to speech communities and individual speakers.

4.4. The Time Courses of Fourteen Changes

At the same time as this section outlines the temporal progression of 14 changes in the CEEC, it also serves as an introduction to the changes and their linguistic embedding. Since our aim is not to offer new linguistic analyses, priority has been given to developments that have been investigated before. Our focus of interest is how they spread in society, in this chapter especially the temporal aspects of their diffusion. This section also provides basic data for further discussions on their transition, evaluation, and social embedding.

The criteria for selecting changes to be studied in this book have mostly sprung from our own previous research on Late Middle and Early Modern English, supplemented with some well-known developments from the period. At the outset, we had some idea about the social embedding of a few changes on the basis of our pilot studies, but in most cases all we knew were the results of studies on textual variation. One of the changes, the decline of multiple negation, was chosen because of its heavy stigmatization in Present-day English. In this case we wished to discover the background of the later development. The original list of changes was shortened for various reasons. Some subjects of our pilot studies, such as variation between BE and ARE, were dropped because of the amount of time the laborious analysis of the whole corpus would have taken. The replacement of THOU/THEE by YE/YOU was not explored, since the use of THOU/THEE concentrated on only a few correspondents (see Nevala 2002). Finally, in some changes the frequency of occurrences was too low for the study of the external factors, e.g. variation between the compound pronouns in -SELF and -SELVES.

Our introductions to the changes presented here will of necessity be short, meaning that all linguistic constraints are not described in detail. In general, great linguistic divergence can be attested in these changes, although, in broad terms, they could be characterized as morphosyntactic. Most of them can be linked with some general drifts in the history of English, such as morphological simplification and the introduction of the SVO word order. The shifts range from central and peripheral pronouns to verbal inflection, from auxiliaries to word order, and from gerunds to multiple negation. Interestingly, these changes also form a testing ground for Labov's argument (2001: 28–29) that speech communities are sensitive to individual linguistic items rather than abstract structural patterns. Our shifts include both since, for instance, the pronoun forms YOU and ITS are individual items, and multiple negation and gerund structure represent abstract patterns.

The changes are expressed as curves, the majority following the S-shape. Some changes are naturally binary, such as the replacement of subject YE by YOU. Some others are presented as binary, for instance the possessive determiner ITS is opposed to the postnominal variants OF IT and THEREOF lumped together. Some shifts are illustrated by three curves (noun subjects of the gerund) or even four (indefinite pronouns with human reference). Some introductions also describe variation across linguistic environments, such as the loss of inversion after initial adverbs and negators. The curves are based on percentages of the innovation except for two, the prop-word ONE, and auxiliary DO in affirmative sentences, which are given as frequencies per 10,000 running words (for the method, see Appendix I).

Our intention to provide a general picture of the developments justifies the use of quite long intervals, namely periods of 40 years. Although we have tried to standardize the temporal frame, it has not been possible in all cases without doing injustice to some rapid shifts. We are well aware that the 40-year scale levels out some peaks and troughs. Detailed discussions of the changes with a shorter time-scale will be presented in later chapters. It is, however, important to bear in mind that all changes are based on the same data, which guarantees a high level of mutual comparability.

In this chapter, the first to deal with concrete linguistic material, we have chosen to give all data as corpus aggregates, tacitly assuming the existence of one language community. This is, of course, a highly idealized picture of reality. However, this choice can be legitimized by the fact that all changes at issue were gradually supralocalized into the literate ranks of the whole of England. Moreover, the linguistic variation we deal with is quantitative, not qualitative or absolute, meaning that the sets of variants are more or less the same throughout the country. Later chapters will dissect this seemingly uniform picture into socially and regionally constrained components and processes.

For a fuller linguistic treatment of the developments, we refer to the literature given in the text (major sources only) and the notes (additional works). The number of occurrences extends from over 15,500 (relative pronoun THE

WHICH versus WHICH) to about 13,000 (both subject YE versus YOU and third-person singular suffix -TH versus -S) to just over 200 (prop-word ONE). Details can be found in Appendix II.

4.4.1. Replacement of Subject YE by YOU

The replacement of the subject pronoun YE by the object form YOU can be associated with the general trend of the disappearance of the case contrast in English. The immediate origin of this change is said to be phonological confusion, since both forms had the same weak forms.

(4.1) whan **ye** come set it in sech rewle as **ye** seme best (John Paston I, 1465; PASTON, I, 135)

(4.2) wyth whom I prey yow to be aqweyntyd as **you** semyth best. (John Paston III, 1472; PASTON, I, 575)

(4.3) Thus Fare **ye** hertely well (Thomas Cromwell, 1537; CROMWELL, II, 94)

(4.4) And thus in hast fare **you** hartely well. (Otwell Johnson, 1545; JOHNSON, 317)

(4.5) I perceave **you** have subskrybed our bylles to Thomas Everton, and that **you** do looke for advise, which I do not understond, for I am sure **ye** know the parcelles that we have bawght bothe of wulles and felles, by my cosyn Richarde's lettre; which yf **you** do not **ye** maie [in] tyme ynowgh hereafter (Ambrose Saunders, 1551; JOHNSON, 1411)

Natural loci for the early stages of this change were ambiguous contexts, such as impersonal structures (examples 4.1 and 4.2) and optative sentences, in

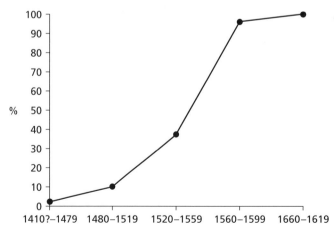

Figure 4.3. The replacement of subject YE by YOU. Percentages of YOU. Impersonal structures included. CEEC 1998 and Supplement.

which the subject follows the verb (4.3) and (4.4). The impersonal expressions have been included in the study, as a survey of THINK, SEEM, LIKE and PLEASE in the fifteenth century showed that there was a great deal of variation between the pronoun forms at this stage. Clauses with the accusative and infinitive pattern were also sites of confusion, especially requests like *I pray ye do something* versus *I pray you do something,* but they were not included in this study.[6] (For further information, see Nevalainen & Raumolin-Brunberg 1996a.)

Example (4.5) illustrates a typical case of mixed usage in the middle of the sixteenth century, when the S-curve in Figure 4.3 had reached its steep mid-course. As the curve shows, the change from YE to YOU was very rapid. The whole process lasted approximately 80 years.

4.4.2. MY and THY versus MINE and THINE

The first- and second-person singular possessive determiners lost their -N inflection in Renaissance English. Examples (4.6)–(4.10) illustrate the variants with and without -N. Schendl (1997) argues that in the first half of the sixteenth century the distribution of the elements was phonologically determined, the forms in -N appearing before words with initial vowels. According to Schendl, the role of nonlinguistic factors grew afterwards.

(4.6) **Myn** lord Chanselere come not here sone I come to Lundun (William Paston II, 1454; PASTON, I, 155)

(4.7) **Myn** herte me byddys euer more to love (Margery Paston, 1477; PASTON, I, 662)

(4.8) hath so assured me of the constancie of fortune in **myne** endevors (Nataniel Bacon II, 1613; CORNWALLIS, 13)

(4.9) and by many others how **thyne** owne credit made (Philip Gawdy, 1593; GAWDY, 78)

(4.10) I beseech you commend me to **my** uncle Charles and **my** Aunt (Arabella Stuart, 1603; STUART, 181)

In order to explore the phonological context of this change, an analysis was made of four different environments. Besides consonants and vowels, we also looked at the possessives preceding an initial <h> and one specific lexeme, OWN. Owing to problems in assessing the pronunciation of individual words, items with an initial <h> were selected mechanically according to the spelling. This class contains both native words, such as HEART in (4.7) and Romance loans, such as HONOUR(ABLE), HONEST(Y). OWN belongs to a small group of lexemes which favoured the N-variant even after the short form had found its way to most other cases. The classification was exclusive, so that neither the words with an initial <h> are included in the consonant class nor those occurring with OWN in the vowel group.

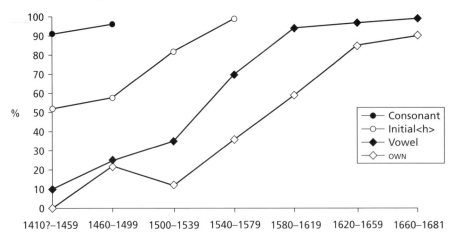

Figure 4.4. MY and THY versus MINE and THINE. Percentages of MY and THY. Use in four linguistic environments. CEEC 1998 and Supplement.

Figure 4.4 illustrates the wave-like pattern according to which the short form diffuses from one linguistic environment to another. In the early part of the fifteenth century, about 90 per cent of words with an initial consonant had adopted the N-less variant, while no occurrences of OWN are found to occur with this alternative. Between them we find forms preceding an initial <h> (c. 50 per cent) and vowels (c. 10 per cent). The consonants have run their course by the end of the fifteenth century, while the forms preceding <h> culminate during 1540–1579. The vowel curve forms the 'best' S-curve, the steepest slope occurring between 1500–1620. OWN at first follows the vowel curve, but takes a turn downwards early in the sixteenth century, and then again rises steeply until the mid-seventeenth century. It does not reach an invariable phase by 1681. Our later discussions will be based on one curve only, consisting of forms preceding vowels, including the word OWN.

4.4.3. Possessive Determiner ITS

The introduction of another determiner, the possessive pronoun ITS, is one of the latest developments within the English pronoun system (Nevalainen & Raumolin-Brunberg 1994a). After the demise of grammatical gender, the old neuter possessive HIS gradually became associated with masculinity and was increasingly avoided in the neuter. Postnominal paraphrases like OF IT and THEREOF were used instead.

For this study, the core paradigm of the seventeenth century was chosen. The introduction of ITS was examined against the use of the two postnominal variants mentioned above. Although HIS was probably a competing though rare prenominal alternative during the earliest years of the seventeenth

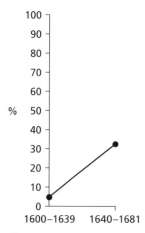

Figure 4.5. Possessive determiner ɪᴛs. Percentages of ɪᴛs as opposed to the postnominal variants ᴏғ ɪᴛ and ᴛʜᴇʀᴇᴏғ. CEEC 1998.

century, it was not included, since it quickly disappeared from the neuter use. Early occurrences of ɪᴛs are illustrated in examples (4.11)–(4.12).

(4.11) my ague dos yet contingu and begines to renew **its** strenght. (Jane Hook, 1631; Bᴀʀʀɪɴɢᴛᴏɴ, 174)

(4.12) wherin nature is forced aboue the simplicity of **its** owne inclynacon. (Thomas Wentworth, 1619; Wᴇɴᴛᴡᴏʀᴛʜ, 127)

(4.13) He had a letter to thee from me. I pray be mindfull of the contents **of it** assoone as you can. (Thomas Knyvett, 1644; Kɴʏᴠᴇᴛᴛ, 144)

(4.14) and on those of the ould faction, whom they suppose the authors **thereof**. (John Holles, 1615; Hᴏʟʟᴇs, I, 76)

Definiteness was the main criterion in the selection of the postnominal variants. Hence phrases without the definite article (e.g. *for prevention of it*) were excluded. We also left out fixed phrases, such as *the worst of it*, ᴏғ meaning 'concerning' (e.g. *the meditation of it*) and cases in which ᴏғ is part of a prepositional object phrase (e.g. *the thought of it*). As regards ᴛʜᴇʀᴇᴏғ, it can refer to both singular and plural noun phrases, but only occurrences with singular reference were included. Examples (4.13)–(4.14) illustrate the postnominal variants.

As mentioned in Nevalainen and Raumolin-Brunberg (1994a: 191–195), the reflexive use (reference to the syntactic subject) and the semantic roles ᴀɢᴇɴᴛ and ᴘᴏssᴇssᴏʀ promoted the employment of ɪᴛs, whereas the nonreflexive use and the semantic role ᴏʙᴊᴇᴄᴛ favoured the postnominal alternatives.

The 80-year period in Figure 4.5 indicates a sharply rising curve. Clearly there was rapid diffusion of ɪᴛs in seventeenth-century England.

63

4.4.4. Prop-word ONE

Although early instances of the prop-word ONE can be found in Middle English, the structure was established in the language during early modern times (Rissanen 1997: 118). Its increasing use seems to be connected with the syntactic need to provide an explicit headword for the noun phrase. This need arose with the simplification and loss of inflectional endings.

(4.15) I with **all your lytell ons** be in helthe, the Lord be prasid (Sabine Johnson, 1546; JOHNSON, 668)

(4.16) with a pen of my Cosine Cooks which I think haue writen many an indenture, it is but **a bad on** and my hast makes it not better (Katherine Paston, 1626?; PASTONK, 92)

(4.17) has already had the villany to write one untruth (and **soe bold a one**) concerning you (Samuel Pepys, 1680; PEPYS, 147)

By Early Modern English, the prop-word had acquired a wide range of uses. It was employed in both the singular and the plural, with personal and nonpersonal, and anaphoric and nonanaphoric reference, as examples (4.15)–(4.17) show. The adjective could be modified in several ways. According to Raumolin-Brunberg and Nurmi (1997), several changes took place in the frequencies of different uses in the seventeenth century. Both anaphoric and nonpersonal reference were on the increase as well as the singular use of the prop-word.

When analysing the prop-word we have followed Rissanen's (1997) principle of including only premodified cases, leaving out instances with only a determiner.[7] Figure 4.6, expressing the frequency of the prop-word ONE per 10,000 words, illustrates a development in which a linguistic item, after existing in the language for a long period, at some point of time begins to increase in frequency. The period between 1540 and 1620 looks like an

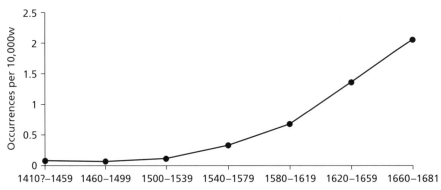

Figure 4.6. Prop-word ONE. Occurrences per 10,000 running words. CEEC 1998.

incipient stage, and the growth in 1620–1681 may be characterized as new and vigorous. However, the fact that the curve has been drawn on the basis of a frequency count and not relative frequency calls for caution in the interpretation.

4.4.5. Object of the Gerund

The next two changes deal with the development of gerund constructions. As a basis of this study, we have chosen Fanego's (1996: 97) definition of the gerund: 'any -ING form having, roughly, the same distribution as nouns or noun phrases'. In order to avoid problematic borderline cases and also for reasons dictated by research economy, our focus here is on gerundial constructions functioning as prepositional complements[8] (examples 4.18–4.22).

> (4.18) And as for **the makyng of that litill hous**, he toke (John Paston I, 1450s; PASTON, I, 74)
>
> (4.19) heyr is dyveres sent to proson for **byeng of grayn** (Richard Preston, 1552; JOHNSON, 1541)
>
> (4.20) I promis myselfe the contentment of **meeting you**; (Lucy Russell, 1614; CORNWALLIS, 23)
>
> (4.21) as you have done by **contynuall charging of monney** (Ambrose Saunders, 1552; JOHNSON, 1610)
>
> (4.22) that might give us some usefull Informations towards **the further discovering this villaine's forgeries** (Samuel Pepys, 1679; PEPYS, 87)

Previous research has established that gerunds underwent a gradual transformation from a full abstract noun to a verbal structure. This long process meant, among other things, that the typical modifiers of nouns, e.g. adjectives, came to be replaced by verbal modifiers, such as adverbs. The part of the gerund phrase (an *ad hoc* term also borrowed from Fanego 1996: 97) that follows the headword offers an interesting vantage point on one of the clearest manifestations of verbalization, the shift from OF-phrase to direct object. According to Fanego, the gerund phrases that first acquired direct objects were of the type that had only posthead elements (examples 4.19–4.20). The use of the direct object became common in the phrases that had modification on both sides of the headword only during the latter half of the seventeenth century. This led to hybrid structures (example 4.22) with a nominal prehead part and a verbal posthead structure. Both types have been included in this study.

Figure 4.7 illustrates a gradual change, which had begun before 1410. The emerging pattern can be recognized as an S-curve, although the slope is not so steep as that of the second-person pronoun, for example.

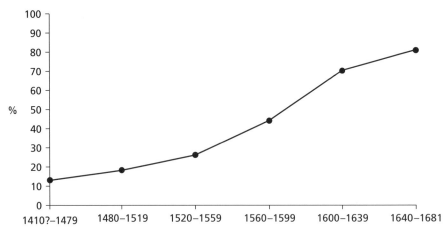

Figure 4.7. Object of the gerund. Percentage of zero forms as opposed to OF-phrases. CEEC 1998 and Supplement.

4.4.6. Noun Subject of the Gerund

The argument linking in the gerund phrase was also looked at from another angle. The preferences in the choice of the form of the noun subject of the gerund also underwent a change in Early Modern English.[9] As pointed out by Fanego (1998), there were three alternative forms: the genitive, the OF-phrase and the common case (examples 4.23–4.25). Gradually the posthead OF-phrase gave way to the prenominal variants. In this way the order of the arguments came to resemble the clausal SVO order.

    (4.23) where they taryed and wayted for **the Queenes commyng to her barge** (Thomas Cranmer, 1533; ORIGINAL 2 ADD, II, 36–37)

    (4.24) The Banqueting-house goith on now well, though **the going of the masons awaye** have byne a great hinderance to it. (Inigo Jones, 1620; HOWARD, 169)

    (4.25) cane well testyfye for **m^r Leake receyving the possession of her** (Francis Cotton, 1590; CLERK, 197)

    (4.26) a fayre picture of **Aeneas flyinge out of Troy** (Thomas Howard, 1621; HOWARD, 196)

The three-curve Figure 4.8 shows that the proportion of 'other', comprising common-case nouns (example 4.25) and ambiguous cases with the subject ending in a sibilant (4.26), varied very little and remained below 10 per cent for most of the time.[10] Consequently, the genitive noun and the OF-phrase formed almost complementary curves.

    Although there seems to be an upward curve in OF-phrases until 1500–1539, there was in fact random variation until 1539. The second crossover (from 1500–1539 to 1540–1579) is statistically significant at the .05 level (chi-

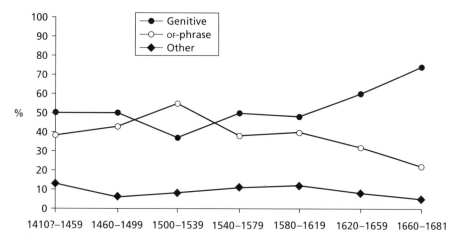

Figure 4.8. Noun subject of the gerund. Variation between the genitive, OF-phrase and the common case. Percentages. CEEC 1998.

square test). From this time onwards the genitive curve assumes the shape of an S-curve, with a clear turn upwards after 1620. The critical period of this change occurs in 1620–1681, coinciding with the decades of the English Civil War and the Interregnum.

4.4.7. Present Indicative Third-Person Singular Suffix -s versus -TH (HAVE and DO excluded)

The replacement of the suffix -TH by -s has been dealt with in numerous studies, most extensively in Holmqvist (1922).[11] Usually this change has been seen as one long process, beginning in the north in the tenth century and ending in the most resistant forms HATH and DOTH in Late Modern English. The focus of attention has been on the final consonant, the shift from -TH to -s.

The puzzling behaviour of this change, i.e. the increasing use of -s in Late Middle English, the subsequent drop for about a century, and the quick growth around 1600, has made us reconsider the traditional approach. In addition to the consonantal variation, it may be useful to discuss this change from the point of view of vowel deletion in the suffix (Nevalainen & Raumolin-Brunberg 2000b). This syncope appears to be part of a long-lasting morphophonemic drift by which English lost the unstressed preconsonantal vowel /e/ in inflectional endings. Both verbal and nominal suffixes were affected, except after a stem-final sibilant. The writings of early modern orthoepists suggest that the form with -s was in fact regarded as a contracted form of the syllabic -ETH.

67

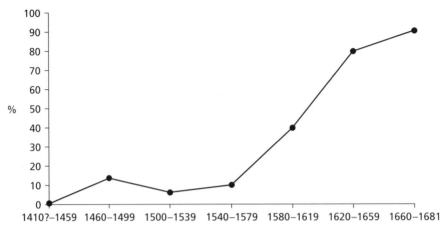

Figure 4.9. The replacement of the third-person singular suffix -TH by -S (excluding HAVE and DO). Percentages of -S. CEEC 1998 and Supplement.

The details of regional variation will be discussed in Chapter 8. Suffice it to say that a considerable difference appears between north and south, as both the suffix -s and the syncope were introduced in the north. It seems that, at least in the south, two different processes are at issue rather than one. In Late Middle English the crucial choice was made between the inflectional consonants (examples 4.27–4.28). As Figure 4.9 indicates, -s did not carry the day. About a hundred years later -s again began to rise. This time the question was more about rivalry between the contracted form -s and the syllabic -ETH than variation between the consonants alone (examples 4.29–4.30).

> (4.27) the next trosty man that **comyth** shall bring hym (George Cely, 1476; CELY, 5)
>
> (4.28) me **semys** it **makys** litell force (Richard Page, 1482?; STONOR, II, 143)
>
> (4.29) by meanes wherof she **resteth** better then she did, **eateth** and **digesteth** her meate reasonably well (John Heveningham, 1624; PASTONK, 66)
>
> (4.30) who **dwells** at Thistleworth (John Chamberlain, 1614; CHAMBER-LAIN, I, 513)

As Figure 4.9 shows, the mid-range of this change occurs between 1580 and 1660. Once again we can testify to a rapid shift, well in harmony with the general idea of changes following the S-pattern.

4.4.8. Periphrastic DO in Affirmative Statements

A great deal of attention has been devoted to periphrastic DO in the literature.[12] Unlike present-day usage with the so-called NICE qualities (Negation, Inversion, Code, Emphasis), DO also frequently appeared in affirmative sentences (examples 4.31–4.34). There were linguistic environments that have been said to promote the use of DO, such as second-person singular subject (example 4.31), past tense (4.32) and preverbal adverbial (4.33). Nurmi (1999b) discovered that, at least in the CEEC Sampler, these features play a rather minor role. For example, DO was only once used with THOU and rarely in the second person at all. Two-thirds of the instances of DO were in the present tense and only one-third in the past. But as Nurmi (1999a: 23–27) argues, the function of DO in the sixteenth century was not grammatical but instead seems to have belonged to the fields of discourse and style. Only later did it acquire the NICE qualities it has today.

(4.31) I se by thy last letter thow **dost desire** much to se me (Katherine Paston, 1625; PASTONK, 82)

(4.32) Allso I have had a great fond myend this iij weckes to dryncke red wyne, for the which I **dyd send** to my brother, hoy sayth (Sabine Johnson, 1545; JOHNSON, 468)

(4.33) Sʳ Jordan & my cosen Collingwood are both here, they **doe** faythfully **promis**, that they will not oppose us tomorrow (Daniel Fleming, 1653; FLEMING, 37)

(4.34) The buyldinges of your noble colledge most prosperouslye and magnyfycently **dothe arryse** in suche wise that (Thomas Cromwell, 1528; CROMWELL, I, 319)

This study counts the occurrences of affirmative DO per 10,000 running words. The results of this method may not be quite as accurate as they would have been if the counting had been performed by using the linguistic variable as a basis. This would have meant counting the occurrences of different variants, including simple forms and possibly other auxiliaries, in clauses where affirmative DO appeared or could have appeared. A methodology test in Nurmi (1999a: 67–69) shows, however, that a frequency count placed twelve CEEC informants practically in the same order as a variable count did.

Figure 4.10. Periphrastic DO in affirmative statements. Frequency of DO per 10,000 words. CEEC 1998. (Based on Nurmi 1999a).

Hence it seems likely that the less laborious frequency count draws a picture that is sufficiently accurate for the description of a general development.

Figure 4.10 shows how the use of affirmative DO increased in the sixteenth century, only to drop after the turn of the century. What is interesting is the timing of the drop during the first decades of the seventeenth century instead of 1575–1600, as argued in Ellegård (1953: 161).

4.4.9. Periphrastic DO in Negative Statements

Another development of DO-periphrasis is its use in negative sentences, in other words one of the above-mentioned NICE qualities. As examples (4.35)–(4.36) from Nurmi (1999a: 141–162) show for the indicative and (4.37)–(4.38) for the subjunctive, negative statements could be produced with or without resorting to periphrastic DO.

> (4.35) Item I **doe not meane** to pase the lease of Redbourne unles I maie have (Nicholas Bacon, 1579; BACON, II, 101)
>
> (4.36) Item I **meane not** to pase eny assuraunce of landes or leases in generall wordes (Nicholas Bacon, 1579; BACON, II, 101)
>
> (4.37) if it **take not** effect according to your mynd (Otwell Johnson, 1546; JOHNSON, 795)
>
> (4.38) if Mr. Cave **do not like** his prices, lett him sett either sorte at xij d more (Otwell Johnson, 1547; JOHNSON, 867)

Figure 4.11 shows the percentage of DO counted from all negated sentences that could have had DO. Clauses with another auxiliary as well as the main verb BE have been excluded as well as some other verbs that never appeared with DO in the CEEC (for details, see Nurmi 1999a: 143).

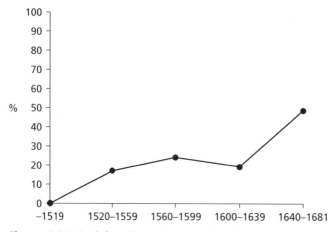

Figure 4.11. Periphrastic DO in negative statements. Percentage of DO from negated sentences where DO could be used. CEEC 1998. (Based on Nurmi 1999a).

As Figure 4.11 indicates, the development of negative DO-periphrasis occurs later than the affirmative: its growth begins only in the first half of the sixteenth century. Its share does not increase to over 30 per cent until the middle of the seventeenth century.

4.4.10. Decline of Multiple Negation

In Middle English sentential negation typically consisted of two parts, NE and NOT. Indefinites in negative clauses were also expressed by negative forms, a sentential negator co-occurring with NO, NEVER, NEITHER, etc. NE, the first element of the sentential negator, was practically lost by the end of the fifteenth century, and multiple negation with indefinites had almost disappeared from most kinds of writing by the end of the seventeenth century.[13] But it did not disappear from the vernacular, and continues to be used in many regional varieties of Present-day English.

In Early Modern English the disappearance of multiple negation is connected with the rise of single negation accompanied by nonassertive indefinites (ANY, EVER, EITHER, etc.). Example (4.39) illustrates a case of multiple negation, and (4.40) single negation followed by the nonassertive indefinite pronoun ANYTHING. Multiple negation could also sometimes appear with nonassertive forms in the sixteenth century, as in the letter by Sir Thomas More in (4.41). The decline of multiple negation was linguistically conditioned: multiple negation was preserved in coordinate and additive structures, typically those containing NOR or NEITHER, much later than in simple constructions; see (4.42).

(4.39) And that sawe y **never** yn **no** place but ther (John Yeme, 1466?; STONOR, I, 78)

(4.40) it hath bene for that I haue **not** hade **anything** to wryt of to your aduauncement. (Thomas Cromwell, 1523; CROMWELL, I, 313)

(4.41) there shall **no** poore neghebore of myne berre **no** losse by **eny** chaunce hapned in my howse. (Thomas More, 1529; MORE, 423)

(4.42) the dewke of Gelder send me **no** vord vat I sale do, **nor** heelpes me **nat** with **notheng**, as Petter sale chove yov. (Edmund de la Pole, 1505; RERUM, I, 254)

Figure 4.12 compares the distributions of multiple and single negation in the CEEC. Instances of single negation only include those with nonassertive indefinites (Nevalainen 1998: 267–272). A further distinction is made between simple and coordinate/additive constructions. As Figure 4.12 shows, multiple negation disappears from simple structures in the course of the sixteenth century, but is retained considerably longer in coordinate and additive constructions. In the last period of our corpus (1660–1681), nearly all simple cases take nonassertive forms, while the corresponding figure for coordinate/additive constructions remains slightly below 80 per cent.

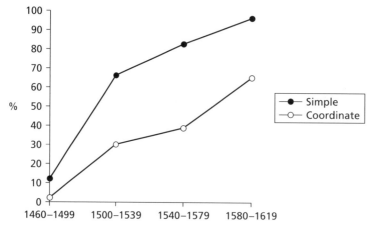

Figure 4.12. Single vs. multiple negation with nonassertive indefinites. Percentages of single negation in simple and coordinate constructions. CEEC 1998 and Supplement.

4.4.11. Inversion after Initial Adverbs and Negators

Unlike Old English, Present-day English is not a verb-second language: sentence-initial adverbials no longer regularly invert the order of the subject and the verb in declaratives. The verb-second order declined in Middle English, but new inversion rules were introduced into the language by later developments. One of them is the renewed grammaticalization of inversion after initial negatives and implied negatives in Early Modern English (Nevalainen 1997).

The loss of the old verb-second rule and the rise of subject-operator inversion after negatives is here studied by contrasting two sets of initial adverbs and coordinators, affirmative (THEN, THEREFORE, THUS, and YET) and negative (NE, NEVER, NEITHER, and NOR). Direct and inverted word-order patterns were both in principle possible with the two sets in Early Modern English. They are illustrated by examples (4.43)–(4.49).

(4.43) **Thus** you perceave what is to be done hierin, etc. (Otwell Johnson, 1548; JOHNSON, 973)

(4.44) and **thus** stande they in altercation, not like to agree, as many thynck. (Henry Southwick, 1545; JOHNSON, 338)

(4.45) thy fathers illnes of his legge haue bine the Cawse of our stay for he was faynt to take Phisike for it: but **yett** it is bigge so that he can not endure on his boote. (Katherine Paston, 1626; PASTONK, 93)

(4.46) I heer so bade newes of the increase of the sikenes at London, that allthough I haue great ocation to haue bine ther, **yett** will I forbear till it shall please god in mearcy to scease it: (Katherine Paston, 1625?; PASTONK, 84)

Figure 4.13. Inversion vs. direct word-order after initial adverbs and negators. Percentage of inversion. CEEC 1996; collection-based search.

(4.47) but **neither** they mowght persuade me to approve that which both faith and my raison condemned: **nor** I mowght dissuade theim from the excusing of that, which all the worlde abhorred. (Thomas Elyot, 1536; ELYOT, 27).

(4.48) I perceyve youre opinion of owre monneyes, which dissentyth not partely from others I have herd of beffore; **neither** dyd I suppose anny better sequele of it. (Anthony Cave, 1551; JOHNSON, 1476)

(4.49) I can now also truly averr, that I have not countenanced any factious persons, **nor** have such persons resorted to me. (Edward Harley, 1665; HARLEY, 241)

When the data are quantified and presented in a sequence of 40–year periods, a striking difference between the affirmative and negative sets emerges in the course of the early modern period. Figure 4.13 presents the relative frequencies of inversion in both sets.

Figure 4.13 shows, first, that inversion after the affirmative items is rare in the correspondence data, and that it all but disappears by the end of the seventeenth century. The opposite is the case with initial negative adverbs and coordinators: they start from zero-inversion in the fifteenth century but reach almost 100 per cent of inversion by the end of the early modern period. The data show that it is the latter half of the sixteenth century that constitutes the steeply rising part of the S-curve.[14]

4.4.12. Relative Pronouns WHICH and THE WHICH

Like the third-person singular suffix, the rivalry between the relative pronouns THE WHICH and WHICH is a development of northern origin.[15] In this

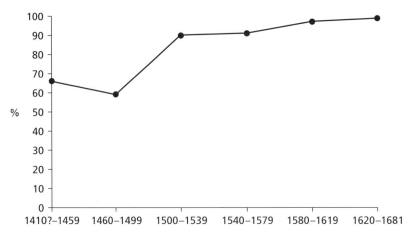

Figure 4.14. Relative pronouns WHICH and THE WHICH. Percentages of WHICH. CEEC 1998 and Supplement.

case it was the northern form THE WHICH that failed to generalize, and its use became marginal as early as the first half of the sixteenth century.

Raumolin-Brunberg (2000) shows that the grammatical profiles of the two pronouns were practically identical until around 1500. Examples (4.50)–(4.51) illustrate the common nonrestrictive use, although restrictive reference also occurred (examples 4.52–4.53). Examples (4.54)–(4.55) represent sentential relative clauses. The relative pronoun in (4.50)–(4.52) is the subject and in (4.53) and (4.55) the object of the relative clause, while (4.54) is an example of adverbial usage. From 1500 onwards, some grammatical specialization took place, so that WHICH was preferred in the subject function and THE WHICH in prepositional phrases.

(4.50) And we shal make a good ende, be þe grace of Oure Lord, **which** haue you in hise gouernance. (Thomas Scales, 1450s; PASTON, II, 196)

(4.51) And as ffor your gownys of chamlet and dublettes of sylke, I have bought hem: **the which** shall plese yow ryght well. (Elizabeth Stonor, 1476; STONOR, II, 19)

(4.52) And Sir, I beseche your maistershipe to delyver to John Burton the moneye **the whyche** is dewe to me. (Godard Oxbryge, 1478; STONOR, II, 49)

(4.53) And I send John Bookyng a copy of the panell **wheche** I shewed yow. (Thomas Howes, 1454; PASTON, II, 106)

(4.54) there com no marchauntys to Caleys for to bye woll nor fellys, for **the weche** ys ryght heuynese for the marchauntys of the Stapyll. (Richard Cely sr, 1477; CELY, 11)

(4.55) it is my part to holde with hym rather than with Danyell in hise right, **which** I wyll do to my pouer. (Thomas Scales, 1450; Paston, II, 34)

4.4.13. Prepositional Phrase vs. Relative Adverb

Another change operating among relative markers is a shift from synthetic adverbs to analytic prepositional phrases.[16] This change did not proceed from synthetic to analytic in a straightforward manner; the pattern was rather analytic – synthetic – analytic. As examples (4.56)–(4.60) show, the prepositional phrases involve pronouns THE WHICH and WHICH, and the adverb has an initial WHERE-element.

The following eight prepositions were investigated for this study: ABOUT, AFTER, BY, ON, TO, UNTO, UPON and WITH. These prepositions were chosen because they did not undergo major semantic or pragmatic changes in Early Modern English. BY, TO and WITH account for the largest numbers of occurrences (examples 4.56–4.60).

(4.56) I recevyd a lettere from you send by Laurens Rede on Fryday laste past, **wherby** I vnderstond that ye had no tythyngys. (Margaret Paston, 1465; Paston, I, 315)

(4.57) she had some twentie of other of lyvelods or of goods, **to the which** my sister, as fare forth as she durst, abode upon; **by the which** they brake and nott concluded. (Godfrey Greene, 1464; Plumpton, 11)

(4.58) with his written & printed intelligence, **wherewith** (& his many other kindenesses) He hath very much obliged mee. (Daniel Fleming, 1670; Fleming, 184)

(4.59) I dout not but I haue satisfied you in honor, as time and comoditie serue, **with wiche** I wil not molest you more. (Elizabeth I, 1594; Royal 1, 109)

(4.60) ther wilbe no more speach of my daughter's parting with her land, **which** she would by no meanes yeald **to**. (Elizabeth Masham, 1629; Barrington, 105)

While the relative adverbs have one form only, the combination of the preposition and the relative pronoun has two alternatives: the preposition may either precede the pronoun (example 4.57) or be stranded (example 4.60).

Figure 4.15 shows that the relative adverbs form the majority of the occurrences until around 1600, with a peak in 1520–1559. The curve of the prepositional phrases is almost a mirror image: a decrease until 1520–1559, then an upward turn, the crossover taking place after 1640. Cases of preposition stranding can be found throughout the data, with a gradual increase from 1560 onwards.

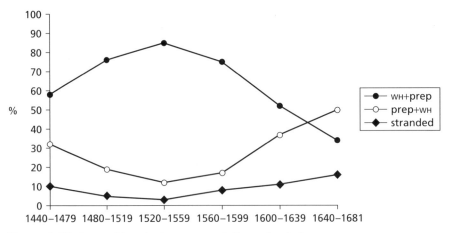

Figure 4.15. Prepositional phrase vs. relative adverb (ABOUT, AFTER, BY, ON, TO, UNTO, UPON, WITH). Percentages. CEEC 1998 and Supplement.

4.4.14. Indefinite Pronouns with Singular Human Reference

Our final example involves as many as four paradigmatic variants. Early Modern English had four alternative types of indefinite pronouns with singular human reference, two of which, the compounds in -BODY and ONE, have remained in the language until our time. Table 4.1. gives the items studied.[17]

The three compound variants have all resulted from grammaticalization. The alternatives in -MAN must have developed very early, since their use as a pronoun goes back to the earliest periods of Old English. On the basis of the *Helsinki Corpus*, the introduction of the other compounds can be timed as follows: EACH ONE and EVERY ONE go back to Early Middle English, NO BODY and SOME BODY to Late Middle English, and the rest, except for NO ONE, were first found in Early Modern English texts (Raumolin-Brunberg & Kahlas-Tarkka 1997: 75). Unlike the *Helsinki Corpus*, a few instances of NO ONE can be found in the CEEC.

Syntactically these compound pronouns share more similarities with full noun phrases than central pronouns. They appear in the genitive and can have a wide range of postmodifiers. The main syntactic difference between the sets of variants is their use in partitive constructions. Unlike the compounds with BODY and MAN, the forms with ONE and the simple variants listed under 'other' could appear in partitive structures, e.g. *none of them, any one of them*. In order to increase the comparability of the material, the partitive structures were excluded from this study.

Examples (4.61)–(4.62) illustrate the alternatives with BODY. Example (4.63) has the most frequent pronoun of the -ONE series, EVERYONE, whereas (4.64) is an example of the MAN variants. Great effort has been made not to in-

Table 4.1. Indefinite pronouns with singular human reference. Compound pronouns and their equivalents

	-BODY	-ONE	-MAN	Other
Assertive	SOME BODY	SOME ONE	SOME MAN	SOME (OTHER)
Nonassertive	ANY BODY	ANY ONE	ANY MAN	ANY (OTHER)
Negative	NO BODY	NO ONE	NO MAN	NONE (OTHER)
Universal	EVERY BODY	EVERY ONE	EVERY MAN	EVERY, EACH
			EACH MAN	

Note: Classification from Quirk *et al.* (1985: 377). Most compounds were spelt as two words in the letters.

clude cases in which MAN refers to a male human being, a human being as opposed to God, or someone's servant. Examples (4.65)–(4.68) illustrate the pronouns classified as 'other'. They show that, contrary to present-day usage, simple pronouns could be employed as independent indefinite pronouns in the singular.

(4.61) I prey yow let Whetley or **some body** spek wyth hym. (John Paston III, 1479; PASTON, I, 616)

(4.62) Thus in hayst, the levyng Lord send youe helthe and **everebode** to His wylle and plesor. (Richard Preston, 1551; JOHNSON, 1243)

(4.63) My dear love to all yours. You must favour me delivering itt perticulerly to **every one**. (Winefrid Thimelby, 1660s; TIXALL, 28)

(4.64) till his 3 last fitts there was no [more] doubt of his safety then of **every man's** that hath an ordinarie tercian ague. (Lucy Russell, 1625; CORNWALLIS, 120)

(4.65) This will I, orelles cawse **some other** to, put into the Secretaryes heade. (Francis Wyndham, 1584; BACON, II, 281)

(4.66) Concerning the mony, it shall be reddy according to your desire, for **any** yow shall appoynt to receave it. (John Holles, 1626; HOLLES, II, 331)

(4.67) Deare Semandra, **none** deserves more love from everybody then you. (Princess Anne, 1679; ROYAL3, 108)

(4.68) that must endure so many chaunges of maisters, and abyde the hazards of **everyes** [SIC] good lyking how good, how faythfull, and how honest soever our service be. (Lodowick Bryskett, 1582; BRYSKETT, 39)

Two curves in Figure 4.16, namely those representing -BODY and -ONE pronouns, gradually rise towards the end of our period. The curve of -MAN forms correspondingly declines, and pronouns classified as 'other' make a rise-fall curve. These trends corroborate the results acquired from the *Helsinki Corpus* (Raumolin-Brunberg 1994: 313).

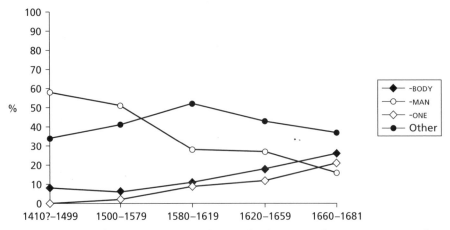

Figure 4.16. Indefinite pronouns with singular human reference. Compound pronouns and their equivalents. Percentages. CEEC 1998.

4.5. Conclusion

Our selection of changes covers all the 270 years under examination, although only one change, the increasing use of the direct object in gerund phrases, was fully operative throughout this period. The fifteenth century attested the first rise of the third-person singular -s, increase in the use of THE WHICH as opposed to WHICH, and growth of relative adverbs. In the sixteenth century YOU replaced YE as second-person subject pronoun, the short forms MY and THY were established, affirmative DO was on the increase, the employment of multiple negation decreased, and WHICH came out as the winner over THE WHICH.

Around the turn of the seventeenth century the use of prop-ONE began to grow, the third-person -s had its second rise, and inversion increased after negative expressions. The second half of the seventeenth century witnessed several changes: the use of possessive ITS expanded, the genitive came to dominate as the noun subject of the gerund, DO-support was increasingly employed in negative sentences, the use of relative adverbs dropped, and the indefinite compounds in -BODY and -ONE increased in frequency. The latest changes, except for negative DO, have in fact not run their course yet, but variation still occurs in Present-day English.

The above compact summary suggests some temporal clusterings of developments. This is probably a result of the interplay of various factors, as changes usually are. However, we would not like to rule out the possibility that their concentration on some specific periods might be associated with specific extralinguistic issues, such as rapid social change. It is worth pointing out that the clusterings we have observed do not follow the traditional period boundary between Middle and Early Modern English around 1500, although, perhaps surprisingly, the S-curves would have looked 'nicer' if our study had begun from the year 1500.

What we have seen in this chapter suggests multiformity of language change rather than uniformity. A great deal depends on the way the changes are analysed, for instance, whether they are discussed in terms of a binary development or as a competition of several rivalling forms. Still, the choice of method can only fine-tune the picture to some extent. What remains, we believe, demonstrates genuine diversity in the way linguistic changes diffuse in speech communities.

Although the S-shaped curve serves as an ideal pattern of the diffusion of language change, several of the fourteen morphosyntactic changes presented in this chapter do not replicate the model in an unequivocal way. Some are more of the roller-coaster type, with rises and falls following each other. In these cases parts of the curves can be related to the S-model. Even with changes complying with the S-pattern, the rate of change varies a great deal. The extremes are the very rapid change from subject YE to YOU and the gradual shift of the object of the gerund from OF-phrases into direct object noun phrases. However, no systematic difference emerges between the behaviour of individual linguistic items and abstract structural patterns.

In the rest of the book our aim is, among other things, to find explanations for the extensive variability attested in this chapter. The changes introduced here form the basis for our discussions but at times these changes will be supplemented with other linguistic material retrieved from the CEEC.

Notes

1. The size of our corpus allows us to assume that for most changes, save the most infrequent phenomena, all linguistic constraints are included and repeated over and over again. On the other hand, it has been argued (Hudson 1996: 202) that linguistic variation tends to be independent of social variation and can be ignored in a study of social variation (see also Labov 1982: 51–52; Romaine 1982a: 193). The interaction between external and internal factors is by no means fully understood yet (e.g. Woods 2001), but our focus on the external can be justified by the need to discover even the most general principles of nonlinguistic conditioning on past varieties of English.

2. We cannot argue that the operation of the S-curve would be fully explained in the literature. It is, for instance, not all that easy to see how the frequency-of-contact argument could be combined with the suggestion that the age by which a person's sound system is stabilized is 17 years (Labov 2001: 447). Taken literally, this claim could exclude all sound changes from adulthood (for the child-based theory of language change, see Croft 2000: 44–53). The accommodation framework, however, has been employed to account for phonological changes made by adults, in particular immigrants (Trudgill 1986). Interestingly, Trudgill (1986: 11) includes language change among the phenomena that carry sufficient salience for becoming a target for accommodation.

3. Words in small capitals are used to cover the spelling variants of the items studied, e.g. ITS for *its, itts, it's*. The forms in small capitals are also used to refer to lexemes such as DO, covering all tenses and inflections.

4. The introduction of the possessive determiner ITS can serve as an example of the time lag. According to the literature, its first attestation goes back to 1598 (Nevalainen & Raumolin-Brunberg 1994a). The first occurrence in the CEEC stems from 1619 (see note 10, Chapter 7).

5. During the compilation process, the *Helsinki Corpus* project team made decisions about the temporal frame of the corpus which came to have a far greater significance for future research than was understood at the time. Concerning the Early Modern English section, as compilers we tried to find texts that would create three periods of contemporary writing (Nevalainen & Raumolin-Brunberg 1989). This was not always possible. We now know that the timespan of 70 years is too long for capturing rapid changes. Nevertheless, the *Helsinki Corpus* has proved its usefulness as structured data for detecting general developments.

6. Although there is also a clausal interpretation of these sentences (omission of the complementizer THAT), they were excluded from our data, as the pronouns in the accusative with infinitive analysis are understood as objects.

   This study has not made any difference between the singular and plural reference of YE and YOU. As most of the letters have been written by one individual to another, the occurrences usually represent singular reference. For research on YE/YOU, see also Kenyon (1914) and Lutz (1998).

7. The letters of one idiosyncratic informant, Dorothy Osborne (1627–1695), have been excluded from this part of the study (see Appendix I).

8. According to Fanego (1996), based on the Helsinki Corpus, prepositional complements account for about 80 per cent of all gerunds. They seem to have led the verbalization process, and hence our figures may be more advanced than the case would have been if we had chosen all gerund phrases. Despite this procedure, some borderline cases remained in the data. -ING forms that had been lexicalized into nouns, e.g. *blessing* 'divine favour', *learning* 'knowledge', *lodging* 'dwelling-place', *painting* 'picture', *reckoning* 'account', and *writing* 'written document' were excluded. Objects which did not vary with the OF-phrase were naturally also excluded, too, e.g. *wishing someone well, giving someone the credit, letting someone know/hear* etc.

   The sociolinguistic literature (e.g. Downes 1998: 99; Labov 2001: 86–90) argues for a long social history of the variation between the alveolar and velar pronunciation of the -ING forms. For this reason we expected to find forms without the final <g> especially in semiliterate people's letters. These cases were infrequent, mostly occuring in functions other than the gerund. Only two people, the lawyer's wife Agnes Paston in the fifteenth century and bailiff John Mounford in the sixteenth, both from East Anglia, used this form with some degree of regularity. Forms in *-end(e), ind(e), ynd(e)* were also checked in the medieval data, but no gerunds were found. See also Raumolin-Brunberg (2002).

   Further studies on the gerund include Houston (1989, 1991) and Moessner (1997).

9. A study of the pronominal subjects was also carried out. Its results showed an overwhelming use of possessive and genitive forms throughout the material (96–100 per cent).

10. It is also possible that some instances of the northern uninflected genitive are included in these figures (see e.g. Klemola 1997).

11. A common approach is to see this change as competition between two suffixes, -TH and -S (e.g. Stein 1987; Ogura & Wang 1996), although there was also a third rival, zero (Holmqvist 1922; Kytö 1993; Nevalainen & Raumolin-Brunberg 2000a; Nevalainen *et al.* 2001). Owing to the laborious search that finding the zero forms in our untagged corpus would involve, this study also comprises the two endings only.

The third-person inflection in a historical context has also been dealt with by Wyld (1936: 332–341), Bambas (1947), Taylor (1987), Stein (1987), Bailey *et al.* (1989), Ferguson (1996), Nevalainen (1996b), Raumolin-Brunberg (1996a, 1996c), and Nevalainen & Raumolin-Brunberg (1998).

It is repeatedly argued in the literature that -S was the ending that was used in spoken language and -TH the one employed in writing. This argument goes back to Holmqvist (1922: 185), who was puzzled by the fact that the northern sibilant, despite not being attested in the Midlands, was found in the writings of Londoners as early as the fifteenth century. This finding contradicted the prevailing idea of the diffusion of language change in dialect contact. It was believed that changes proceeded in a wave-like manner from one adjacent area to another. To solve this apparent problem, Holmqvist suggested that '-S attained general currency in the spoken language . . . probably as early as about 1500'.

It is difficult to understand how people who were barely able to write could have made a grammatical analysis before putting words into writing. They would have had to keep apart nouns with the -S suffixes, which were to be written as spoken, and verbs, for which they should have written -TH where they pronounced [s] at the end of a word. If this is what they were taught to do, we should find at least some hypercorrect -TH endings in nouns. Such occurrences have not been reported anywhere, and they do not appear in our data either. It may be worth adding that discussions of the plural -TH ending do not seem to claim an [s] pronunciation.

The spoken–written dichotomy has also been argued for by referring to seventeenth-century comments on -S occurring in the spoken language and -TH in the written. As our material shows, by the middle of the seventeenth century, -S had become the dominant alternative with an incidence of about 80 per cent of the cases. By this time formality-based textual variation had emerged, so that the conservative -TH was used in more formal types of language, usually written, and -S in informal language, predominantly spoken. For an in-depth discussion of this change, see Nevalainen & Raumolin-Brunberg (2000a, 2000b).

12. We would like to thank Dr Arja Nurmi for letting us use the results of her doctoral dissertation of 1999, based on the CEEC. All examples of periphrastic DO stem from her thesis, and she has redrawn her graphs to comply with the pattern that has been employed here for other changes.

For research on DO-periphrasis, see Rissanen (1985, 1991), Stein (1986, 1990), Tieken-Boon van Ostade (1985, 1987), Kroch (1989), Nevalainen (1991), Gerner (1996), and Klemola (1996).

13. For Middle English, see Mustanoja (1960: 340) and Iyeiri (1999) and for Early Modern English, Singh (1987) and Nevalainen (1998).

14. The spread of negative inversion is also lexically conditioned. NE, which falls out of use in the sixteenth century, fails altogether to catch on with the new rule. NOR is rather slow, too, but does generalize inversion in the seventeenth century. NEITHER, by contrast, clearly favours inversion by the mid-sixteenth century, as does NEVER. This timing pattern partly runs parallel with the decline of

multiple negation, which took a longer time in coordinate and additive constructions than in simple ones.

Parallel results with this study were obtained when these items were analysed in the multigenre *Helsinki Corpus of English Texts* (Kytö & Rissanen 1993; Nevalainen 1997: 207–209) and in a prose corpus covering the periods 1480–1530, 1580–1630 and 1680–1730, discussed in Bækken (1998: 249–275).

15. Studies relevant for this change include Reuter (1937) and Rydén (1966).
16. Relative markers have been the object of numerous historical studies, but the variation between the relative adverb and prepositional phrase has attracted little interest. Schneider (1993) deals with one particular case, OF WHICH.
17. The delimitation of this paradigm with fuzzy edges has not been without its problems. Suffice it to say that we regard the items with MAN as pronouns on the basis of their distribution and semantics. For details, see Raumolin-Brunberg (1994) and Raumolin-Brunberg & Kahlas-Tarkka (1997).

Chapter 5

Apparent Time

Apparent-time studies have the inestimable advantage of making information about temporal developments available in a shorter time
than the developments themselves take. (Chambers 1995: 193)

5.1. Ongoing Change in Relation to Age

In observing **language change in progress**, sociolinguists have had to tackle
the question of time one way or another. As mentioned in Chapter 4, the examination of changes in real time is often impossible for the contemporary
researcher. Developments are so slow that grasping them takes longer than
a researcher's active career or whole lifetime. Useful data on earlier stages
of the language for comparative research are seldom available today, and
they were even rarer 30 years ago when sociolinguistic studies were first
introduced.

An insightful concept to solve this problem is **apparent time**. Tracing a
linguistic change in apparent time means looking at the distribution of
linguistic variables across age levels. In this way conclusions about developments can be drawn from language samples collected within a short period
of time.

Figure 5.1, adapted from Downes (1998: 238), illustrates how the apparent-
time construct is thought to function. The horizontal axis refers to real time,
and the vertical to apparent time. The basic assumption here is that each
generation acquires its language, both use, structure and attitudes, during the
formative years of childhood and youth. Consequently, if a linguistic feature
is observed at a specific point in time, as in Survey 2 in 1950, each generation
uses the form or forms they learnt in their youth. Those who were 60 years
old in 1950 would have acquired their linguistic variants around 1900, a
pattern repeated with each successive younger generation, until we reach
those who were 20 years old and who had only adopted their forms about
10 years before the survey. The 60- and 50-year old informants would have
the same variants in Survey 2 as they did in Survey 1 forty years earlier.

In the case of language change, each successively younger generation
is expected to employ the innovative form more than the previous one; in

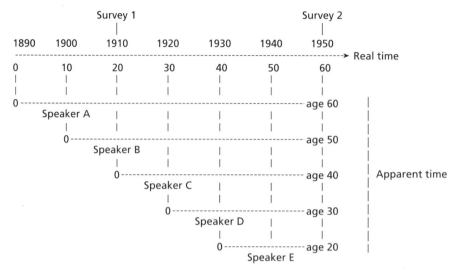

Figure 5.1. Real and apparent time in language change. (Adapted from Downes 1998: 238).

other words, it is not only the variants but also their frequencies that are acquired during the formative years. The emerging pattern[1] then reflects a change in progress, indicating its direction and possibly also its rate of change. If no pattern appears, what we see is most likely **stable linguistic variation**.

The apparent-time construct has proved to be a powerful tool in socio-linguistics. It can give us valuable information about the **transition** of linguistic changes within populations. Several real-time replications of earlier studies have testified to its validity and usefulness (e.g. Labov 1994: 85–112; Bailey *et al.* 1991; Chambers 1998), although diverging results have also been obtained (Trudgill 1988).

There are, however, serious problems connected with the basic assumptions of the apparent-time model. We cannot take for granted that people go on using the same linguistic items all their lives. The literature usually introduces the concept of **age-grading**, i.e. a regular change of linguistic behaviour with age that is repeated in each generation (Labov 1994: 46). For example, middle-aged people have been observed to use the standard language more than the young and old (Downes 1998: 223–224), and teenagers' increased employment of slang and other non-standard varieties is a well-known phenomenon. Labov (2001) argues for an adolescent peak that is especially noticeable in stable sociolinguistic variation. It is clear that the possibility of age-grading must always be taken into consideration when apparent-time surveys are carried out. In addition, it is known that changes in external conditions, such as migration and social mobility, often promote changes in individuals' language.

It is not only **speaker-variables** that explain shifts in peoples' language. The emergence of change has been said to depend on the type of linguistic phenomenon at issue. According to Labov (1994: 83–84), sound change and morphological change typically follow the pattern of **generational change**, while lexical and syntactic changes represent the converse pattern, **communal change**. In the first, individual speakers enter the community with a characteristic frequency of a particular variable, which is maintained throughout their lifetimes. But there are also regular increases in values adopted by individuals and generations, which lead to linguistic change in the speech community. In communal change all members of the community alter their frequencies together or acquire new forms simultaneously. It is obvious that generational change is the pattern that corresponds to the basic idea of apparent time described above. Studies such as Chambers (1998), including apparent-time analyses of some lexical, morphological and phonetic items, suggest that Labov's argument about the connection between type of change and linguistic character may not entirely hold.

Furthermore, the success of apparent-time studies depends heavily on the comparability of the data used. External variables such as gender, socioeconomic background and ethnicity should be kept constant so that the age cohorts all have a similar background (Chambers & Trudgill 1998: 151).

5.2. Apparent Time in Historical Research

An obvious question springs to mind here: why use apparent time when real-time data are available? True, real time definitely forms the basis for diachronic research, as we have seen in Chapter 4. But a combination of real and apparent time can provide exciting information about the manner in which linguistic changes spread among populations. This is where it is possible to take full advantage of the benefit of hindsight, something that present-day studies cannot do.

Here as elsewhere, the application of sociolinguistic methods calls for adaptation in the temporal framework. In this chapter, it is mostly 20-year periods that are considered contemporary. Our real-time data make it possible to conduct several successive apparent-time surveys, providing opportunities for testing of the apparent-time construct in general, and the nature of change, generational versus communal, in particular. New insights into the diffusion of changes will also be acquired by using the time of writing as a starting point. This approach, adapted from Chambers and Trudgill (1998: 164), offers an insight into the role and extent of use of variable grammars in the transition process and into the behaviour of individual informants.

Most problems associated with apparent-time studies in historical linguistics arise from insufficient background data. Even the approximate year of birth of many informants is not available. And as always with long diachrony, external constraints rarely remain constant, as societies tend to change.

5.3. Previous Studies

Traditionally, the concept of apparent time has not belonged to the tools of historical linguistics, although occasional studies using dates of birth can be found. Kemp's (1979) study of headless relatives in Early Modern English made use of the years of birth of the informants. He found a clear correlation between age and an increasing use of WHAT as opposed to THAT, THAT THAT and THAT WHICH. Arnaud (1998) also compared the dates of birth of his informants while investigating the expansion of the progressive in the nineteenth century.

Replications of earlier sociolinguistic studies with the apparent-time model have also become more common, but their time depth hardly exceeds 30 years (Bailey *et al.* 1991; Labov 1994: 85–112). For a historical linguist, Chambers (1998) is more interesting, as it fruitfully combines real and apparent time in a study of changes in twentieth-century Canadian English.

The apparent-time model has been employed in several studies among the 'Sociolinguistics and language history' project team at the University of Helsinki, dealing with issues such as the possessive determiner ITS, second-person subject pronoun, third-person singular inflection, affirmative DO, relativizers and indefinite pronouns.[2] Some of them will be discussed in this chapter.

5.4. Age Cohorts and Individual Participation in Ongoing Changes

5.4.1. Age Cohorts

As mentioned above, one of the advantages of historical studies is the possibility of combining real time and apparent time in a fruitful way. This section gives a survey of a set of ongoing changes among the CEEC informants in both real and apparent time. Let us first have a look at three changes that have been observed over a period of 60 years, broken up into three successive 20-year timespans. The age grouping of the writers is also divided up into 20-year periods.

The changes presented here are relatively late developments, from the end of the sixteenth century and from the seventeenth century. The reason for this choice is the fact that the dates of birth of our early informants are not known as often as for those who lived later. Here again, we shall begin

Table 5.1. Apparent-time analysis of the use of ITS, 1620–1681

Time of writing	1620–1639		1640–1659		1660–1681		Percentage by generation	
	N/Ntotal	%	N/Ntotal	%	N/Ntotal	%	N/Ntotal	%
Year of birth								
Before 1580	0/24	0					0/24	0
1580–1599	1/19	5	0/13	0	3/9	33	4/41	10
1600–1619	1/18	6	17/46	37	7/2	29	25/88	28
1620–1639			12/31	39	30/72	42	42/103	41
After 1639					2/8	25	2/8	25
Total	2/61	3	29/90	32	42/113	37		

Note: N represents the number of occurrences of ITS, Ntotal gives the sum of all instances of the variable (ITS, OF IT, THEREOF). Percentages of ITS. CEEC 1996. Published in Raumolin-Brunberg (1998: 372).

by regarding our informants as members of one language community. However, our subcorpus is socially biased, since the years of birth are better known among the upper and middle ranks than among the lower. The bias is systematic, which in fact leads to an improved commensurability of data in terms of social background.[3]

Our first apparent-time change deals with the introduction of ITS. The possessive determiner ITS is discussed as opposed to its two postnominal alternatives, OF IT and THEREOF, counted together. The totals in Table 5.1. repeat the rapid growth pattern of the use of ITS in real time, with an increase from 3 per cent to 32 to 37 per cent.[4] The right-hand column describes the proportion of ITS in the language of successive generations of informants, in other words in apparent time. It also shows a steady rise, from zero instances to 41 per cent for the age cohort born in 1620–1639. The oldest generation, those born before 1580, do not use the new form at all. Contrary to expectations, the youngest age group has quite a small proportion of ITS, 25 per cent, but the total number of occurrences in their slot, eight, hardly warrants significant conclusions.

The next apparent-time analysis concerns the second rise of the third-person singular suffix -s. Here again, we observe real-time growth in the total use. The choice of the syncopated -s variant increases from 20 per cent for the last two decades of the sixteenth century to 57 per cent and to 75 per cent for the next two 20-year periods (Table 5.2.). The apparent-time column on the right-hand side shows expansion by one generation to the next, from two percent of -s in the language of those who were born before 1530 up to around 80 per cent of people born in 1590 or later.[5]

The above two tables offer interesting results concerning the nature of the progression of changes in language communities. Different usage can be

Table 5.2. Apparent-time analysis of the use of third-person -s vs. -TH, 1580–1639

Time of writing	1580–1599		1600–1619		1620–1639		Percentage by generation	
	N/Ntotal	%	N/Ntotal	%	N/Ntotal	%	N/Ntotal	%
Year of birth								
Before 1530	1/50	2					1/50	2
1530–1549	52/304	17	4/62	7			56/366	15
1550–1569	61/216	28	161/272	59	88/103	85	310/591	52
1570–1589	2/2		139/209	67	161/277	61	302/488	63
1590–1609			26/33	79	278/340	82	304/373	82
1610–1629					58/75	77	58/75	77
Total	116/572	20	330/576	57	585/782	75		

Note: N represents the number of occurrences of -s, Ntotal gives the sum of all instances of the variable (-s and -TH). Percentages of -s. CEEC 1998 and Supplement, quota sample.

observed between the age groups, and hence it seems correct to speak about generational change, which Labov (1994: 84) says is the type of change that occurs in phonology and morphology. All columns in the tables also speak for generational differences in linguistic choices.[6]

On the other hand, if we look at the longitudinal linguistic behaviour of different age groups, the generational pattern does not emerge as expected. The argument that people at an early age acquire the forms and frequencies they will use all their lives does not seem true for these changes, not at least in the quantitative sense. For example, people born 1600–1619 increase their use of ITS with time, as Table 5.1. indicates. Similarly, the age group 1550–1569 in Table 5.2. employs the shorter form -s instead of the syllabic -ETH to a steadily growing degree.

On the basis of this information Labov's argument (1994: 84) about the difference between generational and communal change appears too categorical. It seems that, at least for morphological changes, generational and communal patterns operate simultaneously. Our results do not lend support to Labov's argument (e.g. 2001: 447) that the **critical age** for linguistic change ends at 17, by which age an individual's language has more or less stabilized. However, it is quite possible that phonology, Labov's object of study, differs from morphosyntax in this respect.

In section 5.1 age-grading was discussed, and it was suggested that the possible effects of age-grading should be taken into consideration in apparent-time studies. Tables 5.1. and 5.2. give us an opportunity to compare the linguistic choices of similar age groups, for instance the oldest and the youngest speakers, during different periods. Table 5.2. shows that the oldest speakers hardly choose the new form at all until the last period when

Table 5.3. Apparent-time analysis of the diminishing use of relative adverbs, 1620–1681

Time of writing	1620–1639		1640–1659		1660–1681		Percentage by generation	
	N/Ntotal	%	N/Ntotal	%	N/Ntotal	%	N/Ntotal	%
Year of birth								
1550–1569	12/31	39	3/8	38	0/2		15/41	37
1570–1589	13/37	35	23/45	51	12/25	48	48/107	45
1590–1609	26/44	59	10/31	32	24/59	41	60/134	45
1610–1629	1/2		0/3		19/95	20	20/100	20
1630–1649					7/14	50	7/14	50
Total	52/114	46	36/87	41	62/195	32		

Note: N represents the number of occurrences of relative adverbs (WHERE plus ABOUT, AFTER, BY, ON, TO, UNTO, UPON, WITH). Ntotal gives the sum of all instances of the variable (relative adverbs and prepositional phrases with (THE) WHICH plus ABOUT, AFTER, BY, ON, TO, UNTO, UPON, WITH, either pied piping or stranding). Percentages of relative adverbs. CEEC 1998 and Supplement.

the use of -s almost explodes (from 2 and 7 per cent to 85 per cent). The very youngest generation, those below 30 years of age, do not change their usage between the second and third period at all (79 and 77 per cent). It seems that, whereas in the middle period the oldest informants had not begun to use the new form, during the third period 1620–1639 all age groups had the -s suffix as their major alternative.

Table 5.3. describes a development in which the apparent-time model does not work as nicely as for the other two changes. The object of study is the use of relative adverbs (e.g. WHEREBY) as opposed to prepositional phrases with THE WHICH and WHICH (e.g. BY (THE) WHICH). Relative adverbs decreased in frequency in the seventeenth century, as the real-time totals show.[7] Here we would expect diminishing use by the generation, but that only happens between the age groups 1590–1609 and 1610–1629, and a rise follows this drop. On the other hand, if we exclude this last rise because of the small number of occurrences, and only look at the the middle and the last period, the expected fall can be discerned in the use of adverbs among the younger generations. Although Table 5.3. does not present as neat a development as the other two, it nevertheless indicates the expected direction of change.

The above results as well as earlier studies carried out with the CEEC material data show that the combination of real- and apparent-time analysis increases our understanding of the way linguistic changes progress among populations. It suggests that generational and communal change go hand in hand.

As mentioned above, the most acute difficulty with diachronic apparent-time studies is connected with the data, i.e. the lack of birth dates of a large

Table 5.4. The subject pronoun YOU **vs.** YE **and third-person singular suffix** -S **vs.** -TH **(excluding** HAVE **and** DO**) in London wool merchants' language**

Time of writing	1472–1488 Cely family		1542–1553 Johnson circle	
YOU VS. YE	N/Ntotal	%	N/Ntotal	%
Older generation	0/126	0	29/446	7
Younger generation	5/231	2	336/1073	31
Supplementary corpus	45/222	20	106/107	99
-S VS. -TH				
Older generation	0/14	0	27/127	21
Younger generation	96/136	71	22/400	6
Supplementary corpus	19/93	20	2/78	3

Note: N represents the number of occurrences of YOU and -S, respectively, Ntotal the sum of all instances of the variables (YOU and YE; -S and -TH). Percentages of YOU and -S, respectively. CEEC 1996. Adapted from Nevalainen and Raumolin-Brunberg (1998).

proportion of informants. The missing years of birth can be compensated for by choosing informants from one and the same family, in which case the relative age of the people is known to us. Parents, children and grandchildren as well as masters and apprentices represent different generations, although we do not know their exact lifespans. Even better, the social and geographical settings of families either remain constant or involve changes that can be used in interpretations.

Table 5.4. describes two ongoing changes in the Late Middle and Early Modern English in the language of two wealthy wool-merchant families active in London and Calais. Five people of the medieval Cely family have left letters to posterity: Richard Cely senior, his brother John, and Richard's three sons Robert, Richard and George (for details, see Hanham 1985). As regards the sixteenth-century Johnson family, there are letters by three brothers, John, Otwell and Richard. Their correspondence has been complemented by letters written by Anthony Cave, John's and Richard's master, representing the older generation, and John Johnson's brother-in-law, a wool-merchant called Ambrose Saunders (for details, see Winchester 1955). To make sure that the usage among the Celys and Johnsons was not fully idiosyncratic, the family corpora were supplemented by letters written by other contemporary wool-merchants.[8] (For further details, see Raumolin-Brunberg 1996a.)

As Table 5.4. indicates, the older generation of Celys did not participate in either of the changes at all. The younger Celys seem quite advanced in their use of the -s suffix, but their employment of YOU lagged behind their peers' usage. Seventy years later, both the older and the younger generation of the Johnson circle had higher figures for their use of YOU than the Celys, but they appear quite conservative in relation to their contemporaries. As regards the choice of the third-person suffix, the apparent-time data testify to what we have seen to happen in real time in section 4.4.7. above, i.e. a reversal of the variants. The younger generation have a smaller frequency of -s than the older. In this change, the two Cely generations represent a case in which the apparent-time analysis does not predict correctly the future course of the developments. Seen against the general background of social stratification to be presented in Chapter 7, this shift seems to be linked with Labov's argument (2001: 76) that, in a change from below, a reversal may take place as correction from above. The interior social groups, represented by merchants in our case, are likely to react to changes in the social value of particular linguistic variants.

The range of variation among the younger generation, for both the Celys and the Johnsons, is very broad. As regards the third-person suffix of the younger Celys, the use of -s varies between zero and 95 per cent, while the employment of YOU among the younger Johnson circle extends from 3 to 98 per cent (Nevalainen & Raumolin-Brunberg 1998). This variation is not easy to explain, but some factors might be found in the regional background of the families (see section 8.3.).[9]

Using family members as informants for a close study can be illuminating even if the years of birth are known, since this method lets us keep the external constraints under control. For instance, interesting results have been acquired from a comparison of the language of Lord Keeper and Privy Councillor Sir Nicholas Bacon, born in 1510, with the variants chosen by his two sons Nathaniel, probably born in 1546, and Edward, born in 1548, both country gentlemen from East Anglia. Their letters are available from 1569 to 1594.

All three informants had adopted YOU as their second-person subject pronoun, except that the father had a few instances of YE (2 per cent). Sir Nicholas only used relative adverbs, such as WHEREBY, while both sons frequently chose the analytic alternative, the prepositional phrase, e.g. BY WHICH. Nathaniel's score is 39 per cent (15 out of 39 occurrences) and Edward's 60 per cent (3 out of 5). Similarly, the father was more conservative in his choice of the object of the gerund, as he only used the OF- phrase, like in *for usynge of it*[10], whereas Nathaniel and Edward favoured the zero form, as in *of recovering his money*[11] (53 per cent, 65/123, and 81 per cent, 13/16, respectively). The behaviour of the two generations creates a good apparent-time pattern, the sons preferring the incoming alternatives.

In the use of the third-person singular this pattern is not repeated. Sir Nicholas was the most advanced user of -s in the family, 13 per cent (9 out of 68 occurrences), while Edward had no -s suffixes at all and Nathaniel only used it in the phrase METHINKS. This happened during a time when the use of -s was undergoing a rapid increase (Figure 4.9 in Chapter 4), and an apparent-time pattern could be expected.

It seems that the different behaviour within the Bacon family can be explained by geographical and social differences. Sir Nicholas was a government official who spent much time in London, whereas the sons moved in narrower spheres of life in East Anglia. As London was leading the change from -TH to -S, it was natural of the father to participate in this change, while the sons relied on their local -TH variant. Regional differences will be discussed in greater detail in Chapter 8.

5.4.2. Individuals in Successive Periods of Time

While in the former section informants were grouped in accordance with their age at the time of writing, this section uses their linguistic choices as the criteria for modelling diffusion. In other words, linguistic behaviour is chosen as the independent variable and age the dependent one. This approach, occasionally used in sociolinguistics (Downes 1998: 110), offers here not only a way of bypassing the problem of the undocumented years of birth but also an opportunity for a micro-level examination of ongoing changes.

In this section we shall examine the progression of three changes for a period of 100 years each, divided into five 20-year subperiods. As above, each of these 20-year periods is intended to represent contemporaneous writing. The changes include subject YOU versus YE, third-person singular inflection, and relative pronoun WHICH versus THE WHICH. All informants with 10 occurrences or more during each 20-year period are included, some twice or even three times, if their letters stretch over a time that crosses the period boundaries. The writers are introduced as numbers in the graphs, and the lists of names, years of birth, and individual scores representing the percentage of the new form of the total of occurrences in each informant's writing are given in Appendixes 5.1.–5.3. A similar approach was used in Devitt (1989: 39–46) for modelling the diffusion of changes from one genre to another.

Figure 5.2 describes the replacement of subject YE by YOU. The change begins with a few early adopters, but it takes only 40 years until the majority of the informants have the new form as a variant. As 5.2(d) indicates, during 1540–1559, the time of the letters of the Johnson circle, approximately one-third still used the old form YE, another third had a mixed usage, and the remaining third had begun to use YOU invariably or nearly so. Given this background, it may not be surprising that the younger Johnsons did not favour one and the same form of the second-person pronoun.

With time, more and more people gave up the old form altogether and readopted a grammar with one alternative only, this time the new form YOU. As we have seen before, this is a rapid change, running its course during the 100 years under examination.

Figure 5.3 describes the second rise of the third-person singular -S as opposed to -TH. The pattern we see in the five successive graphs resembles

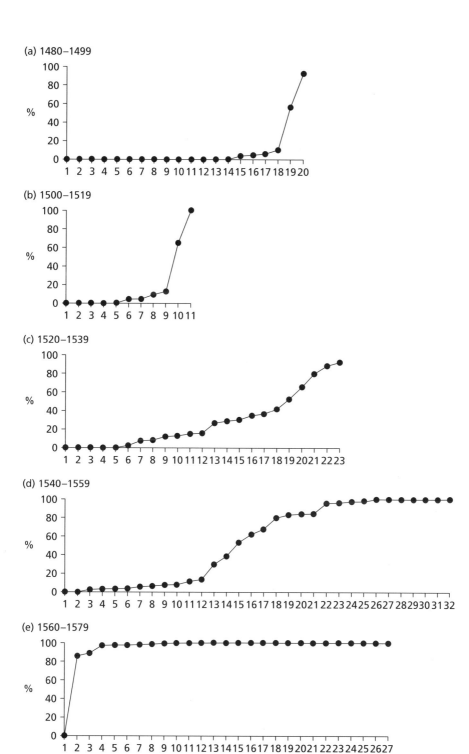

Figure 5.2. Adoption of subject *you* by individual informants 1480–1579. CEEC 1998 and Supplement.

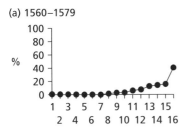

(a) 1560–1579

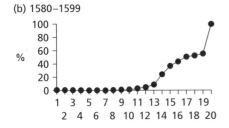

(b) 1580–1599

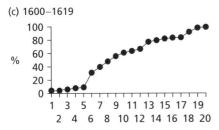

(c) 1600–1619

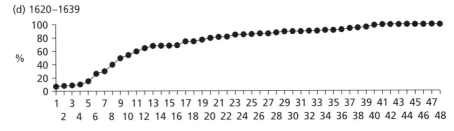

(d) 1620–1639

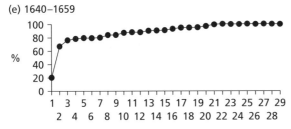

(e) 1640–1659

Figure 5.3. Use of third-person singular -s by individual writers 1560–1659. CEEC 1998 and Supplement.

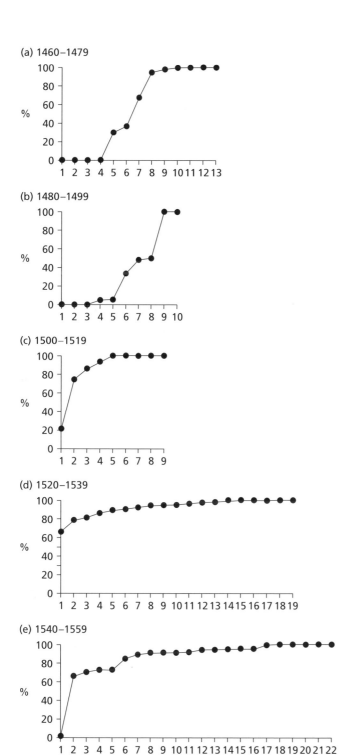

Figure 5.4. Use of relativizer WHICH by individual informants 1460–1559. CEEC 1998 and Supplement.

that shown in the adoption of YOU. Here the early adopters do not reach the 100-per-cent use as quickly as was the case with YOU. On the other hand, during the middle period, presented in Figure 5.3(c), the new -s form appears more popular than YOU in the corresponding Figure 5.2(c). The greatest difference between the shapes of the graphs of these two changes emerges in the fourth period (5.2d and 5.3d), in which early seventeenth-century informants appear to favour the new form -s to a larger extent than their countrymen and -women preferred YOU eighty years earlier. The last figure shows that, despite the high popularity of -s, several writers also use the older suffix -TH as a minor variant.

The third change, variation between the relative pronouns WHICH and THE WHICH, creates patterns that differ from the developments examined above (Figure 5.4.). In the fifteenth century, there was an almost dichotomous choice between the variants. From the third period onwards the situation changes, and the role of THE WHICH clearly diminishes, although during the last period we still find one person who only uses THE WHICH, namely Sabine Johnson, whom we first met in Chapter 1.

A look at the years of birth in Appendixes 5.1.–5.3. offers a new angle on the question of age. According to the apparent-time model, during each period the youngest people could be expected to lead the change. However, our informants cannot be divided into neat age groups according to their choice of linguistic variants. But a closer look reveals that several older informants favour the older variants. For instance, Richard Fox, born in 1447, only used YE in 1500–1519, and Matthew Hutton, born in 1529, preferred -TH as his third-person suffix when writing in 1600–1619. Similarly, the youngest people can be found among those who had adopted the new form as their main variant. For example, those born in 1620 or later all used -s in over 90 per cent of the cases in 1640–1659, and in 1540–1559 the youngest person with a known date of birth, Princess, later Queen Elizabeth I, born in 1533, was a 100-per-cent user of YOU.

Still, there is no unfailing correspondence between the age of an informant and his or her choice of variant. From this we can conclude that the apparent-time hypothesis does not operate uniformly when the whole country is considered one language community. Undoubtedly, many factors other than age play a role here, which is, of course, to be expected. For example, in Appendix 5.2., periods (b) and (c), the domicile, in this case London, seems more important than age. In both periods, the most advanced users of -s are Londoners, Philip Henslowe and John Chamberlain for period (b), and Chamberlain and Robert Daborne for (c). Observations like this call for care in the interpretation of the results of the apparent-time studies in section 5.4.1.

On the other hand, the appendixes also corroborate the trends detected above. When we look at the informants about whom we have data from two or more successive periods, both change and stability stand out. For

Table 5.5. Proportion of informants with variable grammar

	Period (a) %	Period (b) %	Period (c) %	Period (d) %	Period (e) %
YOU VS. YE	15 (1480–99)	18 (1500–19)	61 (1520–39)	34 (1540–59)	7 (1560–79
-S VS. -TH	19 (1560–79)	30 (1580–99)	60 (1600–19)	52 (1620–39)	45 (1640–59)
WHICH VS. THE WHICH	23 (1460–79)	30 (1480–99)	33 (1500–19)	26 (1520–39)	27 (1540–59)

instance, Appendix 5.2. contains several people who did not change their choice of the third-person singular suffix, namely Francis Hastings, Edward Bacon, Francis Wyndham, John Chamberlain, Nathaniel Bacon II, Lucy Russell, Thomas Peyton, and Brilliana Harley (in chronological order). The following people, in turn, did change their usage: Philip Gawdy, John Holles, Thomas Wentworth, Thomas Howard II, Henry Oxinden of Barham, and Elizabeth, Queen of Bohemia.

To some degree at least, the former group supports the idea of generational change, people acquiring their variants in their childhood or youth and keeping them and their frequencies stable all their lives. The second group relates to communal change, people changing their language during their lifetimes, although the present examination does not necessarily testify to their doing it simultaneously. Our material again suggests that generational and communal change proceed hand in hand, some people following one pattern, some others the other, depending on the change.

The three figures and appendixes also allow us to compare the developments in terms of the proportion of informants with a variable grammar. Table 5.5. gives the percentages concerning the three changes. The percentages have been counted as follows: if the individual score falls between 0 and 10, or 90 and 100, the person has been considered to have an invariable grammar. This means that an occasional occurrence of the minority variant does not change the overall impression. The remaining informants are considered to have a variable grammar, using both the old and new variants in parallel.

Different profiles emerge from Table 5.5. In the case of the second-person pronoun, both the increase and decrease in the number of those who have a mixed usage are quite sharp. The third-person singular suffix has the same peak percentage in the (c) period, 60 per cent, but the development is much smoother, and even in the last period the share of people with a variable is 45 per cent. The relative pronoun, on the other hand, behaves differently, as only about one-third of the informants at any stage have a variable grammar in this change.[12]

Why then should the extent of the use of a variable grammar vary between the changes? One obvious explanation is linguistic embedding. As regards YOU versus YE, after the introduction of the change in ambiguous linguistic contexts such as optative clauses (see example (4.4) in Chapter 4), the shift from subject YE to YOU seems to have taken place in all linguistic contexts. The slower progression with the third-person singular finds its explanation in linguistic factors, such as the later introduction of -s after sibilants and the general process of lexical diffusion (Ogura & Wang 1996). In the sixteenth century, grammatical specialization took place in the employment of THE WHICH, which became rare except for prepositional phrases. This nevertheless supported the use of THE WHICH as a minority variant. On the other hand, THE WHICH was never a majority variant in the speech community as a whole (Raumolin-Brunberg 2000).

Other explanations for the maintenance of variable grammars can be found in social contexts. Variation according to social order, gender, dialect, register and genre, especially when elements develop into social markers, certainly supports the preservation of multi-member variables.[13] It is possible for constraints like these to remain in the language for very long periods of time, as the use of YE and the -TH suffix in the King James Bible indicates.

Our final point in this section deals with the relation of the apparent-time construct to the S-curve. As suggested by Chambers and Trudgill (1998: 164), Figures 5.1–5.3 can be interpreted as S-curves, although the patterns are not as smooth as the aggregate graphs in Chapter 4. What is interesting is that the shape of the middle period, the curve in (c), describing a time when the use of a variable grammar is at its highest, varies a great deal. With the second-person pronoun, the slope is gentler than with the third-person suffix. As regards the relative pronouns, half of the informants have reached the 100-per-cent level of the new form at this stage.

Moreover, a comparison of Figures 5.1–5.3 with the real-time curves shows that the middle period falls on different phases of the S-curve. Figure 1 in Appendix I, with corresponding 20-year intervals, suggests that the (c) period represents the new-and-vigorous phase (c. 30 per cent of YOU) for the second- person pronoun (1520–1539), while the corresponding time for third-person suffix (1600–1619) is mid-range (c. 60 per cent of -s). WHICH versus THE WHICH is different again, showing a practically completed state, over 90 per cent of WHICH (Figure 4.14). Although it is difficult to interpret these findings, it may not be ill-advised to connect them with the varying interaction of constraints and the rate of change.

5.5. Conclusion

Age as an external constraint has most often been taken for granted as a factor with a solid biological basis. Its sociocultural context has not been studied much, and, as this study suggests, more information is needed about the linguistic behaviour of people of different ages. Historical data provide opportunities for longitudinal studies of some individuals' language from relatively long periods of time.

This chapter suggests that morphosyntactic changes spread in the speech community in both a communal and a generational manner. It has become evident that some people change their language during their lifetimes while others do not. Why this happens is a challenging research problem. Reasons can be sought in the personal histories of individuals – a matter that emphasizes the role of micro-level studies. A step in this direction has been taken in our analysis of the linguistic behaviour of individuals during ongoing changes. The proportion of people who participate in each change varies with time. The highest incidence of a variable grammar fluctuates and does not coincide with the same area in the S-curve of the different changes.

In this chapter we hope to have shown that the apparent-time analysis of historical data can provide new information about the way linguistic changes diffuse among people, hence addressing the general problem of transition. One advantage of the combination of real- and apparent-time approaches is theoretical: the validity of the apparent-time construct can be tested. Our data show that, although the apparent-time analysis often correctly predicts the progression of an individual change, counterexamples also occur. The existence of counterexamples cannot be explained by age models but has to be analysed with other tools, both linguistic and nonlinguistic. In the end, age is just one dimension in an individual's social space.

Notes

1. The term 'age-grading', which Downes (1998: 238–239) uses in this context, is problematic, since it has been employed with two different meanings. On the one hand, it can refer to the pattern observed in an analysis of the language of successive generations in which younger people use the new form more than older people. This would make it a basic concept for apparent-time studies. However, the term has also been frequently used to refer to changes in which the use of a variant or variants recurs or increases at a particular age in successive generations (Chambers 1995: 188; Labov 2001: 76). This is the meaning we have chosen to use in this book.

2. The apparent-time approach has been employed in the following CEEC studies: Nurmi (1996, 1999a), Raumolin-Brunberg (1996a, 1998), Raumolin-Brunberg & Nevalainen (1997), Raumolin-Brunberg & Nurmi (1997), and Nevalainen & Raumolin-Brunberg (1998).

3. Labov (2001: 77–78) points out that, in comparisons between apparent-time and real-time data, both age and social class distributions should be taken into consideration. Unfortunately, in this respect, our data are not sufficient for crosstabulations. However, upper-rank bias helps in our interpretations. It should also be kept in mind that, although the dates of birth are not known for all informants, all letters included in the CEEC have been dated with an accuracy of one decade.

4. The change from 3 to 32 per cent is statistically significant at the 0.001 level, whereas the difference between the second and third period is not statistically significant. When all data are taken into account, (i.e. including those informants whose years of birth are not known), as is the case in Figure 4.5, the change is statistically significant (see also Raumolin-Brunberg 1998: 373). The differences between the generations are statistically significant.

5. In Table 5.2. all differences in the totals and the generation column are statistically significant except the difference between the last two age groups, those born 1590–1609 and 1610–1639.

6. The fact that the second oldest age group in 1620–1639 used fewer -s forms than the other groups might also be significant. It would be tempting to suggest that this phenomenon reflected the tendency of middle-aged people to employ standard forms to a greater extent than the young and old (Downes 1998: 223–224). However, we must not forget that in the early seventeenth century there was no codified standard language, but the fact that -TH was more common in formal language may be of importance here.

7. In the totals the differences between the adjacent periods are not statistically significant, whereas the difference between the first and the third period is ($p<0.05$). In the generation column the difference between the age cohorts 1590–1609 and 1610–1629 is statistically significant ($p<0.001$) and that between those born 1610–1629 and 1630–1649 is also significant ($p<0.05$).

8. The supplementary corpus for 1472–1488 contains letters by Thomas Betson, William Cely, John Dalton, Thomas Kesten and William Maryon. The sixteenth-century data are supplemented by material written by Robert Andrew, Henry Southwick and Bartholomew Warner. For their backgrounds, see Raumolin-Brunberg (1996a: 94–97).

9. The editor of the Cely letters, Alison Hanham, suggests on the basis of some spellings that Richard Junior might have been educated in the north and hence his frequent use of -s would be dialectal (1985: 8–9). There does not seem to be any external evidence for his stay in the north. Earlier research indicates how difficult it is to locate writers of the late fifteenth century on linguistic criteria, as the origin of the Cely family has been placed both in the west (Malden 1900) and the east (Kihlbom 1926; Wyld 1936: 64).

10. Sir Nicholas Bacon 1572, BACON I, 29.

11. Nathaniel Bacon 1573, BACON I, 95.

12. In a study of language change in 20th-century Canadian English, (Chambers 1998) has also tested the parallel use of old and new variants. The highest percentage Chambers gives is 12. His method is very different, as he has used questionnaires, and so the figures are not comparable with our quantitative results.

13. One of the reasons for allowing a ten-per-cent margin for invariable usage is set phrases. The fact that Sabine Johnson only uses the third-person suffix -TH in the phrase *God knowth* and Nathaniel Bacon -s in *methinks* hardly lets us draw the conclusion that these suffixes belonged to their active inventory of grammatical elements.

Appendix 5.1.

The informants for Figure 5.1. Subject YOU vs. YE

No.	Name	Year of birth	Individual score
(a) 1480–1499			
1	De Vere John	1443	0.0
2	Richard III	1452	0.0
3	Radcliffe John	1452?	0.0
4	Henry VII	1457	0.0
5	Paston William III	1459	0.0
6	Cely Richard I		0.0
7	Cely Richard II		0.0
8	Colet Henry		0.0
9	Elmes Walter		0.0
10	Germyn Richard		0.0
11	Maryon William		0.0
12	Paston Edmond II		0.0
13	Paston Margery		0.0
14	Stallworth Simon		0.0
15	Plumpton Edward		3.9
16	Cely William		4.5
17	Cely George		5.9
18	Percy Henry 4	1446	10.0
19	Dalton John		56.5
20	Kesten Thomas		92.3
(b) 1500–1519			
1	Fox Richard	1447	0.0
2	Wolsey Thomas	1473?	0.0
3	Clifton Anne		0.0
4	Eyre Robert		0.0
5	Killingworth Thomas		0.0
6	Henry VII	1457	4.3
7	Plumpton Robenett		4.5
8	Gascoigne William	1468	9.1
9	Plumpton Agnes		12.5
10	Pole Germayn	1483?	64.9
11	De la Pole Edmund	1472	100.0
(c) 1520–1539			
1	Wolsey Thomas	1473?	0.0
2	Clifford Thomas	1493?	0.0
3	Betts Elizabeth		0.0
4	Brereton Randolph		0.0

5	Godbehere Gilbert		0.0
6	Stanley Edward	1508	2.3
7	Gardiner Stephen	1497?	7.5
8	Radcliffe Alice		8.3
9	Elyot Thomas	1490?	11.4
10	Howard Thomas 3	1473	12.5
11	Percy Henry 6	1502?	14.7
12	Fitzalan William	1476	15.4
13	Darby Thomas		25.7
14	Cromwell Thomas	1485?	28.3
15	Bonner Edmund	1500?	30.0
16	Brandon Charles	1484	34.6
17	Smyttyng Edward		35.7
18	Wyatt Thomas	1503	41.5
19	Henry VIII	1491	52.5
20	Plantagenet Honor	1493?	65.2
21	More Thomas	1478	79.5
22	Willoughby Edward		88.0
23	Grey Henry 3		91.7

(d) 1540–1559

1	Cromwell Thomas	1485?	0.0
2	Garbrand Henry		0.0
3	Breten Christopher		2.5
4	Johnson Richard	1521?	3.1
5	Johnson John	1514?	3.3
6	Preston Richard		3.7
7	Savill Henry		5.6
8	Cave Anthony		6.5
9	Master John		7.1
10	Parr Catherine	1512	7.7
11	Gardiner Stephen	1497?	11.3
12	Wyatt Thomas	1503	13.0
13	Stanley Edward	1508	30.0
14	Coope John		38.5
15	Smith Thomas	1513	53.3
16	Saunders Ambrose		61.8
17	Paget William	1505	67.7
18	Henry VIII	1491	80.0
19	Dodington John		83.3
20	Sandell Richard		84.2
21	Graunt George		84.6
22	Andrew Robert		95.5
23	Johnson Sabine		96.4

24	Johnson Otwell		97.6
25	Saxby Thomas		98.1
26	Elizabeth I	1533	100.0
27	Phillipson Thomas		100.0
28	Saunders Laurence		100.0
29	Saunders Robert		100.0
30	Southwick Henry		100.0
31	Tupholme John		100.0
32	Warner Bartholomew		100.0

(e) 1560–1579

1	Grindall Edmund	1519	0.0
2	Saunders John		85.7
3	Parker Matthew	1504	88.5
4	Robertes Thomas		97.0
5	Harvey Gabriel	1545?	97.1
6	Hastings Francis	1546?	97.5
7	Gardiner George	1535?	98.0
8	Bacon Nicholas I	1510?	98.3
9	Parkhurst John	1511	98.9
10	Gresham Thomas	1519?	100.0
11	Cecil William	1520	100.0
12	Dudley Ambrose	1528?	100.0
13	Dudley Robert	1533	100.0
14	Heydon William	1540	100.0
15	Bacon Nathaniel I	1546?	100.0
16	Bacon Edward	1548?	100.0
17	Allen William	1532	100.0
18	Bacon Anne		100.0
19	Baker John		100.0
20	Barwick Robert		100.0
21	Bentham Thomas	1513	100.0
22	Calthorpe Charles		100.0
23	Mounford John		100.0
24	Stanhowe Edward		100.0
25	Thimelthorpe George		100.0
26	Wood Thomas		100.0
27	Wyndham Francis		100.0

Note to Appendix 5.1. The Arabic numerals following a name refer to the ordinals occurring in titles, such as the fourth, fifth and sixth Earl of Northumberland, who all were called Henry Percy. This type of reference is made to the following members of the nobility:

Grey Henry 3   Third Marquis of Dorset, Duke of Suffolk
Howard Thomas 3   Third Duke of Norfolk

Percy Henry 4   Fourth Earl of Northumberland
Percy Henry 5   Fifth Earl of Northumberland
Percy Henry 6   Sixth Earl of Northumberland

The Roman numerals are used for kings and queens in the conventional manner as well as for two or more untitled people with the same name.

Appendix 5.2.

Informants for Figure 5.2. 3rd sg -s vs. -th

No.	Name	Year of birth	Individual score
(a) 1560–1579			
1	Bentham Thomas	1513	0.0
2	Allen William	1532	0.0
3	Hastings Francis	1546?	0.0
4	Bacon Edward	1548?	0.0
5	Bacon Anne		0.0
6	Becon John		0.0
7	Drury Stephen		0.0
8	Bacon Nathaniel I	1546?	1.7
9	Wyndham Francis		3.2
10	Wood Thomas		3.3
11	Parkhurst John	1511	5.9
12	Gresham Thomas	1519?	7.7
13	Bacon Nicholas I	1510?	13.2
14	Gardiner George	1535?	14.3
15	Baker John		15.4
16	Harvey Gabriel	1545?	39.3
(b) 1580–1599			
1	Hastings Francis	1546?	0.0
2	Bacon Edward	1548?	0.0
3	Edmondes Thomas	1564?	0.0
4	Downing William		0.0
5	D'Oyly Elizabeth		0.0
6	Drury Stephen		0.0
7	Scrope Katharine		0.0
8	Wyndham Francis		0.0
9	Cecil William	1520	0.6
10	Verstegan Richard	1550?	0.9
11	Walsingham Francis	1530?	2.3
12	Bryskett Lodowick	1545?	4.3
13	Bacon Nathaniel I	1546?	8.0
14	Gawdy Philip	1562	23.5

15	Thynne Joan	1558	36.4
16	Cecil Robert	1563	42.6
17	Elizabeth I	1533	50.0
18	Dudley Robert	1533	51.6
19	Henslowe Philip		54.6
20	Chamberlain John	1554	100.0

(c) 1600–1619

1	Hastings Francis	1546?	3.0
2	Fitzherbert Thomas	1552	3.6
3	Hutton Matthew	1529	5.5
4	Littleton Muriel		7.1
5	Bacon Nathaniel II	1585	8.3
6	Stockwell Thomas		30.8
7	Stuart Arabella	1575	39.7
8	Gawdy Philip	1562	47.8
9	Holles John	1565?	55.9
10	Antony Anthony		60.7
11	Pory John	1572	63.2
12	Lambert Hester		66.7
13	Harington John I	1561?	77.1
14	Wentworth Thomas	1593	79.3
15	Howard Thomas II	1585	81.8
16	Hoskyns John I	1566	83.3
17	Jonson Ben	1572	83.3
18	Russell Lucy	1582	91.2
19	Chamberlain John	1554	98.2
20	Daborne Robert		100.0

(d) 1620–1639

1	Lowther Christopher	1611	7.1
2	Bacon Nathaniel II	1585	8.0
3	Heveningham John	1577	8.7
4	Ferrar Batsheba		10.0
5	Montagu Richard	1577	15.1
6	Oxinden Henry of Barham	1608	26.7
7	Gawdy Lettice		30.0
8	Bacon Nicholas III	1617	40.0
9	Chantrell William		50.0
10	Rogers Ezekiel	1584?	54.5
11	Harrison James		60.0
12	Paston Katherine	1578	65.0
13	Ferrar John I	1590	68.4
14	Hoskyns John I	1566	68.4
15	Ferrar Nicholas	1593	68.8

16	Harris Francis		69.2
17	Oxinden James II	1612	75.0
18	Elizabeth of Bohemia	1596	75.0
19	Barrington Judith		77.4
20	Williams Roger	1604	80.0
21	Meux William		81.8
22	Smyth Elizabeth		81.8
23	Holles John	1565?	85.0
24	Masham Elizabeth		85.3
25	Coppin Thomas		85.7
26	Wentworth Thomas	1593	86.7
27	Meautys Thomas I		86.7
28	Meautys Thomas II		88.2
29	Wandesford Christopher	1592	89.7
30	Oxinden James I		90.0
31	Smith Stephen		90.0
32	Russell Lucy	1582	90.4
33	Randolph Dorothe		90.5
34	Barrington Robert		91.7
35	Gerard Gilbert		91.7
36	Knyvett Thomas	1596	92.6
37	Peyton Thomas	1613	94.1
38	Howard Thomas 2	1585	95.1
39	Masham William		95.8
40	Chamberlain John	1554	98.8
41	Poulett John	1586	100.0
42	Harley Brilliana	1600?	100.0
43	Howard Henry F	1608	100.0
44	Barrington Thomas		100.0
45	Bourchier Thomas		100.0
46	Bowes Thomas		100.0
47	Cornwallis Elizabeth		100.0
48	Naylor Oliver		100.0

(e) 1640–1659

1	Oxinden Margaret		20.0
2	Sterry Peter		66.7
3	Jones John		76.1
4	Conway Edward 2	1602	77.8
5	Barrow Thomas		78.9
6	Wharton Nehemiah		78.9
7	Cosin John	1595	80.0
8	Savile Thomas	1590?	83.3
9	Duppa Brian	1589	83.9

10	Elizabeth of Bohemia	1596	86.8
11	Smith Thomas	1615	87.5
12	Oxinden Henry of Barham	1608	87.6
13	Dugdale William	1605	89.7
14	Oxinden Henry of Deane	1614	90.0
15	Peyton Thomas	1613	90.3
16	Throckmorton Baynham		92.3
17	Conway Anne	1631	94.4
18	Basire Frances		94.4
19	Denne Thomas	1622	94.5
20	Isham Justinian	1611	96.6
21	Knyvett Thomas	1596	99.2
22	Harley Brilliana	1600?	100.0
23	Thimelby Winifred	1619	100.0
24	Harley Edward	1624	100.0
25	Finch John	1626?	100.0
26	Osborne Dorothy	1627	100.0
27	Haddock Richard	1629?	100.0
28	Dering Unton		100.0
29	Waynwright James		100.0

For conventions, see Note to Appendix 5.1. This Appendix includes the following members of the nobility:

Howard Thomas 2   Second Earl of Arundel and Surrey
Conway Edward 2   Second Viscount Conway

Appendix 5.3.

Informants for Figure 5.3. WHICH VS. THE WHICH

No.	Name	Year of birth	Individual score
(a) 1460–1479			
1	Betson Thomas		0.0
2	Cely Richard I		0.0
3	Henham Thomas		0.0
4	Maryon William		0.0
5	Greene Godfrey		30.0
6	Stonor Elizabeth		36.4
7	Paston Margaret		67.1
8	Calle Richard		94.4
9	Paston John III	1444	97.6
10	Paston John II	1442	99.2
11	Paston John I	1421	100.0

| 12 | Mull Thomas | | 100.0 |
| 13 | Russe John | | 100.0 |

(b) 1480–1499

1	Cely Richard I		0.0
2	Cely Richard II		0.0
3	Kesten Thomas		0.0
4	Maryon William		4.8
5	Plumpton Edward		5.3
6	Richard III	1452	33.3
7	Cely William		48.5
8	Paston Margery		50.0
9	Paston Edmond II		100.0
10	Germyn Richard		100.0

(c) 1500–1519

1	Pole Germayn	1483?	23.5
2	Fox Richard	1447	74.4
3	Wolsey Thomas	1473?	85.7
4	Henry VII	1457	93.3
5	Dacre Thomas	1467	100.0
6	Boleyn Thomas	1477	100.0
7	Gascoigne William	1468	100.0
8	More Thomas	1478	100.0
9	Tunstall Cuthbert	1474	100.0

(d) 1520–1539

1	Percy Henry 6	1502?	66.7
2	Smyttyng Edward		78.6
3	Cromwell Thomas	1485?	81.1
4	Wilson John		85.7
5	Henry VIII	1491	89.4
6	Dacre Thomas 2	1467	90.0
7	Darby Thomas		92.0
8	Willoughby Edward		94.1
9	Wyatt Thomas	1503	94.4
10	Wolsey Thomas	1473?	95.0
11	Elyot Thomas	1490?	95.8
12	Gardiner Stephen	1497?	97.5
13	Stanley Edward	1508	97.6
14	Howard Thomas 3	1473	100.0
15	More Thomas	1478	100.0
16	Cranmer Thomas	1489	100.0
17	Clifford Thomas	1493?	100.0
18	Brereton Randolph		100.0
19	Godbehere Gilbert		100.0

(e) 1540–1559

1	Johnson Sabine		1.6
2	Cromwell Thomas	1485?	67.7
3	Phillipson Thomas		70.0
4	Dodington John		72.7
5	Saxby Thomas		72.7
6	Elizabeth I	1533	84.2
7	Warner Bartholomew		88.9
8	Andrew Robert		90.9
9	Gery John		90.9
10	Southwick Henry		90.9
11	Sandell Richard		91.4
12	Paget William	1505	94.0
13	Wyatt Thomas	1503	94.4
14	Johnson Otwell	1518?	94.8
15	Cave Anthony		95.3
16	Johnson Richard	1521?	95.3
17	Gardiner Stephen	1497?	99.0
18	Johnson John	1514?	100.0
19	Breten Christopher		100.0
20	Coope John		100.0
21	Saunders Ambrose		100.0
22	Saunders Laurence		100.0

For conventions, see Note to Appendix 5.1. This Appendix includes the following members of the peerage:

Dacre Thomas 2	Second Lord Dacre
Howard Thomas 3	Third Duke of Norfolk
Percy Henry 6	Sixth Earl of Northumberland

Chapter 6

Gender

... whatever the particular sources of the change, and whether they are regarded as vernacular or prestige innovations, women play an important role in establishing changes as components of the standard language. (Holmes 1997: 135)

6.1. The Gender Paradox

Gender differentiation emerges as one of the most robust social variables in present-day sociolinguistics. Women are systematically reported to use high-prestige standard variants more than men, so much so that this **Sex/Prestige** pattern is presented as a sociolinguistic universal in the English-speaking world (Hudson 1996: 195). Language change has been reported to follow a similar pattern, with women leading changes that come from above the level of social awareness.

It is noteworthy that the term often used by sociolinguists to refer to this variable is indeed **sex**. They argue that, since most sociolinguistic research only makes use of the biological distinction, the corresponding term should therefore serve as the label of the speaker variable. Other researchers, including many feminist sociolinguists, however prefer the term **gender**. They identify it as a social variable and argue that it is not biology that ought to be focused on, but the social roles and practices the two sexes typically assume in society. The term is also used to stress that no biological determinism is intended, and that social roles are typically social constructs partly created through language.[1]

The term we shall use throughout this chapter is gender. Like most researchers, we will continue to categorize women and men according to their biological sex, and include monarchs like Queen Elizabeth I in the female category despite their social and political roles. But in order to be able to interpret our findings we need to refer to the typical gender roles assigned to the two sexes in the late medieval and early modern periods. One depended on the other: it was the roles in society they were destined for that determined, for instance, the kind of education given to boys and girls in the past.

A number of explanations have been given for the observed gender variation in modern speech communities. In her review, James (1996) finds that interpretations of the Sex/Prestige pattern are either economic and social or related to status and power. Social and economic factors are approached in terms of 'market forces' and social networks, comparing the two sexes' exposure to standard speech forms. Working-class women may have wider contacts at work with the standard language and more incentive to modify their speech towards it than men (L. Milroy 1987). By contrast, the power-and-status approach relates to the fact that women are generally granted less status and power than men. By using prestige language forms, women wish to assert their authority and position and to gain respect (Eckert 1989; Labov 1990, 2001: 275–279).

Present-day sociolinguists can study language change within fairly limited timespans or solely on the basis of apparent-time patterns. Over the years, a number of generalizations on the role of gender in **language change** have, however, been proposed. Earlier studies associated gender differences with particular social groups and kinds of language change. As an extension of the Sex/Prestige pattern, women in general, and lower middle-class women in particular, were identified as leaders of changes that spread above the level of public consciousness and involved the new **prestige** forms of higher-ranked social groups. By contrast, working-class men were found to predominate in changes in **vernacular** forms which spread below the level of public awareness (Coates 1986: 147–150).[2]

As more research became available, these links proved much less clear-cut: all social classes may be innovative, and women's role cannot be restricted to conscious processes alone – if indeed we can always tell conscious processes from unconscious ones. In a seminal paper, Labov (1990) argues that gender differentiation is independent of social class at the beginning, but that interaction develops later as social awareness of the change increases. He formulates two basic principles connected with increased social awareness (Labov 1990: 213–215, 2001: 274, 292):

1) in linguistic change from above, women adopt prestige forms at a higher rate than men;
2) in linguistic change from below, women use higher frequencies of innovative forms than men do.

The two principles do not preclude changes where men are in advance of women, but these constitute a small minority. Of the two major principles the former is the better documented and almost exceptionless. Both may also be connected with social status. Principle 1 is particularly noticeable in the lower middle class in North America and Western Europe, but it is also observed in societies that are not overtly stratified. As it suggests that women adopt ongoing prestige innovations more readily than men, it is connected to the **diffusion** of linguistic changes.

Especially in phonology, the changes from below referred to in Principle 2 can be traced to the upper working class. In his Philadelphia study Labov (2001: 321–411) relates these processes to social network structures, and identifies as the leading force behind them women of the upper working class who have a high density of interaction within their neighbourhoods but also a high proportion of weak ties outside of them. What Principle 2 is therefore most concerned with is, in the Weinreich, Labov and Herzog (1968) framework, the **actuation** of linguistic changes in relation to their social **embedding**.

The two principles show opposing tendencies in the way men and women promote linguistic change. Labov (2001: 293) calls it the **gender paradox** and formulates it in terms of conformity: 'women conform more closely than men to sociolinguistic norms that are overtly prescribed but conform less than men when they are not'. He assumes that it is the basic nonconformity of some upper-working-class women that makes them the leaders of linguistic change in their communities. In more general terms, however, the two principles state that women are the more active party in promoting linguistic innovations.

Despite the ample evidence supporting Labov's two principles, no consensus has been reached on the relative importance of social class and gender in language change. James and Lesley Milroy (1993), for instance, suggest that 'gender difference is often prior to social class in accounting for sociolinguistic variation'. More specifically, they present evidence on phonological changes in English that suggests that gender difference may override social status as a mechanism by which a change is implemented. Even negatively valued features such as the glottal stop may begin to be generalized once they are adopted by women. The Milroys (1993: 65) conclude that, rather than simply preferring prestige forms, women in fact create them.

There is considerable agreement in recent research suggesting that one pattern of language change that is particularly associated with women is **supralocalization**, i.e., the spread of a linguistic feature from its region of origin to neighbouring areas (see further section 8.1.). In Present-day English supralocal processes are typically witnessed in phonology, as in the diffusion from London to Norwich and the rest of East Anglia of the initial fricative merger in words like *thin* and *fin* (Trudgill 1986: 54). It is observed by Milroy and Milroy (1993) and Docherty *et al.* (1997) that strictly localized linguistic forms tend to be preferred by males, whereas the high-frequency variants used by females typically gain a supralocal status. Janet Holmes's studies of New Zealand English corroborate these findings. Holmes (1997: 131) also subscribes to the view that the success of innovations, both prestige and vernacular, crucially depends on their being adopted and endorsed by women.

No unified explanation is offered in the literature for these gender patterns in supralocal language changes. Lesley Milroy (1999) accounts for the observed differences in terms of gender socialization rather than prestige or mobility. She argues that men's heavier use of non-standard forms could be related to male susceptibility to peer constraint, and their fear of the consequences of any behaviour that sets them apart from their peers. Those looking for historically testable generalizations are offered one in Labov's (2001: 279) conclusion that we are simply 'dealing with a long-standing cultural pattern, an objective social fact.'

6.2. Historical Reconstruction

6.2.1. Gender Inequality

Before discussing some empirical studies that have been carried out on gender and language change with historical English data, we would like to pause to consider some problems to do with historical reconstruction. Most sociolinguists, both historical and modern, would probably agree with the first part of Jennifer Coates's conclusion (1986: 150) when she writes that:

> Societies vary in all kinds of ways, but male and female roles are distinguished in some way in all known societies. It is not surprising, then, that the linguistic variation arising from socially constructed differences between women and men turns out to have a significant role in facilitating linguistic evolution.

It is the second part that creates a challenge for a historical sociolinguist, who has to reckon with social changes both within historical periods and between them. How can we compare male and female social roles today with those found in earlier societies, such as Tudor and Stuart England, so as to be able to interpret their impact on language change? One way of doing this at the macro level is to refer to models developed for cross-cultural comparison. One of them, Allardt's (1989) model for basic human needs, was introduced in Chapter 2. It will provide the framework for our discussion of gender in late medieval and early modern England.

While it would appear that the indicators to do with **loving** have a number of parallels between Tudor and Stuart times and today, those of **having** and **being** yield fewer similarities. 'Loving' refers to the needs people have to relate to other people and to form social identities. It is assessed, for instance, by contacts in the local community, attachment to family and kin, and active patterns of friendship. Although differences between historical periods exist in the satisfaction of these needs, it would appear that they could not be divided by gender as sharply as those based on 'having' and 'being'.[3]

As to **having**, it is evident that in our period women and men did not have the same access either to the material modes of 'having', such as income and wealth, or to the immaterial ones, such as education. It would clearly be an exaggeration to describe Tudor and Stuart women as 'have-nots', however. In macroeconomic terms they could probably be regarded as legally dispropertied: a woman could not inherit her father's estate. But a more varied picture emerges on the microeconomic level, as Erickson's (1993) study based on a large number of probate documents, for instance, clearly indicates, women could and did inherit land and moveable goods.

The two sexes' differential treatment in education typically started at the elementary stage and was reflected in their linguistic repertoires. As shown in Chapter 3, higher education was the prerogative of the social elite, and it remained a masculine one throughout the period focused on in our study. Although some individual women could reach remarkable levels of academic achievement – with Queen Elizabeth I and Margaret Roper, daughter of Sir Thomas More, as two impressive examples – the high achievers came from unusual circumstances (Jewell 1998: 11).

As to **being**, integration into society, gender differentiation could hardly have been more marked. An individual's rights to participate in decisions and activities influencing his/her life were sharply gendered: Tudor and Stuart men ruled every aspect of the public sphere, including national and local politics, the economy, the church and the legal system. The anonymous author of the first exposition of women's equivocal legal position neatly summarized the situation in 1632:

> Women have no voyse in Parliament, They make no Lawes, they consent to none, they abrogate none. All of them are understood either married or to bee married and their desires or [are] subject to their husband, I know no remedy though some women can shift it well enough. (T. E, [Thomas Edgar?] *The Lawes Resolutions of Womens Rights,* 1632: 6)

Even within the domestic sphere, women's social position was derivative, for unmarried women were ranked on the basis of their fathers' status, and married women according to their husbands' (see further Mendelson & Crawford 1998: 256–344).

Whether women constituted a socio-economic class in themselves at the time, as has been argued by writers like Jordan (1993: 103–104), is, however, a moot point. Then as now, there was a great deal of variation within the categories of men and women. What applies to married noble- and gentle-women does not necessarily apply to widows and unmarried women of the same social ranks, and even less so to women coming from lower ranks. According to some estimates, one fifth of the early modern households were headed by women, either by widows or spinsters (Capp 1996: 119). Neither was all women's work limited to unpaid domestic work but could extend to wage-earning outside the domestic setting, for instance, in the cloth and service industries (Fletcher 1996: 223–255).

This 'separate-spheres' model of 'being' also ignores those public spheres where women's presence was prominent: in the street, in taverns, at the market, at church, and – in the case of noblewomen – at Court. The public life that women enjoyed in their networks of friends was particularly lively.

Women's gossip could also work as a powerful means of social control and be feared by men in a society where a man's reputation crucially depended on the opinion of others (Gowing 1994, Foyster 1999: 58). Similarly, it is very difficult to measure gender differences in the positive aspects of 'being' as opportunities for personal growth. Leisure activities were pursued and nature enjoyed by both men and women. Although men clearly ruled the public life, considerations like this may warn historical sociolinguists against casting women as social outsiders in Tudor and Stuart England. 7

6.2.2. Implications for Historical Sociolinguistics

The inequality of gender in Tudor and Stuart times is clearly reflected in the historical record we have of the two sexes. Less than 2 per cent of all the printed works published in the seventeenth century were written by women (Crawford 1985). As shown in Chapter 3, the average proportion of women's letters in the CEEC amounts to about 20 per cent of the total. The overwhelming majority of these women came from the upper ranks. So Sabine Johnson, the merchant's wife discussed in Chapter 1, is an exception, as are the two women merchants whose letters from Calais have survived from the 1540s. With this imbalance in the sources, our access to gender differentiation below the gentry is restricted in the early modern period.

What we do have access to is, however, most valuable. The CEEC allows us to test the hypothesis of gender advantage in language changes that diffused throughout the country during the Late Middle and Early Modern English periods. In social terms, these processes could basically emanate from any social rank. But if we contrast male and female usage in our corpus and women are found to lead the change, three basic alternatives emerge. The change may be spreading:

(a) from the higher social ranks to the lower with women leading the process;
(b) from the lower to the higher ranks with high-ranking women leading the process within their own ranks;
(c) without any obvious directionality based on rank but with women leading the overall process.

Because the social spread of men is wider than that of women in our data, we need to refer to the findings discussed in Chapter 7 to decide whether social stratification is in evidence. If a change is of the first kind (a), we can confidently tell that it is women who lead the whole process. In the second case (b), the process diffuses from the lower via the middle ranks, i.e. professional men and merchants in our corpus. When upper-ranking women are found to promote a change like this, we know they must at least have adopted it earlier than upper-ranking men. The third alternative (c) caters for changes that are gendered but not overtly socially stratified. If female advantage is found in our data, only changes of type (b) leave room for some doubt as to whether women have promoted it from the beginning, or only begun to do so among the upper ranks.

We may, moreover, assume that, for women to favour the incoming forms, the changes themselves cannot be 'from above' in the sense that they were consciously promoted in formal genres by the educated section of the population. As Labov (1990: 213) put it, 'for women to use norms that differ from everyday speech, they must have access to these norms'. This was clearly not the case in Tudor and Stuart England.

But every coin has two sides. The fact that gentle- and noblemen's sons expended a lot of time and effort acquiring their classical education could be seen as an impediment to their proficiency in the mother tongue, as suggested by the author of *An Essay in the Defence of the Female Sex* (1696) (probably Mary Astell or Judith Drake). She rejects maturational differences (*natural forwardness of Maturity*) and attributes girls' better language proficiency to boys wasting their youth learning Latin. Whether these linguistic differences were due to nature or nurture, upper-rank girls in the seventeenth century were clearly exposed to a range of linguistic variation outside their domestic spheres:

> For Girles after they can Read and Write . . . are furnish'd among other toys with Books, such as *Romances*, *Novels*, *Plays* and *Poems*; which . . . give'em very early a considerable Command both of Words and Sense; which are further improv'd by their making and receiving Visits with their Mothers, which gives them betimes the opportunity of imitating, conversing with, and knowing the manner and address of elder Persons. These I take to be the true Reasons why a Girl of Fifteen is reckon'd as ripe as a Boy One and Twenty and not any natural forwardness of Maturity as some People would have it. These advantages the Education of Boys deprives them of, who drudge away the Vigour of their Memories at Words, useless ever after to most of them, and at Seventeen or Eighteen are to begin their Alphabet of Sense, and are but where the Girles were at Nine or Ten. (*An Essay in the Defence of the Female Sex* 1696: 57–58)

Keeping contemporary evidence like this in mind, we could formulate a historical counterpart to Labov's original statement: 'for men and women to use everyday speech norms that differ from their own, they must have access to these norms'. In the following sections we will also refer to information on register variation in the changes discussed.

6.3. Previous Studies

Besides the studies carried out within our project, there is some earlier research on the late medieval and early modern periods to suggest that gender differences may indeed be traced back to times before language standards became codified and prescribed.[4] This evidence on linguistic practices, although patchy, points to women favouring and promoting **vernacular** forms in both periods.

Romaine (1982a: 167–170) finds that women's basic relativization strategies come closer to vernacular norms than men's in her material of Middle Scots correspondence. The notion of women spreading vernacular norms is supported by Meurman-Solin's (2000) study of Aitken's Law in a set of sixteenth-century Scottish English letters. The changes involved in this phonological process can be antedated by decades if these data are taken into account.

Using the Early Modern English part of the *Helsinki Corpus of English Texts*, Kytö (1993) reports that the third-person singular present-tense indicative -s was used more by women than by men in their private correspondence in the two periods, 1500–1570 and 1570–1640. We shall return to this change with more evidence later on in this chapter.

Palander-Collin (1999: 246) shows that women employ first-person expressions of epistemic evidentiality (e.g. I THINK, KNOW, FIND, DOUBT, BELIEVE, TRUST) more than men in the CEEC in the seventeenth century, and that the grammaticalization of I THINK is promoted by female writers. Women are similarly in the vanguard of the diffusion of the progressive form -ING in the personal correspondence of well-known authors in the eighteenth and nineteenth centuries examined by Arnaud (1998).

But counterexamples to this female gender advantage also occur. Rydén and Brorström (1987: 206) find women more conservative than men when mutative transitive verbs change from the older BE-dominated paradigm to a HAVE-dominated one (*they are come* vs. *they have come*) in the course of the eighteenth and nineteenth centuries. These findings are supported by Kytö (1997: 50–51): while female writers use HAVE more than male writers in the latter half of the seventeenth century, they prove more conservative from 1700 onwards. The study is based on the fiction, journal, letter, drama, science and sermon texts in the ARCHER Corpus.

A similar discrepancy between the Early and Late Modern English periods is found in the use of exclusive adverbs discussed in Nevalainen (1991: 178–182). In their sixteenth-century letters, women were found to adhere more closely than men to the colloquial form preferring BUT to ONLY, which was gaining ground in the course of the period (*she's but/only a child*). No gender difference appeared in the seventeenth century, but one surfaced again in the latter half of the nineteenth century: women favoured the by then universal ONLY, while men showed more variation.

Besides these individual cases detected in the late modern period, there were two major areas of linguistic change that can be attributed to men in Tudor and Stuart England: lexical borrowing and regularization of spelling. Early Modern English underwent a period of massive borrowing mainly from Latinate sources. The first monolingual English dictionaries appeared at the turn of the seventeenth century. They mostly consisted of 'hard words', which were 'gathered for the benefit of & helpe of Ladies, Gentlewomen, or any other unskilled persons' (Cawdrey 1604, Preface). Spelling regularization similarly had to do with classroom teaching and the printed word. As H. C. Wyld (1936: 113) amply demonstrates, women were not the dominant force in spelling standardization in the Early Modern English period.

6.4. Gender and Real-Time Linguistic Change

The majority pattern that emerges from the fourteen cases analysed by us is one in which women are found to lead the process of linguistic change. But as pointed out above, these cases, too, require further analysis before we can conclude that gender is a more robust variable than, say, social status in the diffusion of linguistic changes in the periods investigated. When examining the way in which gender differences are distributed we will pay attention to three issues: (1) the point in time at which gender differences become noticeable, (2) the consistency of these differences across time, and (3) the social strata from which the changes emanate. The data are presented following the patterns that emerge: women ahead of men (6.4.1.), switches from male to female advantage (6.4.2.), and men ahead of women (6.4.3.). The distributions are based on the variable totals shown in Appendix II (see also Nevalainen 2000a: 54–55).[5]

6.4.1. Women Ahead of Men

Subject form YOU

Figure 6.1 shows that the replacement of the subject form YE by YOU is not only rapid – the change is plotted in periods of 20 years instead of 40 – but it is also markedly and consistently promoted by women from the early sixteenth century onwards. This systematic gender advantage emerges when the process has exceeded the frequency of 20 per cent.

In the mid-course of the change the male–female margin is at its widest (and statistically highly significant). It may be explained by the fact that at the time the change diffuses from the upper and middle ranks to the lower, with only social aspirers lagging behind. In the latter half of the century these social status differences are levelled out (see 7.4.3.).

We could argue that YOU spread 'from below' in terms of public consciousness on various grounds, not just because of women's general lack of learning. First, the origins of the change suggested in the literature point to a typical vernacular change: similarity of rapid-speech forms of the subject and object pronouns. Second, the change was completed only within a couple

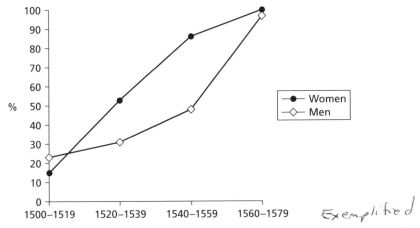

Exemplified

Figure 6.1. The replacement of subject YE by YOU. Gender distribution of YOU. CEEC 1998 and Supplement; quota sampling.

of generations in all the ranks included in the CEEC. In King Henry VIII's official correspondence the majority form switched from YE to YOU around 1535. Mixed usage of the subject pronouns even extended to the 1549 *Book of Common Prayer* (Prins 1933: 72–74). Both cases speak for the wide-ranging acceptability of the incoming form at the time.

MY and THY

A systematic gender advantage also appears in the diffusion of the short possessive determiners MY and THY as opposed to MINE and THINE. Figure 6.2 illustrates the process in prevocalic contexts. The change begins to be

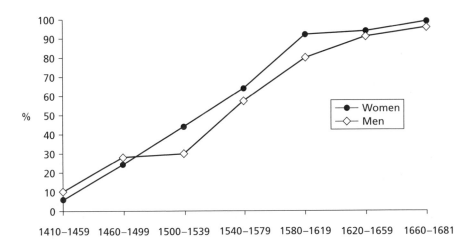

Figure 6.2. MINE and THINE vs. MY and THY. Gender distribution of MY and THY before vowels. CEEC 1998 and Supplement; quota sampling.

promoted by women once it has reached a frequency level of 30 per cent. Looking for the social *locus* of the change, our data show little variability across the social spectrum at the beginning of the sixteenth century, but a clear trend from below can be traced for the rest of the century (7.4.3.). The relatively small difference between women and men may therefore be accounted for by the change progressing from the lower ranks. These are overwhelmingly represented by men, especially for the period 1540–79. Figure 6.2 indicates how consistently upper-ranking women spread the incoming forms throughout the sixteenth century.

Possessive determiner ITS

The new possessive determiner ITS gained ground in the seventeenth century, and just exceeded the frequency of 30 per cent by the 1680s, where our corpus ends. No gender differentiation can be observed if we consider the data in 40-year periods. However, periodization by 20 years reveals that the two sexes have different rates in adopting ITS in the last period, 1660–81 (see Figure 6.3). Although the absolute figures for an incipient change like this are low, the tendency is worth noting. As ITS is also frequent both among high-ranking and professional men (Raumolin-Brunberg 1998), women's lead is in evidence within the higher ranks.

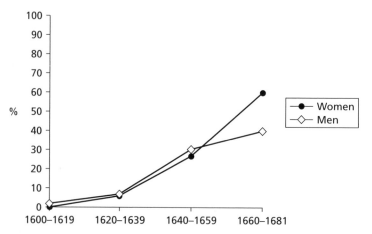

Figure 6.3. Gender distribution of the possessive determiner ITS as opposed to OF IT and THEREOF. CEEC 1998.

Prop-word ONE

The prop-word ONE is one of the innovations that were strongly favoured by women in the sixteenth and seventeenth centuries. It parallels the rise of the subject form YOU in that a considerable gender difference emerges very early on (see Figure 6.4). ONE also parallels YOU in that it appears not to have spread from the lower social ranks (Raumolin-Brunberg & Nurmi 1997).

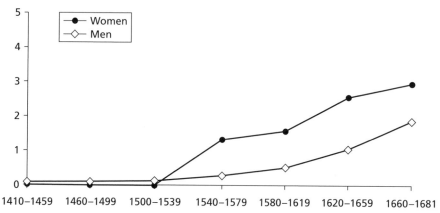

Figure 6.4. Gender distribution of prop-word ONE. Occurrences per 10,000 running words. CEEC 1998; excluding Dorothy Osborne (see Ch. 4, note 7).

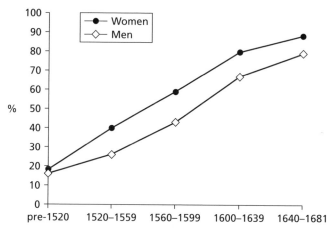

Figure 6.5. Object of the gerund. Gender distribution of zero forms as opposed to OF-phrases. CEEC 1998 and Supplement.

Earlier corpus evidence, however, suggests that the prop-word ONE is yet another change that diffused from below in terms of social awareness: it first occurs in oral genres, including fiction, and is only found in more literate kinds of writing from the latter half of the seventeenth century onwards (Rissanen 1997).

Object of the gerund

Figure 6.5 shows that the 'verbalization' of the gerund was also a process consistently favoured by women in the Early Modern English period. The zero object, as in *the contentment of meeting you* (4.18), was generalized over a long

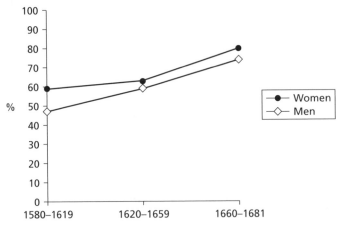

Figure 6.6. Noun subject of the gerund. Gender distribution of the genitive. CEEC 1998.

period of time, and the process was not completed by the end of the seventeenth century. However, a gender difference can already be detected when the incoming form is nearing the frequency of 30 per cent around 1520–59.

This syntactic change shows only weak social directionality in our data. As it spread across the section of the social spectrum accessible to us, the observed gender difference was not as large as with changes led by the higher ranks. But in any given period women use zero objects on average more than men in either the upper, middle or lower ranks.

Noun subject of the gerund

The dominant form of the noun subject of the gerund in the seventeenth century was genitive (the type: *the Queen's coming to her barge* (4.21)). Figure 6.6 suggests that its generalization was also sensitive to the gender distinction, with women showing a higher rate of the genitive form than men. But as the figure indicates, women's advantage was only slight. It points to a tendency but the numbers do not reach a 5 per cent level of statistical significance in the seventeenth century. More material would be needed to confirm the trend at this relatively late stage of the change in progress.

Third-person singular -s

As suggested in Chapter 4, there is good reason to think of the diffusion of the third-person present-tense suffix -s in terms of two waves: one in the latter half of the fifteenth century and the other a century later. Figure 6.7 indicates that this process, too, was gender-sensitive and that women were responsible for promoting the second wave in the sixteenth century.

Figure 6.7 does not, however, tell the whole story about the late fifteenth century. The male advantage suggested by the figure is due to the London

Figure 6.7. The replacement of -TH by -s, excluding HAVE and DO. Gender distribution of -s. CEEC 1998 and Supplement; quota sampling.

data, which consist of men only, while the women in the period 1460–99 mostly come from East Anglia, where the -(E)s form was practically non-existent at the time, among men and women alike (see 8.4.2.).[6]

But the second wave is reasonably well documented for both sexes in our data, and it is led by women. Gender differentiation is evidenced quite early in the process, in the first half of the sixteenth century, before the change has reached the frequency level of 20 to 30 per cent. Women's advantage is statistically highly significant and continues into the early decades of the seventeenth century, when the change is nearing completion in verbs other than HAVE and DO. In these, too, the same gender pattern with women adopting HAS and DOES earlier than men continues in the first half of the seventeenth century (Nevalainen 1996a).

Although the changes run parallel in the first half of the sixteenth century, with -s the difference between men and women is less striking than with the subject YOU – and we are analysing exactly the same set of people here. The reasons for this difference may be found in the social orientations of the two processes. Unlike YOU, which spread from above and from the middle in social terms, -s diffused from below: as shown in Chapter 7, it is one of the few changes in our data to reveal a systematic pattern from the lowest literate ranks to the middle and upper strata. The use of -s also varied according to register: besides private writings, it was typically used in verse drama in the sixteenth century but avoided in more formal registers (Görlach 1990: 113; Kytö 1993).

The rise of -s in the south was therefore a change from below both socially and in the sense that it proceeded from everyday spoken usage. Figure 6.7 reveals a long period, from 1500 till the 1580s, during which nearly categorical grammars, over 90 per cent of -TH, were the rule with men in the south, while moderately variable grammars were displayed by women.

Indefinite pronouns with singular human reference

In the seventeenth century the English indefinite pronoun system contains three types of compound that refer to human beings in the singular. Those in -MAN lose ground, while those in -BODY and -ONE gain it. Figure 6.8a shows the distributions of the three forms in women's data, and Figure 6.8b in men's. The male–female differences are statistically significant in all four periods.

The figures suggest two major trends. Women are most of the time ahead of men in the use of the forms in -BODY and -ONE. By contrast, men continue to use forms in -MAN much later than women. Women's use of -MAN forms had already been much reduced in the course of the previous century. As Raumolin-Brunberg (1998: 376) notes, the most likely reason for this may

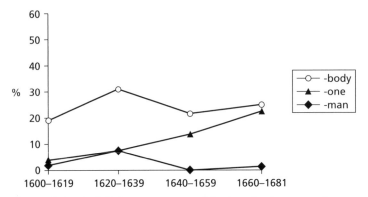

Figure 6.8a. Indefinite pronouns with singular human reference. Female usage of compound pronouns in -BODY, -ONE and -MAN. CEEC 1998; excluding Dorothy Osborne.

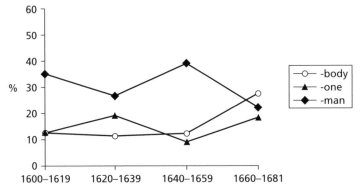

Figure 6.8b. Indefinite pronouns with singular human reference. Male usage of compound pronouns in -BODY, -ONE and -MAN. CEEC 1998.

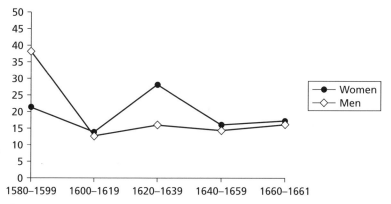

Figure 6.9. Periphrastic DO in affirmative statements. Gender distribution of DO per 10,000 words. CEEC 1998, excluding Dorothy Osborne (based on Nurmi 1999a: 139, 172).

have been semantic ambiguity, the use of -MAN compounds with reference to both the male sex and human beings in general.

6.4.2. Switches from Male to Female Advantage

The CEEC data display a few cases where the gender profile of a change is altered in the middle of the process. However, these cases also have in common that the course of change is arrested or interrupted, momentarily or for good, and does not form a regular S-curve. These changes include the use of the auxiliary DO in affirmative and negative statements.

Periphrastic DO in affirmative statements

When analysed in 20-year periods, two rises can be seen in the use of the auxiliary DO in affirmative statements, the major one peaking in 1580–99 and the minor one in 1620–39. An interesting crossing-over in the gender distribution of DO takes place between these two peaks. Figure 6.9, based on Nurmi (1999a), indicates that the use of periphrastic DO was male-dominated in affirmative statements in the last two decades of the sixteenth century. But it lost ground at the beginning of the next century – as Nurmi (1999a: 179–181) suggests, probably due to the arrival of the Scottish court in London – and has never regained its former position since.

There was, however, a second rise in the use of the auxiliary in affirmatives in the early decades of the seventeenth century. Figure 6.9 shows that DO was favoured in the language of women at the time, while the male usage was almost unaffected by the trend. The CEEC evidence is here ample for both sexes, even when the data are presented in twenty-year intervals. The linguistically most interesting interpretation of these data is to think of the

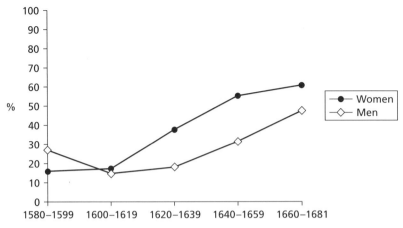

Figure 6.10. Periphrastic DO in negative statements. Gender distribution of DO. CEEC 1998, excluding Dorothy Osborne (based on Nurmi 1999a: 153).

second peak as an attempt to extend the systematic use of DO to affirmative statements. It is supported by the simultaneous rise in the use of DO in negative statements, another process clearly led by women, to be discussed below.

Why DO became generalized in negative statements but failed to do so in affirmatives is another question. Nurmi (1999a: 177) shows that affirmative periphrastic DO was particularly favoured by East-Anglian gentry in the early seventeenth century, men and women who generally did **not** lead supralocal processes. Perhaps DO failed to regain its former position as part of nationwide usage because it was not promoted by the capital. Although an abortive change in purely syntactic terms, there is however some evidence that unstressed DO never fully disappeared from affirmative statements in colloquial speech (Gerner 1996).

Periphrastic DO in negative statements

Unlike in affirmatives, the use of periphrastic DO in negative statements was diffused rapidly in the course of the seventeenth century. However, as indicated by Figure 6.10, negative and affirmative DO behaved exactly alike in that both lost ground at the beginning of the seventeenth century.

The spread of *do* into negative statements was a new and vigorous change promoted by men in the late sixteenth century, but the process had halted by the first decades of the seventeenth. Women were responsible for its revival in 1620–39, when its overall frequency again exceeded 20 per cent. The upward trend continued, and was followed by men, but the gender difference remained statistically significant. It is noteworthy that the men who had promoted the use of DO in negatives in the late sixteenth century were on the whole less educated than those who contributed to its revival

Figure 6.11. Relative adverb vs. preposition plus (THE) WHICH. Gender distribution of the preposition-plus-WH constructions. CEEC 1998 and Supplement.

in the early seventeenth century (Nurmi 1999a: 157). We may therefore assume that, while the former had been a change from below socially, the latter emanated from the middle and upper ranks.

Relative adverb vs. prepositional phrase

The rise of the analytic relative adverbial construction, preposition plus relative pronoun, is included here because it, too, shows an initial male advantage. But, as shown in Chapter 4, the rise did not advance directly from synthetic relative adverbs (*wherewith*) to analytic preposition-plus-pronoun constructions (*with which*), but from analytic to synthetic and back to analytic. Or rather, the U-turn took place in male usage.

Figure 6.11 suggests that women had never really joined in the first analytic tendency shown in the male usage in the first half of the fifteenth century. Women's data form a single rising S-curve, albeit not a smooth one. The saw-tooth pattern may be partly due to the relative infrequency of the study variable in their data. Men begin to revert to analytic forms in the latter half of the sixteenth century. They make steady progress, but retain synthetic forms considerably more often than women throughout the seventeenth century.

This change involves relativization processes, which are typically associated with educated usage (cf. Romaine's findings on Middle Scots mentioned in 6.3.). It is therefore not surprising to see that women do not follow the male pattern in the early data. The relevance of the time factor in processes promoted by men will reappear with the relativizers WHICH and THE WHICH to be discussed in 6.4.3.

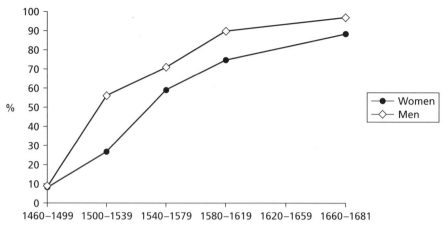

Figure 6.12. Multiple negation vs. single negation. Gender distribution of single negation followed by nonassertive indefinites. CEEC 1998 and Supplement.

6.4.3. Men Ahead of Women

Decline of multiple negation

The disappearance of multiple negation is one of the three changes in our data to be consistently promoted by men. Figure 6.12 presents simple and co-ordinate structures in the aggregate and shows that the change was as good as completed by men around 1600 but only nearing completion in women's data. As will be shown in detail in Chapter 7, the process was socially stratified. The gender difference, however, also prevailed among the higher ranks: although the process was led by professional men, and especially by social aspirers, upper-rank men used multiple negation significantly less than upper-rank women throughout the period under examination (Nevalainen 2000a: 49–52, and 7.4.3., below).

Because of paucity of data, few generalizations can be made on the middle and lower ranks. That Sabine Johnson was a more frequent user of multiple negation than the male members in her family does suggest that the male advantage was equally pronounced in the merchant circles at the time. As single negation with nonassertive indefinites was promoted by professional men – it was already a feature of late-fifteenth-century legal texts such as the Statutes of the Realm (Rissanen 2000: 125) – it therefore looks like a change from above the level of social awareness.

We know that, in those present-day speech communities where it is found, multiple negation is more sharply stratifying for women than it is for men, and women use it less than men in all social classes (Romaine 1994: 79–80). When multiple negation became a stable social variable in the late modern

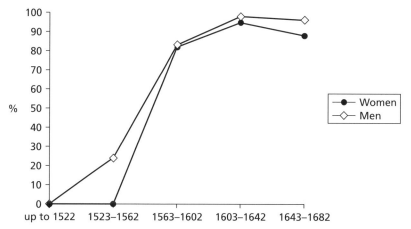

Figure 6.13. Inversion vs. direct word-order after clause-initial negators. Gender distribution of inversion. CEEC 1996; collection-based search.

period, a switch in its gender affiliation must have taken place resulting in the Sex/Prestige pattern that we know today.

Inversion after initial negators

Interestingly, no social marking seems to be attached to inversion, or lack of it, after initial negators today. The inversion process, too, was led by men in the Tudor period. Figure 6.13 suggests that women did not catch up with it until the latter half of the sixteenth century. Unfortunately, there is not enough data to analyse the process further in social terms.

But it is possible to connect multiple negation and inversion after initial negators linguistically: they provide alternative ways for marking the scope of sentential negation (Nevalainen 1998: 283–284). As multiple negation disappears as a scope marker, inversion comes to replace it. The linguistic connection lends support to the systematic gender affiliation, male advantage, shown by the corpus data with both innovations.

Relative pronoun WHICH

The generalization of the relative pronoun WHICH is another case of male advantage in our data. The dip in the second half of the fifteenth century in the S-curve in Figure 6.14 is also associated with men. It is explained by social facts: WHICH was preferred by upper-rank and professional men in 1460–99, while THE WHICH was clearly favoured by London merchants, who are well represented in the period (see 7.4.3.). THE WHICH is also the form preferred by women, who differ from the men of their own ranks until the middle of the sixteenth century. Figure 6.14 excludes Sabine Johnson, the merchant's wife: she continues to prefer THE WHICH almost 100 per cent of the time, and so deviates from all her contemporaries in 1540–79 (see Appendix 5.3.).

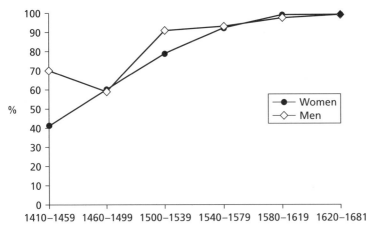

Figure 6.14. Relative pronoun THE WHICH vs. WHICH. Gender distribution of WHICH. CEEC 1998; excluding Sabine Johnson.

As the diffusion of WHICH was well under way in the early fifteenth century, we cannot say when the gender difference first emerged. We can, however, surmise that it was related to women's restricted access to the professional usage of the day: WHICH is common in fifteenth-century statutes and official correspondence (Raumolin-Brunberg 2000).

6.5. Conclusion

The three issues we have paid attention to in this chapter are the timing, consistency and social directionality of the gender differences observed. As to the first, it appears that gender affiliation can only be detected when a change has passed its incipient phase and reached the 20–30 per cent level of overall frequency. This is what we shall call, following Labov (1994), the new and vigorous stage in the life cycle of a change in progress. It reveals the gender affiliation of YOU, MY/THY, ITS, the object of the gerund, third-person singular -S, DO in negative statements and the prepositional WH-phrases, all with female advantage. But in a couple of cases, gender differentiation may also be detected earlier. This is the case with two male-dominated processes, the loss of multiple negation and inversion after initial negators. More data are needed to confirm the trend but it is not unexpected at a time when supralocal changes led by men are typically channelled through learned and professional usage.

Another clear trend that emerges from the data is that the gender affili-ation of a process remains constant from the new and vigorous stage on until its (near-)completion. This is the case with all except three of the changes we have examined. Crossing-over is only seen with the changes involving periphrastic DO and, much less clearly, with relative adverbs. A simple crossing-over from male to female advantage may not, however, be what happened with DO either. A sudden break is put on its diffusion in the first decades of the seventeenth century when it is curbed in both affirmative and negative statements. In negatives DO is later revived and becomes generalized, but in affirmatives the brief revival in 1620–39 is followed by its slow demise. In both cases women take the lead after the disruption of what had been male-oriented processes. Some scholars have argued (e.g. Kroch 2001) that whatever major disruption there was in the diffusion of DO must have been a reflection of a sudden restructuring in its syntactic properties. Following Nurmi (1999a) we have offered dialect contact as a likely cause for the changes in the sociolinguistic profiles of the two processes in the early seventeenth century.

The third trend that appears from the data is female advantage in language change regardless of the social embedding of the process. Some of the changes we have examined, such as the determiners MY and THY and the third-person singular -s, proceed from the lower literate end of the social hierarchy rather than from the topmost ranks. The gentle- and noblewomen leading these processes in our data must have adopted them early and diffused them further within their own ranks. In certain cases their usage was even more advanced than that of middle- or lower-rank men. This could also be observed with the object of the gerund, which did not show any distinct pattern of social embedding. Interpreting these findings following Milroy and Milroy (1993), who regard gender as a socially more decisive variable than social class, we could argue that gender difference came before social status in Tudor and Stuart England, too. But before we can really make this claim, we shall have to account for the possible effects of register variation. This is a topic that we shall return to in Chapter 9.

In cases like the spread of subject YOU and prop-word ONE, with no great difference between the upper and middle ranks, female advantage is even more pronounced. These processes appear to have progressed from below in terms of social awareness: there is no difference between the City of London and the Court in the rise of YOU, for instance (see 8.4.1.).

Where the opposite is the case, however, and evidence from other genres suggests that a conscious process was under way, the change was consistently led by men. A case in point is the disappearance of multiple negation, which was promoted by male professionals and systematically led by men in the upper and middle sections of society. Here emerges the chief difference between Tudor and Stuart England and the present day: late medieval and early modern Englishwomen did not promote language changes that emanated from the world of learning and professional use, which lay outside their own spheres of 'being'. However, with this major exception confirming the rule, Labov's 'long-standing cultural pattern' was already clearly in evidence.

Notes

1. According to one definition, gender roles are those expected attitudes and behaviours which a society associates with each sex (Lindsay 1994: 4). **Sex** is the term used e.g. in Coates (1986), Eckert (1989) and Labov (1990); both sex and gender are considered and compared in Chambers (1995); **gender** is preferred e.g. by Milroy and Milroy (1993), Coates (1998), Bergvall (1999) and Labov (2001). On the different traditions in gender research, see Wodak and Benke (1997). A great deal has been written on social and biological conditioning in linguistic behaviour, but the issue remains far from settled. Interdisciplinary issues to do with the sex vs. gender debate – nature vs. nurture – are addressed in Walsh (1997).

2. By the term **vernacular**, sociolinguists typically understand the language used by speakers when they are not being observed by the field-worker: 'structure that exists independently of the analyst', 'the language used by ordinary people in their everyday affairs', 'the style in which the minimum of attention is given to the monitoring of speech' (Labov 1972: 62, 69, 208). Milroy (1992: 66) defines the term as 'real language in use'. Throughout this book, we use the term in Labov's second sense 'the language used by ordinary people in their everyday affairs'.

3. Here we need to consider, in particular, the research carried out on family and childhood; for surveys, see Houlbrooke (1984), Burke (1992a: 47–55), O'Day (1994). Apart from issues such as extended vs. nuclear family, two topics have received particular attention in the literature: the role of the individual in earlier societies and, ever since the publication of Ariès's *Centuries of Childhood* in the 1960s, the notion of childhood across time.

4. Our team's publications include Nevalainen (1996a), (1999b), (2000b), Palander-Collin (1999), (2000), and Vuorinen (2002).

5. Gender differences are statistically significant (chi-square test, $p<0.5$) in subperiods two and three in Figure 6.1; in subperiod five in Figure 6.2; in subperiods four, five and six in Figure 6.4; in the last two subperiods in Figure 6.5; in all subperiods except the first and the last in Figure 6.7; in all four subperiods in Figure 6.8; in the first and the third subperiod in Figure 6.9; in the last three subperiods in Figure 6.10; in the first, fourth and sixth subperiod in Figure 6.11; in the second, fourth and final fifth subperiod in Figure 6.12; and in the first and third subperiod in Figure 6.14.

6. An additional factor here is the mediating role of the amanuenses used by women in the late medieval period. Many of the late medieval changes examined by us show gender differentiation in the fifteenth century, thus suggesting that a number of women's letters must have been taken down from dictation; see Norman Davis' preface to his edition of the Paston letters (1971: xxxviii–xxxix).

Chapter 7

Social Stratification

> Different social grades have different standards of what is becoming in speech, as they have in dress and manners, or questions of taste and fashion. (Wyld 1936: 4)

> In studies of urban dialects to date, social class has proved to be the most likely independent variable to correlate with linguistic innovation. (Chambers & Trudgill 1998: 153)

7.1. Social Order in Sociolinguistics

Although **social class**[1] is regarded as one of the major – if not *the* major – external constraints in much of the sociolinguistic literature, it is not an issue that has attracted much attention recently. Unlike the recent research on gender, most of what we know about the role of social status in language change was investigated a couple of decades ago. However, although not a fashionable area of study today, linguistic differences between social classes are generally taken for granted in sociolinguistic research. With time it has also become evident that the stratification patterns discovered by Labov, Trudgill, Wolfram, etc. in western cities are not universal. Sociolinguistic differences vary according to the type of society and culture people live in.

The general fact that social background is a factor that conditions people's linguistic choices is interesting in its own right. Quite in the same way as there are geographical differences in language use, better known as **regional dialects**, there are also differences between people of different social standing, often called **social dialects** or **sociolects**.

The criteria used in determining age and gender depend on human biology, and are usually regarded as unidimensional. As the previous chapters show, this does not make their interpretation uncomplicated. Social class as a speaker variable is not only complex in interpretation but also in definition. In sociolinguistic studies, classifications have been borrowed from sociologists, and the main determinants for assigning social-class membership have been occupation, income and education. In some studies these components have been supplemented by type of housing, location and father's occupation (for a recent discussion, see Labov 2001: 60–68, 113–119). It is clear that placing a multidimensional phenomenon on one scale creates problems, but if one succeeds in singling out groups that are real, the emerging sociolects will also be real. The pursuit of representative composite scores has met with criticism for different reasons, which all basically go back to the fact that 'individuals are notoriously hard to classify by using objective criteria' (Wardhaugh 1994: 147). Alternative models, such as life-modes (Milroy 1992: 214–220), have proved difficult to operationalize.

In speech communities there are varying levels of awareness concerning sociolects, in particular the use of individual linguistic forms. Three concepts, **indicators, markers** and **stereotypes**, have been introduced to classify linguistic elements in terms of their identification as preferred variants among different social strata (e.g. Labov 2001: 196). Indicators are not commented on or even recognized by native speakers. Unlike markers, they represent socially stratified linguistic items, in other words, elements whose choice and frequency vary across social class but not style. Markers, i.e. variables with both a social and stylistic dimension, have some degree of social awareness. Stereotypes are variables that are so well-known in language communities that they become objects of overt comments.

The whole issue of social-class variation becomes more intriguing when the focus is directed towards linguistic change. Change is usually also connected with the indicator–marker–stereotype system and it is markers in particular that represent change in progress.

On the whole, it is argued that social class differences belong to the driving forces for the diffusion of new linguistic elements among populations. For this to happen, there must be variation in the social value that is associated with varying usage (Downes 1998: 109). To put it simply, people are supposed to imitate those whose language they find prestigious and subsequently accommodate to their usage. **Overt prestige** is usually connected with standard languages, while there may be **covert prestige** in vernacular forms (Chambers 1995: 221–226). In the end, it all boils down to the social identities, aspirations and interactions of individuals and groups, which make prestige a complicated issue.

Directionality of language change in terms of pressures from below and above has been mentioned in Chapter 3. In previous research, this classification only involved processes emanating from below and above the level of conscious awareness, and were not usually associated with social status. Labov (1994: 78) combines both types by arguing that 'changes from above are introduced by the dominant social class, often with full public awareness'. Changes from below, on the other hand, can be 'introduced by any social class, although no cases have been discovered in which the highest-status social group is the innovating group'. It is generally held that linguistic innovations follow the **curvilinear pattern,** meaning that people who introduce new elements into the language are found in the interior social groups and not at the top or the bottom of the social hierarchy (Labov 2001: 31–33). In the context of directionality we can speak of a vertical diffusion of changes (Görlach 1999) as opposed to a horizontal one, i.e. the spreading of changes among people of the same social standing. This chapter will focus on origin and direction in terms of social stratification, but in actual analysis social awareness also needs to be taken into account.

Social mobility belongs to those phenomena that are considered essential for the spread of linguistic innovations. Present-day studies of the behaviour of the **upwardly mobile**, also called **social aspirers**, show that these people are sensitive to both **prestige** and **stigma** (Chambers 1995: 52–57). Their linguistic choices not only differ from those of the people who they grew up with, but they have also been found to overuse forms they find prestigious. This can be manifested in the analogical extension of specific linguistic features to 'wrong' words or phrases. One of Labov's well-known examples is the insertion of a postvocalic [r], a prestigious sound in New York English, into the word *God*, where, of course, it has no place.

This behaviour of the social aspirers, called **hypercorrection**, is an extreme form of an ambition to sound socially 'better' than one really is. It is often a reflection of the **linguistic insecurity** people feel when they adopt external norms which differ from their own vernaculars (Downes 1998: 193). Besides hypercorrection, insecurity can generate **avoidance strategies**, i.e. the non-use of forms whose social value the speakers are not sure of. Avoidance not only applies to uncertain cases but also to stigmatized forms.

Labov (2001) includes social mobility among the main forces of linguistic change. He discovered that the leaders of sound changes in Philadelphia are upwardly mobile upper-working class women who do not conform to prevailing social norms. He also suggests that linguistic changes from below spread from the interior social groups only in communities with a reasonable degree of social mobility (Labov 2001: 518). As we shall see in section 7.4., the linguistic behaviour of social aspirers diverged from the rest of the inhabitants of Tudor and Stuart England, and their role seems essential in some linguistic changes.

As an issue of ideological nature, researchers' views on social class have necessarily played a role in their approach to this variable. Sociolinguistic theory based on stratificational social analysis and hence shared social values has been the target of criticism especially by adherents of Marxist theories on class (e.g. Lesley Milroy 1987: 97–101, see also Chapter 3). In this chapter, as elsewhere, our aim is to test the applicability of modern sociolinguistic methods to historical data. The correlation between the social order and the use of specific linguistic forms is one of the issues to be tested, and it is natural for us to choose the approach that has the strongest tradition.

7.2. Reconstructing Social Order

Chapter 3 has already provided general information on Tudor and Stuart England. This section explores different ways of operationalizing the social structures for the study of language change.

As we have seen above, determining social class membership is not an uncomplicated issue in present-day sociolinguistics. As far as historical linguistics is concerned, the challenge is even harder. To find linguistically relevant social divisions a decision must be made about which model or models to use. Section 3.3.2. has presented varying views on social differences, both synchronically and diachronically. Against this background, we have had to make a choice between the models, i.e. hierarchy, tripartite or dichotomy, keeping in mind that longitudinal comparisons were required. In addition, the poor availability of data from the lower orders had to be taken into consideration.

In our pilot studies on social stratification based on the CEEC,[2] we used relatively fine-grained models of social hierarchy. It has become obvious by now that coarser divisions often highlight linguistic differences more clearly than the detailed models. For the present study this means that, in addition to presenting some data in terms of the hierarchy model, we have used a model of our own involving four strata, with the advantage of making temporal comparisons more reliable by levelling out fluctuations in primary data.

Model 1 in Table 7.1. represents the delicate social division we have used in our Sender Database (for details, see note 22 in Chapter 3). This model keeps apart upper and lower gentry, upper and lower clergy, and also distinguishes between nonprofessional and professional gentlemen. The latter

Table 7.1. Models of social stratification

Model 1	Model 2	Model 3	Model 4
Royalty	Royalty	Upper ranks	'Better sort'
Nobility	Nobility		
Gentry	Gentry		
– Upper/Prof			
– Lower/Prof			
Clergy	Clergy		
– Upper			
– Lower			
Social aspirers[3]	Social aspirers	Social aspirers	
Professionals	Professionals	Middle ranks	'Middling sort'
Merchants	Merchants		
Other non-gentry	Other non-gentry	Lower ranks	'Poorest sort'

After Nevalainen (1996b: 58).

group comprises gentlemen in high government offices, such as Sir Thomas More, the son of a knight, a lawyer, and the King's Secretary and Lord Chancellor, and Sir William Cecil, later Lord Burghley, Elizabeth I's chief administrator. This model follows the social hierarchy presented in Table 3.2., Chapter 3, with the exception of a separate category for social aspirers. On the basis of the well-documented importance of the language of the upwardly mobile, keeping this group apart seemed vital. To be placed in this category, a person must have climbed at least two rungs on the social ladder. The group includes men who advanced to gentility or the upper clergy from their merchant, professional or other non-gentry backgrounds.

However, Model 1 proved to be too detailed for our analysis, and a simpler version of the hierarchy model, Model 2, was chosen for the description of the full range of social variation in section 7.4.2. This hierarchy model also includes social aspirers as a separate category.

Model 3 is the basis for the dynamic examination of changes in 7.4.3. All orders above the professions have been lumped together as the upper ranks, the professions and merchants forming the middle ranks, and the other non-gentry the lower. Here, too, social aspirers have been kept as a separate category. Model 4, based on contemporary views on social differences, has been introduced to lend support to the basically tripartite division in Model 3. Our choice of four categories complies with Labov's position (e.g. 2001: 31) that three and preferably four divisions of the social hierarchy should be distinguished in order to acquire a reliable picture of linguistic changes in progress. It is noteworthy that divisions into four categories have also been used in studies of local social history, such as Wrightson (1984) on Terling, Essex.

We are well aware that our long timespan is a problem. Late medieval England and Restoration England were indeed different societies, and one and the same model hardly does justice to the differences. As Wrightson (1991) shows, the hierarchy models best describe the sixteenth century, while the tripartite pattern applies to the seventeenth. As a compromise, we chose Model 3, believing that it was simple enough to allow long-term temporal comparisons.

A further issue to be tackled was gender. As Chapters 3 and 6 have shown, there is considerable disparity between the social backgrounds of the sexes in the CEEC. Most female informants belong to the upper ranks, while men represent a broader social spectrum. This imbalance was felt to be so strong that women were excluded from the analysis of social stratification, leading to the fact that all data in this chapter represent men's language only.

Finally, if we like to see the social differences between men of varying social status in terms of the three dimensions 'having', 'loving' and 'being', the results certainly differ from those presented in Chapter 6. In this case our attention focuses on having, on the inequality that can be assessed with objective measurements. The greatest differences occurred in what one possessed, both materially and immaterially. The privileged upper ranks had estates and educational opportunities which the lower orders could only dream of. On the other hand, most men irrespective of social status had access to family life and a meaningful existence in a local community. This is not to say, however, that for instance there would not have been differences in the ability to influence decisions concerning one's life and neighbourhood, or that poverty would not have affected family life.

7.3. Previous Studies

Although philologists have not been ignorant of social differences in language use, systematic empirical studies of these differences in a diachronic perspective are rare.

There is one area in which attention has been paid to social order, namely forms of address. In addition to Finckenstaedt's relatively early monograph (1963), several articles have emerged in this field. Breuer (1983), Replogle (1987), Brown and Gilman (1989), and Kopytko (1993) all use Shakespeare's plays as their source of data. These studies testify to the significance of social status in the choice of the address form. Leith (1984) is a study of the pronouns of address in Early Modern English, unfortunately mostly based on secondary data. In their separate studies of court records, both Hope (1993) and Nevalainen (1994) find evidence of THOU becoming a marked form earlier than in literature.

The CEEC offers an unprecedented opportunity for examining address forms in letters over a 270-year period. Studies published in this area (Nevalainen & Raumolin-Brunberg 1995; Raumolin-Brunberg 1996b; Nevala 1998) prove that prevailing power relations tend to direct the choice of address forms. Further studies in interactional sociolinguistics based on the CEEC include Palander-Collin (1999), who, among other things, argues for social differences in the use of markers of evidentiality in Late Middle and Early Modern English.

As far as research on phonological and grammatical change is concerned, Wyld (1936) is still a rich source of information, especially if we ignore his outdated value judgements. An important early article in the contemporary sociolinguistic tradition is James Milroy (1983), discussing the sociolinguistic history of /h/-dropping. Most often, however, social stratification has only been brought up as one external factor among many in studies within the variationist framework, and is not necessarily taken into account in a systematic manner.

A number of the changes discussed in this book have been dealt with in our pilot studies based on the CEEC. In order to avoid unnecessary repetition, results that will be given later in this chapter are not presented here (see note 2 to this chapter).

7.4. Social Order in Language Change

7.4.1. Empirical Diachronic Research

Capturing the social stratification patterns of diachronic language changes is a demanding task, perhaps more so than an analysis of gender variation depending on the writer's sex. On the basis of what we know of the relationship between social order and language change in present-day societies, there is every reason to believe that similar phenomena existed in the past. The question is how to trace them, how to find evidence.

Our first challenge is connected with the nature of the social stratification of linguistic developments in general. Although we readily subscribe to James Milroy's argument (1998: 41) that 'all changes diffuse socially', it is not necessarily the case that all changes should correlate with social order, although they may do so with some other extralinguistic factor or factors. As we have seen in Chapter 6, gender is a constraint that seems to be relevant for practically all changes that we have taken up for analysis. In contrast, this may not be the case with social order.

This leads us to our second concern, which, as explained in Chapter 3, is the unbalanced social representation in our corpus. In fact only some periods provide material for catching more than a glimpse of the linguistic choices made by non-gentry writers. A third problem may be added, namely the general scarcity of material for the social analysis of our less frequent changes. What is enough for a gender analysis is not necessarily sufficient for a study of social differentiation, at least when a more fine-grained scale is used.

After dwelling on the problems, let us look on the bright side: we have been able to investigate half a dozen changes with satisfactory accuracy. Our main questions are (a) the existence of social stratification at all, (b) the phase or phases of the S-curve in which stratification appears, (c) origin and direction of change, and (d) contemporary evaluation of ongoing changes.

Although most of the above questions have been addressed in present-day sociolinguistics, their longitudinal aspects have not been considered owing to the lack of long-term real-time data. We have not only looked at individual 20- or 40-year periods, but plotted changes along the S-curve. This analysis draws on both statistical significance and consistency, as was done in Chapter 6.

7.4.2. Full Range of Social Variation

The empirical part begins with a comparison between two phases of one change in a detailed social hierarchy according to Model 2 in Table 7.1., above. The change under scrutiny is the third-person singular suffix -s vs. -th, which will be examined in two 40-year timespans, 1520–1559 and 1640–1681. The

Table 7.2. Third-person singular indicative suffix -s vs. -TH. Percentage of -s. HAVE and DO excluded. Male informants. Quota sample (Excluding Sir Thomas Browne)[4]

	1520–1559				1640–1681			
	-TH	-S	%	Total	-TH	-S	%	Total
Royalty	17	0	0	17	0	55	100	55
Nobility	58	13	18	71	10	158	94	168
Gentry	274	25	8	299	45	635	93	680
Clergy	86	4	4	90	35	217	86	252
Social aspirers	177	5	3	182	23	170	88	193
Professionals	56	1	2	57	36	200	85	236
Merchants	304	33	10	337	8	107	93	115
Other non-gentry	30	42	58	72	3	39	93	42
Total	1002	123	11	1125	160	1581	91	1741

CEEC is socially representative in both periods, offering a statistically significant distribution of variants (p<0.001).

The left-hand columns in Table 7.2., covering the period 1520–1559, indicate a marked social stratification in the choice of -s. The representatives of the royal family, King Henry VIII and Edward VI, did not use -s at all. The gentry, including Sir Thomas More, the clergy, social aspirers and professional men all predominantly used -TH. Merchants, mostly members of the Johnson circle, also chose -TH in nine cases out of ten. By contrast, the lower end of the social scale, other non-gentry writers, favoured -s up to 58 per cent of the occurrences.

The behaviour of the nobility strikes the eye, with a share of -s as high as 18 per cent. A closer look at the informants helps us solve this puzzle. Many of the noblemen have a northern background in the Clifford collection, and, as we will see in Chapter 8, -s was not only introduced in the north but the north also remained the geographical stronghold of this suffix.

A century later the situation looks very different. The change from -TH to -s is practically completed. The highest and the lowest social strata chose the new ending over nine times out of ten, while the intermediate ranks used it somewhat less frequently. The leading role of the lower ranks in the use of -s had been levelled out.

Some speculations about the relative conservatism of the middle ranks may be advanced. The clergy might have been influenced by the religious, especially Biblical usage, which retained the old suffix. Since the group of social aspirers at this time includes three elderly bishops, their score may have something to do with both religious language and old age (for the role of age, see Table 5.2. in Chapter 5). Professional men, lawyers in the forefront, may have been affected by the conservative language of legal documents.

Our early pilot studies examined social stratification in two 30-year periods, 1520–1550 and 1590–1620 (Nevalainen & Raumolin-Brunberg 1996a; Nevalainen 1996b). Variation was attested in the use of subject YOU versus YE, indicative plural ARE versus BE and relative pronoun WHO versus WHICH in an earlier version of the CEEC. Owing to the limited size of the corpus and the perhaps unnecessary detail in social divisions, all distinctions were not statistically significant but, nevertheless, the results suggested that at least a number of ongoing changes stratified socially in Early Modern English. Similarly, Nurmi (1996: 160–161) argued that the use of periphrastic DO was socially stratified in 1590–1620.[5]

Table 7.1. confirms the results of our pilot studies by presenting a relatively fine-grained social stratification of an ongoing language change in Early Modern English. In the middle of the sixteenth century the third-person suffix -s was most likely limited to the language of the lower social strata. Although we cannot conduct a similar stylistic testing as sociolinguists have done in Present-day English, Kytö's argument (1993) that -s was more common in informal writing suggests that it might have been a social marker. Whether or how far it was stigmatized is difficult to say, as we are dealing with a speech community with no explicit codified standard language. We will return to the issue of evaluation in section 7.4.6.

7.4.3. Changes along the S-Curve

After these two photolike still pictures we shall move on to a more dynamic way of examining changes. In this section our focus is on the second issue mentioned above, i.e. the phase or phases of the S-curve in which stratification occurs. For the purposes of this investigation we shall only use Model 3 from Table 7.1. including four categories: the upper, middle and lower ranks plus social aspirers. The temporal scale is mostly 40 years. The changes are given as graphs, and the division into five stages is the same as in Chapter 4: incipient below 15 per cent, new and vigorous 15–35 per cent, mid-range 36–65 per cent, nearing completion 66–85 per cent, and completed over 85 per cent.

Subject YOU versus YE

Previous chapters have shown that the replacement of subject YE by YOU was a rapid development. Figure 7.1 portrays three periods that can be placed on various phases of the steep S-curve depicting this change. The percentages given under the period boundaries represent the total proportion of YOU for each timespan.

The social differences in Figure 7.1 are statistically significant. By 1560–1599, however, the three ranks, but not the aspirers, had practically reached the same level so that their differences lost significance.

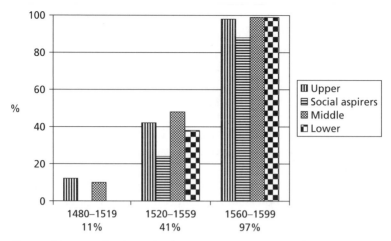

Figure 7.1. Introduction of subject YOU. Percentage of YOU. Male informants. Quota Sample. CEEC 1998.

What is remarkable for 1480–1519 is that YOU is not attested at all among the lower ranks. During the next period of very rapid growth, the middle ranks led the change and social aspirers lagged behind.

Figure 7.1 suggests that the introduction of subject YOU stratifies socially at the early stages of the change, in the incipient and new and vigorous phases, but only to a limited extent in the completed phase.

MY and THY versus MINE and THINE

The next change, the disappearance of -N- from the first- and second-person singular possessive determiners, is also given as three 40-year periods in Figure 7.2. All three periods contain social differences that are statistically significant. A closer look reveals that, excluding the upwardly mobile, the usage is homogeneous during the first period, but in the other two periods the ranks behave differently. In 1540–1579, mid-range in Labovian terms, the change is led by the lower ranks, the middle and upper following at a close distance, leaving the social aspirers far behind. During the nearly completed phase, which the last set of columns represents, the aspirers have almost caught up with the lower and middle ranks, the upper ranks showing the lowest usage.

Object of the gerund

The interpretation of our third change, the increasing use of the direct object in prepositional gerund phrases instead of an OF-phrase, e.g. *of recovering his money* versus *for usynge of it*, is less straightforward. Figure 7.3 gives four sets of columns covering altogether 160 years. The first, 1520–1559, and the third, 1600–1639, are statistically significant (p<0.01 and p<0.05, respectively). This inconsistency calls for caution in the interpretation of results.

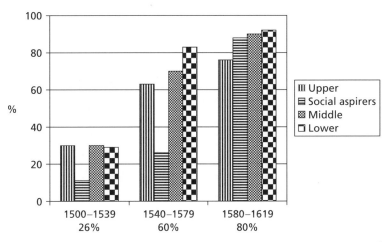

Figure 7.2. Possessive determiner MY/THY vs. MINE/THINE. Percentage of MY/THY. Male informants. CEEC 1998.

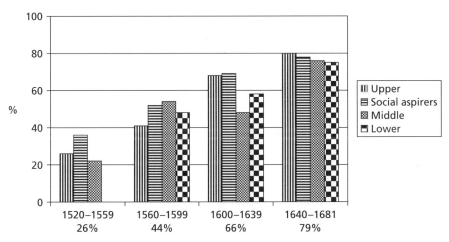

Figure 7.3. Object of the gerund. Percentage of zero forms. Male informants. CEEC 1998.

The rather limited amount of data poses our first problem here. Unfortunately, the absolute numbers of lower-rank usage are quite small (4–12 occurrences per period). Secondly, as Figure 7.3 shows, the roles of the different strata vary without forming a consistent pattern. If we compare the mutual order of the ranks, the series begins with aspirers–upper–middle–lower in 1520–1559, during the next period it is middle–aspirers–lower–upper, then aspirers–upper–lower–middle, and finally in 1640–1681 upper–aspirers–middle–lower with small margins.

In the case of this change, we cannot say more than suggest that the upper ranks and social aspirers might have favoured the zero form in the

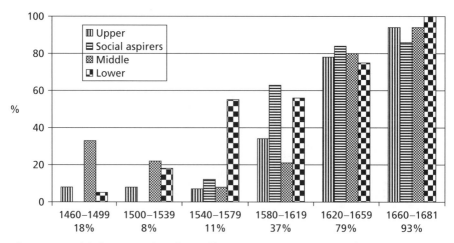

Figure 7.4. Third-person singular suffix -s vs. -th. Percentage of -s. Have and do excluded. Quota sample. Male informants. CEEC 1998. (Excluding Sir Thomas Browne for 1620–1659 and 1660–1681)

new and vigorous and late mid-range phases, but to confirm this more research is needed.

Third-person singular -s versus -th

This section deals with the process of change of the third-person singular indicative suffix almost for its entire duration, covering 220 years from 1460 to 1681. It not only bridges the gap between the two periods analysed in Table 7.2., but also looks at the medieval increase in the use of -s. As in earlier chapters, the change is presented as competition between two consonants, -th and -s, although, especially in later times, it is most likely that the deletion of the suffix vowel played a crucial role in the process.

Of the six sets of columns in Figure 7.4 the first four show statistically highly significant differences between the social ranks. In 1620–1659 the differences are not significant, but during the last period the significance level is 1 per cent.

During the first rise of -s, in a new and vigorous phase, the middle ranks clearly lead the development. Afterwards the overall employment of -s drops at the same time as its use increases among the non-gentry ranks. As Table 7.2. showed, in the middle of the sixteenth century the lower ranks were the only section of the population that preferred -s to -th. At the turn of the seventeenth century, the general usage approaching mid-range, the upwardly mobile led the way with over 60 per cent of -s, the lower ranks close at their heels. The upper echelons had acquired a level of 34 per cent of -s, while the middle orders still lagged behind. When the change approached its completion after 1620, the social differences more or less levelled out. In sum, we

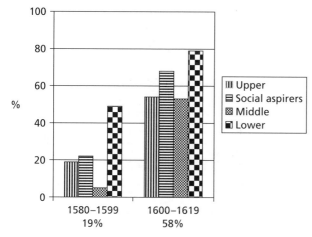

Figure 7.5. Third-person singular suffix -s vs. -TH. Percentage of -s. Have and do excluded. Quota sample. Male informants. CEEC 1998.

could say that, after an unsuccessful attempt to diffuse among all echelons of Englishmen, -s lived on as a common suffix among the lower orders until it gained new popularity after 1620.

Since the 40-year temporal frame, despite offering a good overview, seems somewhat crude for this rapid process, the most crucial period, 1580–1619, was divided into two 20-year sections. This division is all the more interesting, as other scholars, such as Stein (1987), have argued that the year 1600 formed a dividing line in the choice of the suffix. Indeed, only a glance at Figure 7.5 is enough to confirm this argument: the use of -s grows from 19 to 58 per cent between the two subperiods. The preference for -s is not only conspicuous among non-gentry informants but also among social aspirers. What is even more interesting is that just around 1600, as -s becomes the majority variant in all ranks, the social differences begin to fade away.

Decline of multiple negation

Depicting one 20-year and three 40-year periods, Figure 7.6 shows a very clear case of social stratification: the lower strata lag far behind in the change from multiple negation to single negation (*I haven't done nothing* vs. *I haven't done anything*). Unfortunately, no data are available of the upwardly mobile in the first two periods.

The earliest usage being led by the highest strata, the upwardly mobile and the middle ranks take over in mid-range and stay at the top until the completion of the change. Previous studies have shown that this change in fact was led by professional people such as lawyers and administrative officers (Nevalainen 1998). Here it is important to notice that the social differences do not disappear even in the latest phases of the change.[6]

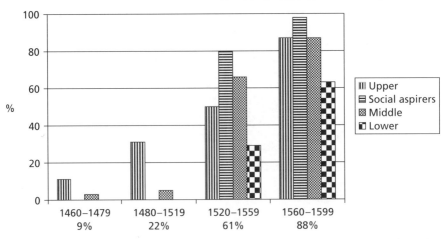

Figure 7.6. Use of single negation vs. multiple negation. Percentage of single negation. Male informants. CEEC 1998.

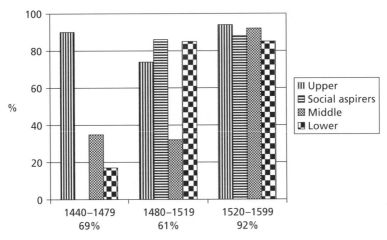

Figure 7.7. Variation between the relative pronouns WHICH and THE WHICH. Percentage of WHICH. Male informants. CEEC 1998.

Relative pronoun WHICH versus THE WHICH

The last change taken up for closer examination is variation between the relativizers WHICH and THE WHICH. All three periods in Figure 7.7 represent statistically significant variation.

This change differs from the others, as it only describes developments in the late mid-range or later. The picture we get is inconsistent. While in 1440–1479 the upper ranks clearly lead the process, favouring WHICH, by the next period the social aspirers and lower ranks have surpassed the upper. The only consistency observed is the approximately 30-per-cent proportion of WHICH in the language of the middle ranks during the first two periods.

146

Table 7.3. Social stratification of changes along the S-curve. Four social strata. Statistically significant variation at 5% level or better[7]

	Incipient below 15%	New and vigorous 15%–35%	Mid-range 36%–65%	Nearing completion 66%–85%	Completed over 85%
Subject YOU vs. YE	x	–	x	–	x
MY/THY vs. MINE/THINE	–	x	x	x	–
Object of gerund, zero vs. OF	x	o	x	o	–
Third-person -S vs. -TH	x	x	x	o	x
Single vs. multiple negation	x	x	x	–	x
WHICH vs. THE WHICH	–	–	x	x	x

Note to Table 7.3. x = stratification, o = no stratification, – = no data.

This change once more confirms the fact that social differences do occur in mid-range and nearly completed phases. However, since our material from the early part of the corpus is socially not as representative as from the later sections, the results have to be interpreted with caution. As we have seen in Chapter 6 and as we will see in the next chapter, gender and region appear to play a more important role in this change than social status does.

It may also be of interest to point out that this change makes a record in terms of the differences in use between the social strata. In 1440–1479 the upper ranks chose WHICH in 90 per cent of the cases, whereas the corresponding percentage in the lower ranks is only 17.

Returning to the question of the connection between social stratification and phase of change, our six changes prove that stratification may emerge at any stage of diffusion. Table 7.3. summarizes the stratification patterns that have come to light in this section.

On the basis of Labov's Philadelphia study (2001), one would expect clearer stratification in the new and vigorous phase, but this does not seem to be the case.[8] The curvilinear pattern in the early development will be discussed in the next section.

Finally, a look at the linguistic nature of the changes does not seem to reveal much regularity. The typical morphological changes, such as third-person inflection and second-person pronouns, do stratify socially, but so does a more syntactic change as well, the loss of multiple negation. It is worth noticing that the overall frequency of a variable, which might be expected to play an important part, is not decisive after all, since the incidence of the six variables varies a great deal (see Appendix II).

7.4.4. Origin and Direction of Language Change

In addition to issues concerning origin, this section explores the directionality of change, a topic already introduced in Chapter 6. We shall have a close look at four changes with different patterns of social origin and direction. Besides our main topic, the dichotomy between change from above and from below, the curvilinear hypothesis is also tested in the broad divisions of our data.

For reasons of representativeness, the same four-stratum model is used as in the previous section. This means that our discussion necessarily remains on a general level and does not encompass the behaviour of individual ranks. This also means that the ends of the social scale, in which changes are not supposed to originate (Labov 1994: 78), cannot be analysed separately. Unfortunately, the lower end is beyond our reach and the highest ranks are not well represented in all periods.

Although the very nature of actuation makes the first stages of a change elusive to an observer – the more so as we deal with written language in a historical context – some evidence can be found concerning the early users of innovations.

Most changes under examination in this study had already passed their earliest stages in Middle English before becoming the objects of our analysis. During the 270 years that this study covers, only one entirely new grammatical element emerged among the changes we have investigated. As mentioned in section 4.4., the possessive pronoun ITS came to be used as a variant to the neuter form HIS and the postnominal alternatives OF IT and THEREOF around 1600. According to the OED (*s.v.* its, poss. pron. A), ITS was first recorded in 1598[9]. In the CEEC, the first occurrence can be found in an upper-gentry letter from 1619. From the period 1620–1639 there are altogether five instances of ITS in men's letters[10], four in the upper ranks and one in the middle. This places our earliest adopters among the highest or middle echelons of society. Unfortunately, nothing can be said about the behaviour of the lower ranks, since there are only five occurrences of the whole variable in the lower-order letters in the CEEC.

The rest of this section will be devoted to the early stages of a further three changes which offer a broader range of data from the incipient phase. The introduction of YOU in subject function was already under way when the analysis for Figure 7.1 begins, in 1480. According to Mustanoja (1960: 125), the first occurrences go back to the fourteenth century. Our earliest instances stem from a wide social spectrum, from royalty to merchants but not the lower orders.

Table 7.4. gives the stratification for three early 20-year periods, all statistically significant. What strikes the eye is the nonoccurrence of YOU in the lower ranks, even during the third period, when high-ranking men chose the new form in almost a quarter of the cases. During the incipient phase in 1460–1499, the middle ranks seem to lead the development. Unfortunately, we have no knowledge of their behaviour in 1500–1519, but Table 7.4. clearly shows that by then YOU had become established among the upper ranks. As Figure 7.1 has indicated, this firm position remains in 1520–1559, although the lower ranks catch up with the highest stratum.

Table 7.4. Replacement of subject YE by YOU. 1460–1519. Male informants. Quota sample

	1460–1479				1480–1499				1500–1519			
	YE	YOU	%	Total	YE	YOU	%	Total	YE	YOU	%	Total
Upper	540	19	3	559	319	9	3	328	187	60	24	247
Middle	353	29	8	382	242	27	10	269	–	–		–
Lower	84	0	0	84	24	0	0	24	18	0	0	18
Total	997	48	5	1025	585	36	6	621	205	60	23	265

To conclude, it seems that the promotion of subject YOU at early stages took place in the middle ranks, from which it found its way to the language of higher social orders. How we should interpret this in terms of direction of change is not quite straightforward. We seem to be dealing with a change from below in terms of social awareness but not of social status. The awareness interpretation is supported by the origin of the change in phonological confusion (see section 6.4.1., above). Previous studies also testify to the higher frequency of YOU in informal language (Raumolin-Brunberg & Nevalainen 1997; for further discussion, see Chapter 9). This analysis is in harmony with Labov's claim (1994: 78) that changes from below can be introduced by any social class.

The next shift to be dealt with is the third-person singular inflection. According to the literature (Holmqvist 1922: 2), the earliest occurrences of -s were found in the tenth century. Consequently, we cannot go back to the innovative stages of this suffix, but what we can do is look at its first attempt to generalize and, in particular, its second rise in the sixteenth century.

Figures 7.4 and 7.5 serve as bases for the analysis. Like YOU, the medieval use of -s was led by the middle ranks. We cannot, of course, claim that they would have been the innovating group, but it is evident that they had adopted the new form as a serious alternative in the new and vigorous phase. What makes the progress of the third-person singular suffix different from the introduction of subject YOU is the failure of -s to diffuse into the upper ranks. On the contrary, it spread into the lower ranks and remained there throughout the sixteenth century. As Figure 7.5 shows it is only after 1600 that the higher echelons began to employ -s more than occasionally.

It is this second wave of the change from -TH to -s that invites a directionality analysis in social terms. What we see is a change from below par excellence. It is interesting, though, that the process does not follow the sequence lower–middle–upper, but looks like jumping over the middle section in the critical period around the turn of the century.

As regards the third change, the decline of multiple negation, we have seen in Chapter 6 that this was one of the few changes led by men. Previous research has suggested that professional writers, in our social division members of the middle ranks and social aspirers, were the men who promoted the use of single negation with assertive pronouns instead of multiple negation (Nevalainen 1998).

Figure 7.7, above, confirms this development, but only after 1520. Before that the upper ranks seem to have been in the lead. This fact alone might warrant an interpretation of this shift as a change from above in social terms. To find out the earliest developments, a closer analysis of the behaviour of the upper strata was carried out. Table 7.5. shows that it is not only during the later stages of diffusion but also earlier that professional writers led the way. Before 1520, gentry professionals did not use the multiple negation as often as other high-ranking men.

It is most likely that the model for the non-use of multiple negation derived from administrative language. Rissanen (2000) has shown that multiple negation was rare in early legal English. This type of language was well-known not only to professionals, such as lawyers, but also gentlemen, who often held high administrative offices. It seems that the loss of multiple negation qualifies as change from above in Labovian terms, being introduced by 'the dominant social class' and borrowed from a prestigious formal variety. Its rapid diffusion, however, took place because it came to be preferred by professional writers and administrators, especially social aspirers – all of them professional men – who led the change from the 1520s onwards.

This change shows that the composite nature of social-rank division causes problems in history as it does in present-day studies. In this case it seems that, rather than a high rank as such, it is a high level of education and an administrative position that promoted a new type of expression.

What we have learnt from this section is the crucial role of the upper ranks. It seems that for a new form to be generalized and supralocalized it had to be adopted by the upper strata (see also Chambers 1995: 251). After an introduction in the middle ranks, subject YOU spread to the upper ranks and quickly won the race against YE. The first attempt of third-person -s probably failed because it did not spread into the upper strata, but, when it finally did so around 1600, the road was open for rapid diffusion. Multiple negation was first dropped among the upper ranks, especially by government officials, and, although the middle ranks and social aspirers later came to lead the change, it is high-ranking men who at all times resorted to single negation far more than the lowest ranks. The possible curvilinear pattern of change, in our case middle-rank leadership, emerges at some stages of change but not systematically.

7.4.5. Evaluation: the Behaviour of Social Aspirers

Unlike present-day sociolinguists, historical linguists cannot carry out interviews to investigate values associated with linguistic choices. We have two

Table 7.5. Decline of multiple negation: gentry professionals. Percentage of single negation. CEEC 1998

	1460–1479				1480–1519				1520–1559				1560–1599			
	+MN	–MN	%	Total	+MN	–MN	%	Total	+MN	–MN	%	Total	+MN	–MN	%	Total
Non-prof nobility+gentry	111	11	9	122	18	6	25	24	42	36	46	78	32	298	90	330
All gentry professionals	57	10	15	67	29	15	34	44	98	68	41	166	30	133	82	163
Social aspirers	–	–	–	–	–	–	–	–	27	109	80	136	1	54	98	55

Note to Table 7.5. +MN = multiple negation, –MN = single negation.
The category nonprofessional nobility and gentry includes all autograph letters by those high-ranking informants who were not holders of administrative offices. The professional category consists of gentlemen who held administrative offices or worked as lawyers. They had usually acquired a high level of education at a university and/or Inn of Court. This category also includes non-autograph letters of the gentry, in other words, letters written by scribes and secretaries, i.e. well-educated professionals.

indirect ways of acquiring information, viz. reading contemporary comments and literature, and studying empirically the behaviour of people whose linguistic sensitivity is believed to be exceptionally high.

Contemporary comments, extremely valuable as they are, have a special characteristic: they tend to refer to stereotypes. They are not very useful for a linguist interested in changes from below conscious awareness. General comments, such as Puttenham's (1589) well-known passage on the best speech found in London, which we will come back to in the next chapter, are better in the sense that, in principle, they may refer to any linguistic feature and not only specific words or pronunciations, such as are characteristically employed in literature (e.g. Blake 1981).

For this section we have chosen the empirical method. Linguistic choices made by social aspirers are taken up for analysis. Our point of departure is the observation that upwardly mobile people tend to be sensitive towards the social connotations of linguistic variants. They are likely to choose overtly prestigious forms and avoid alternatives associated with low social status. In his early research, Labov (1972: 286) remarks that 'the social mobility of speakers provides as good or better correlation with linguistic behaviour than the analysis based on the speakers' socioeconomic positions.'

This analysis includes the following changes:

1. Subject YOU versus YE
2. MY/THY versus MINE/THINE
3. Third-person singular suffix -S versus -TH
4. Affirmative periphrastic DO
5. Decline of multiple negation
6. Third-person plural ARE versus BE

Our focus is on the behaviour of social aspirers in relation to both the lower and upper ranks. If the aspirers only seldom employed a variant that was common among the lower ranks, the form might have carried a stigma. On the other hand, high frequency among the upper ranks speaks against stigmatization.

In three of the changes, subject YOU vs. YE, MY/THY vs. MINE/THINE, and the third-person plural of the verb BE (see Figures 7.1, 7.2, above, section 8.3., below, and Nevalainen 1996b: 67), social aspirers used the incoming forms less than the lower ranks. Consequently, these forms might have carried a stigma. On the other hand, the upwardly mobile also employed them less often than the upper ranks did, which contradicts the idea of stigmatization. As regards the affirmative periphrastic DO, Nurmi (1999a: 99–109) only compared the behaviour of the upwardly mobile with all other informants, finding that the aspirers chose the affirmative periphrastic DO less often than other people. Hence the development of DO may resemble that of the first three changes. Rather than stigmatization, the behaviour of the aspirers in these cases may reflect avoidance strategy as a sign of linguistic insecurity.

The third-person singular inflection is a stronger candidate for stigmatization. During the first period in which the upwardly mobile are represented, 1500–1539, -s is not found at all in the language of these people. Until 1600, unlike the lower ranks but similar to the upper echelons, they rarely used -s. In the period between 1600 and 1619, the situation changed, -s becoming the majority variant in all ranks. As Figure 7.5, above, shows, it is as if a stigma had been lifted from -s. In our scenario, the social aspirers might have been quick to sense the new, nonstigmatized quality of -s and consequently surpassed the upper and middle ranks in the use of the new variant. According to Figure 7.5, compared with the upper strata, social aspirers somewhat overdo the change, a pattern well-known from present-day studies (Chambers 1995: 56).

While third-person inflection shows the possible course of events in a shift of social evaluation, the decline of multiple negation (Figure 7.7, above) is very different. In this change, ever since the social aspirers entered the scene in 1520–1559, they led the way. Again, they appear to be linguistically sensitive so as to follow the prestige model of the administrative language, and overextend it in comparison with the upper ranks. The fact that the lower ranks lagged behind can be compared with women's slow adoption of the incoming expression, based on the lack of access to the language of well-educated professionals.

Finally, a look at later developments interestingly points to a further difference between these changes. The rival of -s, the suffix -TH, the upper-rank favourite in the sixteenth century, has not become stigmatized but kept its position in special registers, such as the language of the King James Bible. By contrast, multiple negation, common in vernacular varieties throughout the English-speaking world, has become highly stigmatized in Standard English.

The behaviour of the social aspirers suggests that two types of change may involve stigmatization of lower-rank variants: (1) change from below both in terms of social status and social awareness, (2) change from above, in particular with a correlation between a high level of education and the frequency of the new form. In the first, the stigma may be lifted at some stage, but, in the second, it may be preserved for centuries. As this information is based on two developments only, more research is needed on the role of the upwardly mobile. However, what we know from Present-day English rather supports than contradicts our findings.

7.5.   Conclusion

The empirical research in this chapter has been based on the linguistic behaviour of male writers. The whole country has been treated as one language community, on the same grounds as in previous chapters. This approach offers a general view – certainly sufficient for a rough outline

– which can be sharpened by combining it with information on regional variation. In the next chapter, it is especially the dichotomy between the Court and London that provides further information on the social differences in the capital of the country.

We have mostly addressed questions pertaining to the social embedding of linguistic changes, to some extent also to transition. Actuation has been explored as far as possible, by tracing the social stratum that yielded the earliest occurrences of an innovative form during the years our study covers.

In addition to showing that social stratification of ongoing changes existed in early modern England, this study has emphasized the role which the upper ranks played in the diffusion of elements that were to become part and parcel of Standard English. If a form was not adopted by the upper echelons, as was the case with the first introduction of third-person singular -s and the relativizer THE WHICH, it did not spread in the country. As expected, we have seen changes from below social awareness percolate through all ranks. It also seems to us that stigmatization of the recessive variant was likely if the incoming form was introduced by highly educated professional men. In this case people without adequate education had no access to the prestigious variant.

The concept of prestige, not an uncomplicated one in the studies of Present-day English, is all the more complex in describing the linguistic behaviour of people for whom there was no codified standard model of language use. It is difficult for us as modern scholars, who have learnt a standard language at school and been exposed to its written variety for years, to imagine a situation without explicit rules for 'good' English or any other standard language. However, there is no reason to believe that the language of the upper ranks would not have carried prestige in the highly hierarchical late medieval and early modern societies. As is the case today, vernacular varieties certainly had their covert prestige, and not everyone tried to imitate the upper ranks. Our data confirm that upwardly mobile professionals, i.e. lawyers, government officials, army officers and doctors, often acquired their linguistic models from their social superiors and consequently played an important part in the diffusion of new variants.

In general, we hope to have shown that many of the concepts and models of present-day sociolinguistics can be applied in diachronic research. Although analyses based on reconstructed social structures and patchy data cannot be as refined as those on modern societies and controlled linguistic material, concepts such as social order and social mobility as well as direction of change from above and below, even in social terms, have proved to be valuable tools in the historical study of language change.

Notes

1. In this section, following the widespread practice among sociolinguists, despite their different meanings, the terms *social class*, *social stratum* and *social status* are

used practically interchangeably. As mentioned in Chapter 3, in discussions related to late medieval and early modern societies, the debatable concept *class* is avoided and contemporary or less theory-bound terms, such as *rank, order* and *degree*, are used. In reference to other scholars' works we naturally follow their usage.

It is worth noticing that sociolinguistics has followed the general trend of declining interest in social class. Cannadine (1998: 1) offers a pertinent quotation: 'the once fashionable and widely accepted view that class structure and class analysis provide the key to understanding British history and modern British life has been disregarded by many historians and abandoned by almost all politicians'. Reasons for this have been manifold, ranging from the political events in Eastern Europe undermining the interest in the Marxist social theory to redirecting the focus to other areas, such as gender studies and the role of language in creating social identities. Labov (2001: 58–60) comments on this development, but shows convincingly that socioeconomic class plays a significant role in sociolinguistic variation.

2. The following studies based on the CEEC have dealt with social status in a systematic way: Nevalainen (1996b, 1998, 1999a, 2000b), Nevalainen & Raumolin-Brunberg (1996a, 1998), Nevala (1998), Raumolin-Brunberg (1998), Nurmi (1999a), and Palander-Collin (1999).

3. In previous research, we often used the category name *social climber*. Although appropriate in reference to many of the upwardly mobile people whose correspondence is included in our corpus, the negative connotation of this phrase has made us reconsider the terminology. In this book we use the expressions *social aspirer* and *upwardly mobile* in reference to people who climbed more than two rungs on the social ladder. Unlike in present-day sociolinguistics (e.g. Chambers 1995: 95–96), these terms refer to people who not only aspired to a higher social position but also reached their goal.

4. The social aspirers in this table include Stephen Gardiner, Thomas Wolsey, Thomas Cromwell and William Paget in the first period, and Brian Duppa, John Cosin, Richard Haddock, William Petty, Joseph Williamson, William Scroggs, Gilbert Sheldon and Benjamin Newland in the second. Another social aspirer, Sir Thomas Browne (1605–1682), seemed very idiosyncratic in his use of -TH and was excluded from the statistics (see Appendix I).

5. Nurmi (1996: 160–162) also looked at the stratification of BE + ING, but the number of instances proved to be very low.

6. The high overall percentages of the last two sets of columns, indicating a nearly completed phase, reflect the fact that the lower ranks are relatively poorly represented. This is caused by the infrequency of negated sentences.

7. In Chapter 7 the chi-square testing of the six changes was carried out with available data for tables containing all four strata. For statistical significance it was basically sufficient that only one stratum deviated from the rest. An alternative method would have been contrasting each stratum with the others one at a time.

8. It is important to bear in mind that, although we have borrowed Labov's division into the five phases, the percentage criteria have been created by us. Hence, there is no immediate correspondence between Labov's analysis and ours.

9. The OED records the first occurrence of ITS in Florio's Italian-English Dictionary *A Worlde of Wordes* in 1598. In this book ITS does not form an entry but occurs in the text (Nevalainen & Raumolin-Brunberg 1994a).

10. The following informants used ITS 1619–1639: Sir Thomas Wentworth, from York-shire 1619, Nathaniel Bacon, gentleman, from Suffolk 1624, Thomas Bourchier, gentleman, from Yorkshire 1631, James Holt, scholar, from Surrey 1631, Thomas Smyth, gentleman, from Somerset 1634, and Sir Thomas Peyton, from Kent, 1639. On the basis of this list, it is impossible to identify any particular region as the provenance of this innovation.

Chapter 8

Regional Variation

And it would be foolish to deny that there *has* been some antagonism, with dialectologists feeling somewhat defensive about the 'newer' discipline of sociolinguistics, and sociolinguists being somewhat scornful about the 'older' discipline of dialectology. It is now apparent, however, that much of this is now past, and that we are moving into a new era of co-operation, integration and synthesis in the field. (Trudgill 1999b: 3)

8.1. Regional Dialects in England Today

In modern linguistic discourse, **sociolinguistics** has commonly come to be associated with the social axis of linguistic variation to do with social groups and structures. **Dialectology**, by contrast, is associated with the regional axis and equated with dialect geography. The divergent foci of the two disciplines have also been expressed by such terms as 'vertical' vs. 'horizontal' and 'urban' vs. 'rural'. But as suggested by Peter Trudgill (1999b: 3–4), despite their differences in emphasis and methodology, the disciplines share important macro-level objectives, such as improving our understanding of the nature of linguistic change. In this chapter we will see that, when it comes to historical processes of change, a hard-and-fast line between regional and social dialects is difficult to draw.

As regional dialect research in England goes back to the nineteenth century, there is a wealth of information, both historical and modern, on English rural dialects and the mechanisms of their diffusion. This chapter will draw on this research in order to be able to account for the processes of **supralocalization** of the 14 changes examined in this book.

The English spoken in England today can be divided into several regional varieties. All these varieties do not, however, have equally long histories. Trudgill (1999a: 5) makes a distinction between **traditional** and **modern** mainstream dialects. Traditional dialects are mostly spoken in the more remote rural and peripheral areas of the country. Some of the phonological features that characterize the traditional Northern, Central and Southern dialects are ancient, and can be traced back to Anglo-Saxon times. They

157

include the regionally variable pronunciations of the vowels in words like *long*, *night* and *land*.

In Trudgill's account modern mainstream dialects are represented by Standard English, on the one hand, and modern nonstandard dialects, on the other. In England the latter cover the majority of the population and are found in most urban areas, in the southeast of the country and in western Cornwall; in the speech of most younger people; and of middle- and upper-class speakers everywhere. The differences between modern nonstandard dialects are mostly phonological. The major dividing line runs between the North and South, but certain northern pronunciations now extend to the Midlands as well (e.g. the vowel in words like *but* and *cut*).

One recent development is the growth of the Home Counties as a large dialect region centred on London. This **Estuary English** is typically but not exclusively associated with lower-middle class speakers (Coggle 1993, Trudgill 1999a: 80–82). It serves as an illustration of the process of supralocalization in language change. As a result of dialect contact, new dialect areas are similarly developing in other urban areas and spreading out of large urban centres such as Birmingham, Liverpool and Newcastle. New levelled dialects have also come into existence in smaller towns such as Milton Keynes, which was designated a new town in 1967 and has since attracted industry and a wealth of new inhabitants from different parts of the country.[1]

The basis of dialect mixing and levelling lies in **dialect contact** and the way speakers of different dialects accommodate to each other in order to ensure successful communication. As contacts can be only short-term, they need not, of course, result in any permanent language changes or anything as radical as the rise of a new stable linguistic variety. Long-term contacts and consequently long-term accommodation, by contrast, are apt to lead to changes under the right social conditions. There are a number of demographic factors that have been found to influence the outcome of dialect contact by either promoting or retarding linguistic **focusing**, that is, the formation and consolidation of a new dialect. The following four are listed by Kerswill and Williams (2000: 75):

1) if adults predominate in the immediate post-settlement years, simplification will occur and focusing will be delayed, while an unusually high proportion of children may have the opposite effect.
2) a high degree of linguistic difference between the contributing varieties will also retard focusing.
3) the possibility of forming new social networks among children and younger people: high density, a 'critical mass' of population and universal schooling will promote rapid focusing.
4) a highly normative approach to mother-tongue literacy will hinder 'natural' processes such as simplification, and delay focusing.

In this list, the rise of dense, new **social networks** among children is one of the major factors promoting focusing and new dialect formation. Generally speaking, the kinds of social networks contracted by speakers are capable of inducing both language change and resistance to change.[2] Sociolinguists have shown that a dense, multiplex network structure is apt to impose linguistic norms on its members, whereas a loose-knit structure is conducive to diffuse language patterns and increased variation. This model, derived from the work of James and Lesley Milroy, suggests that people are likely to accommodate to each other linguistically in a weak-tie contact situation, and that contacts of this kind are therefore likely to lead to dialect diffusion and language change.

Kerswill and Williams' list also suggests that pronounced linguistic differences will retard focusing in a dialect-contact situation. All modern English mainstream dialects differ from each other phonologically more than grammatically. This is also basically true of the differences between modern mainstream dialects and traditional dialects. For a very long time, speakers of English may therefore have perceived variation in phonology as regionally more distinctive than variation in grammar.[3] A number of grammatical features shared by modern mainstream dialects go back to the early modern period.

Tudor and Stuart England was of course characterized by pervasive use of what Trudgill and other dialectologists label as traditional dialects. But, as we have seen in the previous chapters, the period also witnessed the spread of a number of supralocal grammatical features, which in the centuries to come were to supply grammatical underpinnings for modern mainstream dialects, including Standard English. In this chapter we will analyse their progress in regional terms drawing on data from London and the Royal Court, East Anglia and the North. What also interests us are the basic mechanisms propelling these processes.

8.2. Reconstructing Regional Differences in Tudor and Stuart England

8.2.1. Stating the Problem

While there is a multi-volume dialect atlas of twentieth-century English dialects, the *Survey of English Dialects*, and one of Late Middle English, none is available for the early modern period. The authors of *A Linguistic Atlas of Late Mediaeval English* (LALME) state the situation as follows:

> In the course of the fifteenth century [. . .] regional diversity gives way increasingly to Chancery Standard, the official language of the London administrators and the direct ancestor of modern Standard English. By

> the end of the same century, moreover, the establishment of printing was instrumental in the redevelopment of a national literary standard. The dialects of the spoken language did not die out, but those of the written language did; and although there are some late survivals, they are no sufficient basis for a dialect atlas. (McIntosh, Samuels & Benskin 1986: 3)

The reason why there is no Early Modern English dialect atlas is partly that all that has come down to us from this period is written data. The situation is particularly complicated in phonology because, as also observed by Montgomery (1996: 231) with respect to early American English material, dialect levelling is witnessed earlier in writing than in speech. We will return to the problem of gaining access to early modern regional data in 8.2.4., below. Apart from the 'bad-data' problem, two other issues are involved: (1) lack of systematic research on grammatical variation and (2) focus on varieties as distinct entities rather than bundles of linguistic features which constitute them.

As to the first issue, historical dialectology has traditionally centred on orthography and phonology, with less attention paid to morphology, and almost none to syntax. We might therefore wonder whether regional variation could not be detected by looking at linguistic systems other than spelling and the extent to which pronunciation is reflected in spelling. Regional differences in syntax and morphology have largely remained unexplored in Early Modern English and, as Blake (1992: 14–15) notes, this is also true of syntax even in Middle English.[4] One of the major concerns in this book has been to investigate the diffusion of a number of morphological and syntactic changes. As diffusion implies a centre from which the process proceeds, our data can serve as a testing ground for regional variation in language change.

The second issue raised, focus on varieties, is closely connected with language standardization in Late Middle and Early Modern English, and the tendency to overlook any variation in language that is not directly related to the rise of Standard English. The point is made in no uncertain terms by James Milroy:[5]

> At the Middle English stage, the description of divergence is still very salient (partly because the states attested in writing are unquestionably divergent states), but we also begin to notice attempts to launder the data retrospectively in such a way as to focus on those features that lead to modern 'standard' English and to ignore, reject and explain away those features that deviate from it. (J. Milroy 1992: 50–51)

While Milroy's point is partly well taken, there is certainly more to the issue than a political agenda. It has been identified as a problem of the level of abstraction in Nevalainen (2000c) and labelled the SAD (single ancestor-dialect) hypothesis by Hope (2000). It derives from the notion that dialects are distinct entities rather than simply shorthand for bundles of linguistic features, some of them shared by all, some by most varieties of the language in question, with others being of highly limited currency. The SAD hypothesis argues that this notion has typically been extended to promote a view of Standard English as a variety that once was selected to become the standard and subsequently developed on its own, sealed off from other linguistic influences.

Projecting the history of Standard English back to a 'Chancery Standard' arises from this variety fallacy. The fact that regularization of spelling is detected in documents issued from departments of state in the fifteenth century does not mean that spelling became fully standardized on the basis of these models, or that the process was completed in the fifteenth century. Nor does it mean that all aspects of written English were similarly regulated according to the 'Chancery Standard' of the time.[6] Chancery practices were not followed by the scribes who copied the manuscripts of Chaucer's *Canterbury Tales* in the last quarter of the fifteenth century, for instance. They continued to use the 'colourless' written language that had been well established in Late Middle English, and did not adopt the Chancery forms even for common items like THESE, THEIR, GIVEN and THROUGH (Smith 1996: 73–75). Although these Chaucer texts have variation in usage, they, too, were written in a levelled dialect which shows no particular dialectal distinctiveness.

So displacement of local usage is certainly visible in fifteenth- and early sixteenth-century texts to the extent that they can rarely be localized on the basis of linguistic features. While the 'Chancery Standard' may be taken as the first nationwide model, it was not the only supralocal one. Others included the colourless literary language mentioned above, and a Midland-type variety found in the Wycliffite texts (Samuels 1963; Smith 1996: 68–77). It is also to be noted that, although a number of supralocal usages may have been associated with the King's writing offices in the fifteenth century, their later development was not. In the regulation of spelling, an active role was assumed by printers and educators in the early modern period. On other levels of language, the rise of supralocal usages was an even more complicated process involving dialect contacts and varying degrees of focusing.[7]

While we agree that there is really no adequate basis for a dialect atlas of Early Modern English, it is nevertheless not impossible to trace the progress of many **processes of supralocalization** across the country at the time. As will be shown in the next section, the contrast between regional dialects and nonlocalizable language was also recognized by contemporaries in the sixteenth and seventeenth centuries.

8.2.2. Contemporary Views

The capital was often singled out in sixteenth- and seventeenth-century commentaries as having a special position on the dialect map of England. The language spoken in and around London was proposed as a model for literary composition in the sixteenth century. In his *Arte of English Poesie*

(1589), George Puttenham explicitly warned aspiring poets against using certain regional and social dialects. He remarks that undesirable language mixing took place in port towns, at frontiers and in the two universities, and strictly dialectal usage was associated with rural areas, including the north. The language of the lower ranks, 'the inferior sort', was similarly to be avoided, regardless of region, as uneducated. For the aspiring poet, Puttenham recommended neither the official documents nor the printed books of the time, however, but the language of the 'better-brought-up sort' of London, and of the Royal Court in particular. Similar comments can be found, for instance, in the writings of John Hart, the London orthoepist, some 20 years earlier (Dobson 1968: 64).

In the early modern period, nonlocalizable usages were called the 'usual', 'customary' or 'common' language. As was the case with Hart and Puttenham, reference was usually made to the spoken idiom. In his *Logonomia Anglica* (1619 [1972: 102, 104]), Alexander Gil combines regional and register criteria when he divides the dialects of England into 'the general, the Northern, the Southern, the Eastern, the Western, and the Poetic'. His 'general' dialect, *communis dialectus*, is identified as the language of 'persons of genteel character and cultured upbringing'. What Gil, the headmaster of St Paul's school, had in mind were the sociolects spoken by the wealthier sections of the population, in particular, in the capital region.[8] These comments suggest that there was in Early Modern English a difference between traditional dialects and what count, at least grammatically, as predecessors of modern mainstream dialects, Standard English among them. Moreover, London and the Royal Court emerge as having played an important role in the formation of the supralocal usages considered worth imitating by people like aspiring young poets in search of patronage.

8.2.3. The Variability of London English

But what was the English spoken in Tudor and Stuart London like? Many writers on the topic agree on one thing: the strong impact of migration on London English at all times. To begin with Late Middle English, Burnley (2000: 17) points out that a distinct London dialect is identifiable in a few documents in the fourteenth century but that most of them will have to be labelled dialectally as 'diverse *mischsprache*'. In other words, there were very few distinct London features to be found in writing at the time. This continues to be the case in the fifteenth century (Samuels 1981: 48–52).

But many researchers also argue in favour of detectable dialect ancestry for London English. One of the classic studies is Eilert Ekvall's work based on surname evidence. Ekvall (1956: lx–lxi) suggests that in the thirteenth century London immigrants largely came from the Home Counties, but that the pattern changed in the fourteenth century, when a sizable number of immigrants to the City came from the Midlands, from the East Midlands in particular. This East Anglian presence in London, it is then argued by Kristensson (1994: 107), among others, gave rise in the late fourteenth century to a London sociolect that was associated with both wealthy merchants and government officials. But unfortunately our information on the immigrant input into London English suggested by the surname data remains incomplete. Ekvall never published his extensive material on the southern counties (Wright 1996).

There are also those scholars who, on the basis of textual evidence, detect both Southern and East Midland influences in London English in the fifteenth and sixteenth centuries. One of them is H. C. Wyld (1936), who argues in favour of two distinct spoken varieties in London, one for the Court and the other for the City:

> It seems likely that there were at least two types of English actually spoken at London, one strongly tinged with E. Midland and South-Eastern characteristics, the other possessing less of the former, at any rate, and more of purely Southern features. [. . .] I am inclined to hazard the hypothesis that the spoken language of the Court and upper classes belonged rather to the Southern type of London English, that of the lower, and to a slightly less extent perhaps, that of the middle classes, to the Eastern type. (Wyld 1936: 84)

Wyld was, however, more interested in tracing the history of Received Pronunciation (RP) than observing patterns of linguistic variation, and detected a Standard Spoken English in London as early as the sixteenth century. Unlike RP today, which is not associated with any geographical area in Britain, Wyld's early speech norm not only allowed a good deal of variation but was also practically confined to those who frequented the Court or were under the influence of Court speech (Wyld 1936: 103).

The argument in favour of social dialect differences in London is taken further and generalized by Görlach (1999). He, too, assumes the existence of a standard norm quite early on:

> regional features had no great chance of being accepted into the standard after 1500; such 'influences' are rather to be expected, especially as far as pronunciation and syntax are concerned, in 'vertical' diffusion, i.e. they reflect an interchange of coexisting social and stylistic varieties within London English. (Görlach 1999: 473)

But what remains an open question here is the regional input into the various sociolects of London English. As demonstrated in Chapter 3, migration to London continued in Tudor and Stuart times with a large number of the immigrants coming from the north in the late fifteenth and sixteenth centuries. It is this continued magnetism of London which was instrumental in increasing the population of the capital. Combined with a higher-than-average death rate, it also speeded up the population turnover in the capital throughout the early modern period. John Stow writes in his famous *Survey of London* (1598) that London's population was 'by birth for the most part a mixture of all counties, by blood gentlemen, yeomen, and of the basest sort without distinction' (cited in Rappaport 1989: 86).

This constant flow of variable inputs into London English across time suggests that we cannot talk about focusing in the sense understood by present-day sociolinguists who study new towns like Milton Keynes. We may perhaps distinguish the City from the Royal Court on the basis of previous research – and this is what we shall do in the empirical part of this chapter – but we cannot take dialectal continuity for granted. Basing their argument on court records, Coleman and Salt (1992: 27) report that no more than 15 per cent of Londoners had in fact been born in the capital in the sixteenth and seventeenth centuries, and that over two thirds came from at least 50 miles away. Adult population therefore predominated in London. As we saw in section 8.1., this is a feature that may accelerate linguistic simplification but at the same time delay focusing. Despite a number of literate young adults such as apprentices, lack of universal schooling could also have retarded linguistic focusing.   ? P. 158

Population movements of all kinds give rise to changes in the communities' social network structures. We may therefore assume that the rapid urbanization and phenomenal growth that took place in early modern London despite the high mortality rate increased loose-knit and single-function social networks among the population. As suggested by Milroy and Milroy (1985b: 375), circumstances like this are particularly apt to promote language change: 'linguistic change is slow to the extent that the relevant populations are well established and bound by strong ties, whereas it is rapid to the extent that weak ties exist in populations'. Although London English influenced wider regional and nationwide use from the Late Middle Ages onwards, these demographic developments suggest that the influence need not have remained stable dialectally.

8.2.4. The Scope of Our Study

The point made by Wyld about a difference between two major kinds of London English in the Tudor and Stuart period is something that will be tested below. The linguistic features to be analysed consist of the 14 changes that we have discussed in the previous chapters. It is noteworthy that linguistic atlases of both historical and modern dialects suggest that, despite typical majority variants, alternative expressions 'for saying the same thing' commonly occur in different regions. This is also the case with our data. The features we study are usually not strictly confined to a given area at the time when their diffusion begins but may sporadically occur elsewhere, too. However, once it begins to gain momentum, the incoming feature typically diffuses faster in a particular region or locality, not everywhere at the same rate.

Some hypotheses may be proposed as to how a change in progress diffuses. The process can in principle follow the **wave model**, that is, changes spreading gradually outwards from a centre. This is the basis for linguistic similarities between neighbouring dialects. Dialects typically constitute continua, 'a series of systems where those nearest and most in contact show only slight differences' (Samuels 1972: 90). As suggested in the Görlach quotation, above, the principle also applies 'vertically', to sociolects. But the wave model can only be expected to apply normally when the population is distributed equally. There may be geographically isolated or otherwise self-sufficient areas that are bypassed by changes in progress. With supralocalizing features it appears that some of these basic assumptions of dialect diffusion may be specified further on the basis of modern dialect data: the new urban dialects discussed in section 8.1. all diffuse out of large urban centres.

One of the hypotheses advanced in this chapter is that London was instrumental in both promoting dialect mixtures and spreading linguistic innovations. The population of the metropolis grew rapidly, and social networks were looser and more uniplex in London than in small towns and in the countryside. They must have typically been based on a large number of continual contacts between nonadjacent dialects rather than on stable and continuous interaction between adjacent regional or social varieties (Samuels 1972: 92–93). The diffusion of changes is therefore expected to have been faster in London than elsewhere. In order to study this claim empirically, a point of comparison will be established between the capital city and one of the more peripheral dialect areas, East Anglia. The reason for selecting East Anglia rather than, say, the West Country is simply the amount of extant material. East Anglian letters are available throughout the period covered by us, while material from areas such as Somerset and Dorset is harder to come by, especially in an edited form.

The second part of our argument is related to linguistic innovations spreading from urban centres to the surrounding rural areas. In modern language communities these processes have also been found to involve a mechanism of diffusion that differs from the wave model, namely **dialect hopping**. Trudgill (1986) has shown in detail how language changes may first hop from one urban centre to another, bypassing the countryside in between. This model is based on the population sizes of the communities in interaction and the distances between centres (Chambers & Trudgill 1980: 189–204). Dialect hopping may be a powerful means of promoting and speeding up supralocalization: when the urban centres in a given area converge on the use of a particular form, it may diffuse to the countryside from several directions simultaneously.

In our case, migration in sufficient quantities can also constitute a form of dialect hopping. When a process of dialect diffusion following the classical wave pattern is under way percolating from the north to the south, it can be greatly accelerated by the immigration to the capital of a large number of northerners – or of people from the intervening regions already in possession of the feature. This is an aspect of dialect diffusion that can be tested by including a third point of comparison in addition to London and East Anglia. The North, consisting of the counties north of Lincolnshire, was selected because we wanted to explore the mechanisms by which supralocal features spread across the country.[9]

In their study of the diffusion of the third-person singular -s, Ogura and Wang (1996) propose a refinement to the traditional wave model by suggesting that the rate at which a change diffuses may vary in different localities. More precisely, they propose that those localities that are later in adopting the change in progress will, when the process advances, not only catch up with the ones that started earlier, but surpass them. One of the aspects of dialect diffusion that we shall pay particular attention to in our analysis is whether we can observe a **snowball effect** of this kind or whether the changes progress at a constant rate.

However, as shown in Chapter 7, a real success story in supralocal terms also had to involve vertical diffusion in Tudor and Stuart England. This social aspect of dialect contact will come into the picture when we compare the City of London and the Royal Court. While the two other regions, East Anglia and the North, are normally accounted for in dialect research – East Anglia including Norfolk and Suffolk – the capital is not included as a matter of course, or at least not divided into localities. But as we have seen, there is good reason to try to find out whether there were linguistic differences between Westminster and people associated with the Royal Court, and the City of London.[10]

In this chapter, we have included all people living in the City and in Southwark as Londoners. On the social scale they tend to occupy the ranks from the lower gentry downwards with a considerable merchant contingent, though the odd nobleman letter writer could be found living in the City. At Court, by contrast, there is a heavy concentration of the uppermost ranks from the royalty down to the upper gentry. Those who constituted the Royal Court in the Tudor and Stuart periods were mostly resident in Westminster and consisted of courtiers, members of the royal household, high-ranking government officials and diplomats directly reporting to the ruling monarch or the Lord Chancellor. In East Anglia and the North no similar social divide can be found. The high overall literacy rate of London discussed by social historians like Cressy (1980: 72–76) may be reflected in the number of lower-ranking letter writers in the City and Southwark; they included men like Philip Henslow and his theatrical circle, writing around 1600.

Unlike in Chapter 7, both men and women writers are included in our regional subcorpora. As nonmobile older rural males, the 'NORMs' of Chambers and Trudgill (1980: 33), have traditionally served as English regional dialect informants, including women in our data ought perhaps to be justified.[11] There is some research suggesting that females typically migrated shorter distances than males in early modern England (Clark & Souden 1988: 19). In this respect women might be thought of as better regional dialect informants than men. But, for several reasons, this need not be the case.

Especially in the Tudor period, it was customary among the higher ranks to send both boys and girls away to complete their education in the households of family friends or relatives. Women also typically moved house when they got married. In the seventeenth century, the higher ranks became increasingly mobile and attended the London social season on a regular basis. All these facts suggest that those who were fully literate in the early modern period were not typical rural dialect informants: they were either socially privileged and travelled for business and pleasure, or their training and occupation, such as apprenticeship or the merchant's trade, were apt to promote their regional mobility. It is these kinds of people that one would expect to be exposed to supralocal tendencies in the language community, to be in a position to adopt ongoing changes, and by doing so to contribute to dialect levelling.

For all these reasons our classification is not aimed to make a basic distinction between those inhabitants of a locality who had migrated from elsewhere and those who were born there. Nor does it include those who had emigrated from their native area and permanently settled somewhere else. All that matters is where they had settled down to live and work on a permanent basis. It is nevertheless telling of the migration history of the period that three quarters of our Norfolk and Suffolk writers whose place of birth is known to us were native East Anglians. Also, as far as we can ascertain, more than 80 per cent of the Northerners in our data were born in the North. But the picture of London is very different: out of all the writers included in the CEEC who permanently lived and worked in London, and whose place of birth has been documented, about one fifth are recorded as having been born there. This is also the case with only one quarter of those who were attached to the Royal Court. These figures come close to the estimates of the proportion of native Londoners based on the sixteenth- and seventeenth-century records discussed above.

8.3. Previous Empirical Studies

Systematic empirical studies of regional differences in Tudor and Stuart English are not very numerous. Many of them are chiefly concerned with spelling variation in relation to scribal practices or pronunciation, fewer with morphology. In the following some findings directly relevant to our concerns will be presented. They indicate that it is possible to detect the influence of London in the language of immigrants to the capital. Some of them may, however, retain their original dialect to the extent of being regionally localizable. It has also been shown that the North–South divide can to some extent be reconstructed in morphology and grammar but that it is a question of more-or-less rather than either-or: in this period before linguistic prescriptivism, originally northern features even crop up in the language of well educated southerners. However, cases of regular dialect diffusion have also been documented.

The social profile of those who spread Chancery forms in the late fifteenth century can be characterized as male, educated, and socially and geographically mobile (see Hernández-Campoy & Conde-Silvestre 1999; Conde-Silvestre *et al.*, forthcoming). A clear contrast emerges between representatives of the London legal profession or those closely connected with it, and the urban non-gentry, typically London merchants, the latter exhibiting the least accommodation to Chancery practices. Gómez-Soliño (1981) documents the impact of Chancery spellings in the early sixteenth century on two notable individuals both active at Court, Sir Thomas More and Thomas Wolsey. He comes to the conclusion that both of them show idiosyncratic but incomplete accommodation to Chancery usage.

A more general London influence on the language of migrants is detected by Davis (1954) in his study of the Paston family in the fifteenth century. He compares those members of the family who stayed in Norfolk with John Paston II, the courtier and soldier, and his younger brother John Paston III, who became the trusted servant of noble families. Both were mobile and spent considerable time in the capital in the latter half of the fifteenth century. Davis (1954: 130–131) concludes that:

> the writers who [. . .] seem nearest to the general development of the language are not, as we might have expected, those educated at Eton or Oxford, still less the Cambridge men; [. . .] But it must have been from London – no doubt from Londoners 'off worshyp'– that he [Sir John the elder] and some of his brothers learnt to adopt new forms and spellings; so that even at this date one type at least of London speech must have acquired something of the prestige of an incipient 'standard' language.

But apparently not everybody accommodated to the same extent. Britton (2000) reopens the case of Henry Machyn, a merchant-tailor and funeral undertaker, whose diary (1550–63) has often been presented as a source of the London English of the lower orders of the period. Wyld (1936: 141) identifies him as an Elizabethan Cockney. Britton uses the LALME questionnaire and includes high-frequency function words and lexical items as well as inflectional and derivational affixes in his study. Comparing his findings systematically with Late Middle English dialect material, he is able to produce compelling evidence for Machyn having migrated to London from South-West Yorkshire and having retained a large part of his northern linguistic identity.

There is, however, evidence of northernisms and other regional dialect-features in London, something that Bailey *et al.* (1989: 287) take to represent 'the kind of mainstream vernacular that has been important in the evolution of standard English'. In their study of the letters of the Cely family (1472–88; see 5.4.1.), two generations of London merchants, they come across some salient non-southern patterns of subject–verb concord. They find that the subject category to a large extent regulates the use of third-person present-tense suffixes both in the plural and in the singular: full NP subjects favour the use of suffix, either -TH or -s, while pronoun subjects favour -0. Besides this Type of Subject Constraint, which had spread as far south as the Chester–Wash line in the Late Middle English period (McIntosh 1989: 117), the originally northern third-person suffix -s was expanding at the expense of the traditional southern -TH among the younger Celys at the time (Bailey *et al.* 1989: 288–293). This apparent-time change is also discussed by Raumolin-Brunberg (1996a: 105).

The subject-NP constraint is found to operate even in writers like Shakespeare. As shown by Schendl (2000), over 10 per cent of the NP subject cases have -s in the plural in the First Folio. But Shakespeare did not provide evidence for the other requirement of the original Northern Subject Rule, viz. the Proximity of Subject Constraint, which requires -s to be inserted into the second verb of a co-ordinated VP when the subject pronoun is not repeated (*'they V and Vs'*). Schendl concludes that there is no direct proof of northern influence in Shakespeare. This appears to be true of the Northern Subject Rule in general in southern Early Modern English. Schendl (1996) finds the Type of Subject Constraint and even the Proximity of Subject Constraint operating in a number of printed sources, including Queen Elizabeth's translation of *Boethius*, but their incidence remains sporadic. Fascinating evidence though these findings provide for dialect mixing in Tudor English, they also suggest that the Northern Subject Rule was a variable rule and never gained the same supralocal status as the northern suffix -s, for instance (Schendl 1996: 150, Nevalainen & Raumolin-Brunberg 2000a,b).

The other northern features that made their way to the supralocal stock of Early Modern English include ARE, the present plural indicative form of the verb BE. Traditional forms continue to occur in the fifteenth and early sixteenth centuries in the CEEC (Nevalainen 2000c). Apart from ARE, the Scandinavian variant ER is found in the North (8.1a) and ARN in East Anglia (8.1b), while BE is used in London and in the South (8.1c).

> (8.1a) and Sir Roger Fenwike with ccc. men burnt the Town of Langton and distroyed all the cornes therein: which Townes **er** in the hert of the countre two myle beyond Jedworth opon the watere of Chevyot. (Thomas Dacre, 1513; CLIFFORD, 94)
>
> (8.1b) I haue be there with youre tenauntys for here areragys, and they **arn** better plessid to pay you þe mony thanne Master Will P. (William Pecock, 1470s; PASTON, II: 412)

(8.1c) All your menservauntes have bene of counsaill with hym, for they **be** of no les opynion, declaring that your breid is not good ynoghe for dogges, and drincke so evill that they cannot drinck it. (John Johnson, 1545; JOHNSON, 250)

When the distribution of ARE out of the variable total of BE plus ARE was studied in the four regions discussed in 8.2.4., the following results were obtained: London accepted ARE earlier than the Court, and East Anglia earlier than London. The North, not surprisingly, manifested the highest proportion of ARE throughout the period (Nevalainen 2000c: 347–349). These results can be interpreted in terms of dialect diffusion: as ARE was percolating southwards in the fourteenth and fifteenth centuries, it first had a stronger impact on East Anglia than on London. The process also counts as a change from below in social terms: the Court was slower in adopting ARE than the City of London.

Finally, there is some evidence of features that retreated from the supralocal variety of English and only remained in use in some regional dialects. They include the second-person singular pronoun THOU, which became increasingly rare by the eighteenth century. As shown by Nevala (2002), in the seventeenth century the use of THOU was typically restricted either to intimate correspondence between spouses or to letters written by parents to their children. In both cases, the most typical users of THOU came from rural areas, such as East Anglia, Kent and the West Country, and even in these intimate family letters the use of THOU was highly variable.

Second-person pronouns have also been studied in court records. Hope (1993) analysed the Durham consistory court depositions from the 1560s, and came to the conclusion that THOU was the marked form used for emotion and affection rather than as a marker of solidarity. The extent to which regional usages might also have been involved in the records is not, however, addressed. In present-day traditional dialects, there are two major THOU-preserving areas. The northern area covers the Lower North, Lancashire and Staffordshire areas and parts of South Yorkshire, and the western area consists of the Northern and Western Southwest (Trudgill 1999a: 92–93). How much larger these areas were in the Early Modern English period is difficult to tell, but one may assume that the capital was the leading influence in the wholesale adoption of YOU.

8.4. Regional Variation in Late Middle and Early Modern English

The regional analysis of our 14 changes will operate on three levels of delicacy depending on the frequency of occurrence of the linguistic variable and the regional data available. With high-frequency variables, the fourfold distinction between the Court, London proper, East Anglia and the North will be established and quantified. It is particularly relevant with changes that diffuse from the North southwards. But there are also changes with which the division into four regions turns out to be too fine, and the significant dividing line falls between the capital and the two more northern regions.[12]

With some less frequently occurring variables we shall have to content ourselves with a threefold regional division, and analyse London and the Court separately, but East Anglia and the North in the aggregate. All these changes spread from the capital region to the rest of the country, and in all of them the differences between London and the Court proved significantly greater and more consistent than those observed between East Anglia and the North. Distributional differences of this kind will be taken as indicators of the social rather than purely regional character of these processes.

Finally, there are some low-frequency variables whose regional distributions could not be analysed reliably in quantitative terms. So the noun subject of the gerund will only be considered by contrasting the capital with the two more northern regions in the aggregate. Changes that will receive a more summary treatment include the determiner ITS, the prop-word ONE, inversion after clause-initial negatives, and DO-support in negative declaratives. Indefinite pronouns with human reference provide perhaps the most intriguing case among these low-frequency phenomena. They will all be discussed in subsection 8.4.3.

8.4.1. Changes Led by the Capital Region

Most of the linguistic processes we examine in this volume first started their diffusion in the capital area. The distinction between London and the Court turns out to be significant in a number of cases, but not in all.

Subject form YOU

There is little evidence as to the regional origins of the spread of YOU to the subject function. The fact that the historical form YE is preserved in the traditional dialect in Northumberland (Trudgill 1999a: 93) suggests that it never fully supralocalized throughout the North. Figure 8.1 shows the CEEC data, which indicate that the innovation was adopted earlier in the capital than in the rest of the country.

Tracing the change back to the third quarter of the fifteenth century we can see that it was already incipient in London and the North but not totally absent from East Anglia either. However, there is no evidence of it at Court in this period. At the turn of the sixteenth century, the innovative form is also sporadically attested in the language of a few individuals at Court. There is one man among them, Edmund de la Pole, Earl of Suffolk

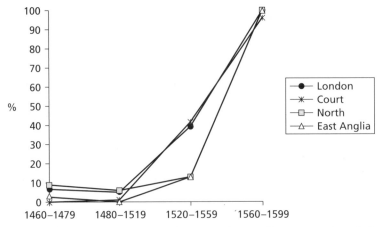

Figure 8.1. The replacement of subject form YE by YOU. Regional distribution of YOU. CEEC 1998 and Supplement; quota sample (excluding Edmund de la Pole).

Lexical Transp
most

(1473–1513), who is exceptional in that he uses YOU 100 per cent of the time. The extracts in (8.2) and (8.3) come from letters exchanged by de la Pole and a servant of his, Thomas Killingworth. H. C. Wyld (1936: 83) suspects that many aspects of de la Pole's 'queer lingo', as he calls it, may have been affected by the years he spent abroad. As far as de la Pole's use of YOU is concerned, the explanation might be found in his frequent contacts outside the Court.

> (8.2) **Yov** have done viesle to send Parrelebene to my cousene Nevele to povt me to more coostes. Yt vas nat my commandment that **yov** chovld do so. Me thenke **yov** do nat viesle nor honestele. I have notheng bovt bovt **yov** have yt, and **yov** povt me to ale the coste, ... (Edmund de la Pole to Thomas Killingworth, 1505; RERUM I, 256)

> (8.3) And if **ye** sende me to the court, Sir, if it please you, this is best: cause a lettre of credence to bee made there in Frenche, or a lettre of your mynd to bee made to my Lord Shyvers aswele as to the other two, and fele asmuche of his mynd as **ye** cann. (Thomas Killingworth to Edmund de la Pole, 1505; RERUM II, 382)

In the next four decades, 1520–59, the change is nearing mid-range in the capital, and no difference can be found between London and the Court. In the two other regions the use of YOU as a subject is still in its incipient stage: it is used less than 15 per cent of the time in both East Anglia and the North. The difference between these two regions and the capital is polarized and statistically highly significant. In the next 40-year period, 1560–99, regional differences are levelled out in the data, and the change is completed.

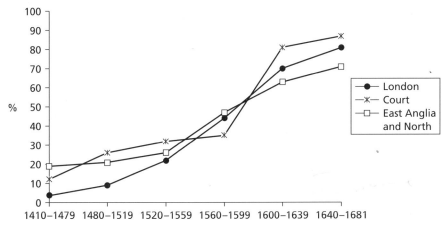

Figure 8.2. Object of the gerund. Regional distribution of zero forms as opposed to OF-phrases. CEEC 1998 and Supplement; percentages.

Object of the gerund

The diffusion of the direct object of the gerund is a less dramatic process than that of YOU. It takes a much longer time and shows a different kind of regional patterning in the capital: London and the Court progress at different rates. The variable is also not frequent enough for the data to yield a reliable picture of the North and East Anglia in the fifteenth and early sixteenth centuries. These two regions will therefore be treated in the aggregate for the entire timespan presented in Figure 8.2.

In the first period studied, 1410–79, when the change was incipient, a slight East Anglian and Northern advantage could be detected over the Court and London. This may suggest that the feature did not originate in the capital region, though it soon found its way there. From the second period on, the Court was in the vanguard of the process throughout the timespan examined, except for the period 1560–99. The regional patterns were not, however, statistically significant until the tail end of the process in the seventeenth century.

Figure 8.2 indicates that the regional distribution of the direct object form remained relatively stable when the change was new and vigorous: the form was mildly favoured at Court in 1480–1559. In mid-range, 1560–99, the North, East Anglia and London progressed faster than the Court. This may be partly due to the age profile of the courtiers in the corpus at the time: they included a number of prominent men like Nicholas Bacon, William Cecil, Thomas Gresham and Francis Walsingham, who were all born between 1510 and 1530, and hence on average older than the rest of the writers in this period (see Chapter 5).

Figure 8.3. Noun subject of the gerund. Regional distribution of the genitive. CEEC 1998; percentages.

The Court regained its leading position in the seventeenth century, as the change was nearing completion. London followed suit and began to show signs of the snowball effect. The relative order of the two localities, however, remained the same in the last two periods.

Noun subject of the gerund

The data on the noun subject of the gerund are too scarce to present any accurate regional breakdowns. But some trends can be perceived that may later be checked against a larger database. The combined figures for London/the Court and East Anglia/the North suggest that the change was promoted by the capital area. The drop in the Northern regions in 1660–81 shown by Figure 8.3 may well be a corpus artefact with the variable total of only 24 instances in that cell. But it is noteworthy that by 1580, when our record begins, the change had already advanced to mid-range. It is therefore impossible to tell whether what looks like a systematic lead of the capital region represents a long-standing metropolitan advantage or is merely a reflection of the snowball effect.

Periphrastic DO in affirmative statements

As shown in Chapter 4, the use of affirmative periphrastic DO began to decline in the seventeenth century. The turning point in the process can be traced to the first two decades of the century. A polar contrast emerges between the four regions, with East Anglia and the North on the one side, and London and the Court on the other (Figure 8.4).

The frequency of DO drops radically in London and at Court in the first two decades of the seventeenth century – according to Nurmi (1999a), due to the influence of the arrival of the Scottish Court of James I in London

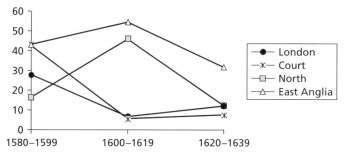

Figure 8.4. Periphrastic DO in affirmative statements. Regional distribution of DO per 10,000 words. CEEC 1998 (based on Nurmi 1999a: 177).

– while it continues to rise in East Anglia and in the North. The change follows the model set by the capital. The overall declining trend can be perceived in all four regions during the next 20 years shown in Figure 8.4. The frequency of the form continues to be low in affirmative statements (below 20 instances per 10,000 words) throughout the century, and DO never becomes grammaticalized the way it does in negative and interrogative clauses (Nurmi 1999a: 166).

Decline of multiple negation

The disappearance of multiple negation is another process favoured at the Royal Court. As shown by Figure 8.5, a sharp contrast arises between the Court and London proper around 1500, when the change is only incipient in London but already in mid-range at Court. As the variable is not of high frequency, our data do not allow detailed comparisons with the North and

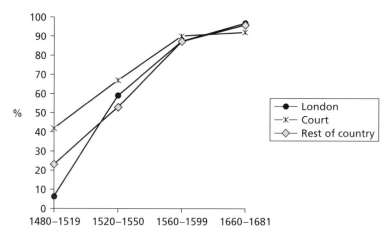

Figure 8.5. Multiple vs. single negation. Regional distribution of single negation followed by nonassertive indefinites. CEEC 1998 and Supplement; percentages.

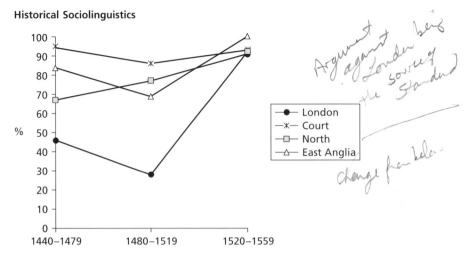

Figure 8.6. Relative pronoun THE WHICH vs. WHICH. Regional distribution of WHICH. CEEC 1998 and Supplement; percentages.

East Anglia. Figure 8.5 therefore plots the mean frequency of the variable in the rest of the country against London and the Court.

The Court advantage continues until the middle of the sixteenth century but, as the process advances rapidly, no significant regional differences can be detected from the second period onwards, when the change is past mid-range at Court. The last period to be measured a century later, 1660–81, shows that the change has practically run its course by that time.

Relative pronoun WHICH

By the middle of the fifteenth century, the spread of the relative pronoun WHICH had been nearly completed in all the four regions examined here, and between 1440 and 1560 little happens anywhere except in London. As shown by Figure 8.6, WHICH is practically the only form used at Court throughout the period. The use of the incoming form steadily increases in the North and, after some minor fluctuation, also in East Anglia.

Throughout the latter half of the fifteenth century, London stands out from the rest. It is the London wool-merchant community in our data, the Celys in particular, which prefers the use of the longer form. But by the time we get to the middle of the sixteenth century, 1520–59, the usage of the section of the merchant community we have access to is substantially altered and now in full agreement with the majority pattern. Only a few individual exceptions persist, including Sabine Johnson, the merchant's wife, who despite her frequent contacts with London continues to prefer THE WHICH in the 1540s.

Relative adverb vs. prepositional phrase

The synthetic relative adverb (WH- plus preposition) dominates the usage across the country in the fifteenth century. The first signs of the slow rise of

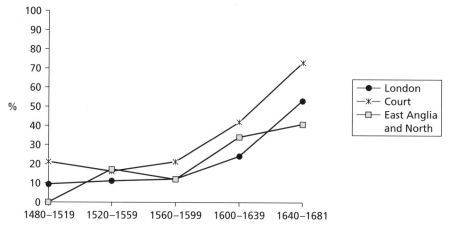

Figure 8.7. Relative adverb vs. preposition plus (THE) WHICH. Regional distribution of the preposition-plus-WH constructions. CEEC 1998 and Supplement; percentages.

the analytic form (preposition plus WH-) can be traced to the capital. As the corpus is not large enough to have separate breakdowns for East Anglia and the North for the first 100 years of the process, they are presented in the aggregate in Figure 8.7. These figures should therefore be considered only suggestive of the trends to be found outside the capital region.

The major pattern that emerges in Figure 8.7 is similar to the one found with the object of the gerund, with the exception that the whole change only reaches mid-range by 1681. When the analytic form is new and vigorous, it is promoted by the Court. London begins to catch up when the change is nearing completion at Court, thus snowballing towards the end of the process. The differences between the regions are not marked; only in early seventeenth century do they reach statistical significance.

8.4.2. Changes Spreading from the North

As pointed out in section 8.3., there are several forms that spread from the north to the south in the Late Middle and Early Modern English periods. One of these processes, the generalization of the third-person plural form ARE, was discussed in 7.4.5. and 8.3. The other two, which are presented below, show partly similar but partly divergent patterns of diffusion. All three, however, suggest that northern features supralocalized from below in social terms.

Third-person singular -s

The northern origins of the third-person singular indicative suffix -s are clearly in evidence in the CEEC data. As shown by Figure 8.8, it is the majority form in the North in the latter half of the fifteenth century. The form is also found in one third of the cases in London. But it does not

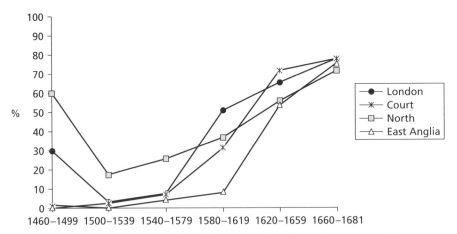

Figure 8.8. The replacement of -TH by -s in verbs other than HAVE and DO. Regional distribution of -s. CEEC 1998 and Supplement; quota sampling (excluding Thomas Browne).

occur in either our East Anglian or Court data. The most plausible way to explain the presence of -s in London but not in East Anglia is to appeal to 'dialect hopping': the form must have found its way to the City and the London merchant community, which displays it, as a result of migration: a large number of migrants to the capital came from the north at the time (Nevalainen & Raumolin-Brunberg 2000a: 290–295).

As noted in Chapter 4, the supralocalization of the northern suffix is not a straightforward process. In the first half of the sixteenth century, the data show a sharp drop in the frequency of -s in London and a sudden dip in the North as well. As we have a fair amount of data from the four regions in the period 1500–79, the 'bad-data' problem cannot explain the trough in the S-curve. We could therefore argue that it was simply caused by the supralocal diffusion of the southern -TH. The spread of -TH to the north was a change from above socially: in the northern Plumpton family circle (1470–1520), the southern form was most frequently attested in the upper ranks, the highest ranking men in particular (Moore 2002).

But the supralocalization of -TH does not explain the subsequent development of the variable: in the latter half of the sixteenth century -s makes a comeback, most conspicuously in London. We argued in Chapter 4 that this comeback may have been phonologically motivated and related to the spread of the syncopated suffix -s (as in *he sings*) as opposed to the unsyncopated -(E)TH, which was preferred in sibilant-final contexts (*she danceth*). Phonological motivation could suggest a change from below in terms of social awareness. As section 7.4.3. indicates, while the change clearly proceeded from below in social terms, it was also promoted by social aspirers, who are usually sensitive to marked variants.

The fact that the Royal Court was slow in adopting the incoming form strongly supports the argument in favour of a change from below socially. But when the supralocal diffusion of -s is nearing completion in the second quarter of the seventeenth century, the Court exhibits a steeper rising S-curve than the rest of the regions, thus displaying the snowball effect discussed earlier.

However, Figure 8.8 indicates that the process was the slowest not at Court but in East Anglia, where -TH persisted into the early decades of the seventeenth century. The reasons as to why this should have been the case range from a three-competing-forms hypothesis (the third being the zero form: Trudgill 2001) to the relative isolation and self-sufficiency of East Anglia at the time. In Late Middle English, it had clearly adhered to the southern form (McIntosh *et al*. 1986; maps 645 and 646). The zero form had also been attested in East Anglia in the fifteenth century – but so had it in London, too (Bailey *et al*. 1989). It is difficult to assess what role it played in the supralocalization of -s apart from possibly slowing it down regionally. The zero form was a viable alternative in East Anglia in the seventeenth century, and continues in the regional dialect well into the present day. A mix of all three forms is found in the extract in (8.4) from Lady Katherine Paston's letter to her 14-year-old son.

> (8.4) thy father **remembers** his loue to the and **take** thy wrightinge to him very kindly: thy brother **remember** his louingest loue to the [. . .] I had thought to haue written to mr Roberts this time. but this sudene Iornye of this mesinger **affordethe** me not so much time. (Katherine Paston, 1626; PastonK, 90)

As shown in Chapter 5, there are always some individuals who markedly deviate from their contemporaries. In the last period, 1660–81, Thomas Browne, the author of *Religio Medici*, who settled in Norwich at the age of 32, continues to use the traditional -TH with many lexical verbs in his personal correspondence in the East Anglian subcorpus. He used mixed endings even in his private letters to his son, as shown in example (8.5).

> (8.5) Tommy **hath** had it with some hooping and vomiting, butt now **vomits** butt seldome, butt **sleepes** prettie well in the night and at any time when hee **lyeth** downe in the day. (Thomas Browne, 1681; Browne, 193)

It is difficult to tell whether this is evidence for regional usage or simply an educated man's conservatism. However, most people restricted the use of -TH to the two verbs HAVE and DO at this time (Nevalainen 1996a). The fact that these two verbs, auxiliary and main verb alike, lagged behind the rest may strengthen our point about phonological motivation behind the rise of the syncopated -s: HAVE and DO both lack any such motivation. As late as 1619 in his *Logonomia Anglica*, Alexander Gil refers to HAS as the northern

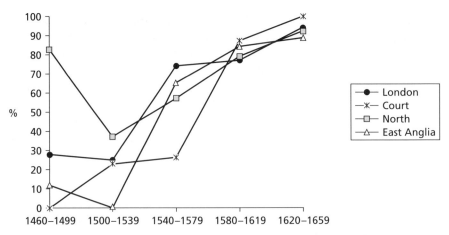

Figure 8.9. MINE and THINE vs. MY and THY. Regional distribution of MY and THY before vowels. CEEC 1998 and Supplement; percentages.

variant of HATH – a reminder that individual lexical items may keep their regional connotations well after the distinction has generally disappeared.

MY and THY

The regional diffusion of the short determiners MY and THY resembles that of the third-person singular -s in some important respects, but the two processes also show marked differences. As the determiner variable has a lower overall frequency than the third-person suffix, our data on it are less plentiful. They nevertheless clearly indicate that the determiner change basically consisted of one process, not two (Figure 8.9).

As our northern data are scarce in the first subperiod, 1460–99, the high frequency of the short forms in the North is therefore likely to be a corpus artefact. But the second period, 1500–39, is quite well represented, and strengthens the supposition that the change diffused from the north. With East Anglia the case is reversed: the first period is representative but the second is not. Put together, these figures offer support for Mustanoja's observation (1960: 157) that the loss of -N occurred earlier in the north than in the south.

As far as the south is concerned, a significant difference emerges between the Court and London in 1540–79: the process was then nearing completion in London, but only approaching mid-range at Court. This suggests a change from below socially, also observed in Chapter 7, which analysed male writers in the entire CEEC.

8.4.3. Low-Frequency Seventeenth-Century Processes

There is too little data to analyse the regional distribution of some of the processes discussed in Chapter 4 in any detail. A few comments may, however, be made on their regional progression. These low-frequency changes include subject–operator inversion after clause-initial negatives. If it is connected with the disappearance of multiple negation and the rise of DO-support, as we have reason to believe, one would expect it to have spread from the capital. This notion is supported by the similarity of the gender distributions of the two processes (see 6.4.3.).

The spread of periphrastic DO into negative statements is a low-frequency phenomenon with a complex pattern of diffusion. Just like DO in affirmative statements, it suffered a remarkable drop in frequency in the early seventeenth century. At the time it appears to have been used in some quantities only in East Anglia – a region that lagged behind the rest in the case of affirmative periphrastic DO as well (Figure 8.4). Regional differences in negative statements are mostly too small to be statistically significant, but the strikingly similar regional patterning of affirmative and negative DO speaks for their co-evolution (Nurmi 1999a: 177–178).

The possessive determiner ITS is attested in the North and in East Anglia earlier than in the capital region in the CEEC. But, as pointed out in 7.4.4. (note 10), the first instances of the form are scattered throughout the country, and it is impossible to identify any one locality as its region of origin. Our data, however, clearly suggest that London was the centre of its subsequent diffusion: in the period 1640–81, the innovative form appears at a 20 per cent frequency in the North, East Anglia and at Court, but twice as frequently in London. The prop-word ONE is similarly attested in all four regions in the early part of the seventeenth century. But in 1640–81, when the change was picking up, it was promoted by the metropolitan area, particularly by the Court.

An interesting pattern emerges with the indefinite pronouns with singular human reference. There is a clear trend in the CEEC suggesting that the forms in -BODY were favoured in London, at the Royal Court, and in East Anglia in the first part of the seventeenth century, but were hardly used at all in the North (well over 20 per cent vs. below 5 per cent, respectively). All the innovative forms preferred in the North were -ONE compounds. While -ONE is found in all four regions in the period from 1640 to 1681, forms in -BODY are much slower to make their way to the North. Although the CEEC does not have enough data to suggest anything more than a trend, it appears consistent with the forms in -BODY. This is obviously one of the many topics in historical dialectology that calls for further research.

8.5. Conclusion

There are a number of conclusions to be drawn from these analyses. They can be focused on (a) the regional origins of the changes analysed, (b) the regional embedding of their diffusion, including the contrast between the

Court and London, and (c) the consistency across time of the distributions of the linguistic variables. One generalization can be made to begin with: most of the supralocalizing features followed the lead of the capital city. In the vast majority of the cases the incoming element was also recorded in small numbers in other localities when the change was in its incipient stage. But the region promoting the process was readily discernible when the process started to gather momentum.

Two of the incoming items hailed from the North, the third-person singular indicative suffix -s, and the short possessive determiners MY and THY. Both reached the City of London earlier than either East Anglia or the Court, and this happened in the fifteenth century. The third-person -s and the short possessive determiners may both be viewed as instances of 'dialect hopping' rather than steady dialect diffusion – East Anglia being initially bypassed by both processes. In other cases, such as the object of the gerund, the possessive determiner ITS and the prop-word ONE, the process may also well have been initiated outside the capital, but its subsequent development was closely associated with the metropolitan region.

The diffusion of the changes revealed certain consistent patterns. With the two forms of northern origins, the City of London continued to lead the process in the south until it was past mid-range. The lead could also be assumed jointly by London and the Court. This happened with the rise of the subject form YOU and the decline of DO-support in affirmative statements. Both were very rapid processes and created sharp momentary contrasts between the capital and the more northern regions.

Interestingly enough, a Court advantage proved the single most common pattern in the data, and it typically continued as a tendency until the change was completed or nearing completion. It was attested with the object of the gerund, the loss of multiple negation, the relative pronoun WHICH, and the preposition-plus-WHICH construction. In these cases, the change usually spread in the more northern regions faster than in the City of London. This would not be expected if the horizontal wave model were the only one operating in supralocalization. Our data show, however, that vertical diffusion was typically combined with horizontal. Many Londoners may only have had delayed access to Court developments. In Chapter 7 we reached a similar conclusion concerning the influence of the higher ranks in the social embedding of changes.

In the more prolonged processes an advanced form of the snowball effect could be traced: a region that had started a process later surpassed the leading area before the process was completed. This happened when the Court surpassed London in the two processes of northern origin, and London overtook the North and East Anglia in the spread of the object of the gerund and of the analytic preposition-plus-WH-relative constructions. Although not all the changes that we have examined were completed in the early modern period, the case argued by Ogura and Wang (1996) can be supported that the snowball effect forms part of the regional diffusion of historical language change.

To present our findings in a nutshell, supralocalizing features do not have any **single** path of transmission. This generalization supports our argument that it is individual linguistic features rather than fully-fledged varieties that get selected, accepted and diffused across the country. The people who do the selecting, accepting and diffusing may vary even with simultaneously spreading features. It is, however, equally evident that the City of London and the Court, in particular, had a key role to play in the processes that we have studied. This only goes to show that it is hard, if not impossible, to keep the horizontal axis of historical language change apart from the vertical one, and to separate historical dialectology from historical sociolinguistics.

Notes

1. As in Chapter 6, we use the term *supralocalization* to refer to the spread of a linguistic feature from its region of origin to neighbouring areas. When it involves the reduction of marked or minority forms, the process is called *dialect levelling* or *koinéization* (Trudgill 1986: 107; Milroy & Milroy 1993; Montgomery 1996; Holmes 1997). The paucity of systematic empirical research on syntactic and morphological variation in nonstandard dialects is discussed by Cheshire *et al.* (1993), and the rise of a levelled dialect in Milton Keynes by Kerswill and Williams (2000).

2. See, for instance, Milroy and Milroy (1985b), L. Milroy (1987) and J. Milroy (1992); for a different interpretation, cf. Labov (2001: 325–365). The effects of social networks in the history of English are discussed in the special issue of the *European Journal of English Studies* 2000, 4/3.

3. In Ihalainen's (1994: 248–249) overview of dialect criteria in four treatments of the topic, only two out of nineteen were not phonological (finite BE and periphrastic DO in affirmatives). In a language rich in inflectional and derivational morphology such as Finnish, morphological differences constitute significant regional dialect features on a par with phonological differences.

4. More attention has recently been paid to grammar, and especially to the North–South divide, in Middle English studies (Kroch *et al.* 2000). For a general criticism of variety-based approaches, see Mazzon (2000).

5. Similar complaints have been expressed by a number of historical linguists in the 1980s and 90s (Crowley 1989; Hogg 1998; Leith 1983). Traditional scholarship is charged with historicizing Standard English in general and RP in particular.

6. Samuels (1981: 44, 48) classifies fifteenth- and early sixteenth-century texts into five types according to their spelling and morphology: (A) localizable dialect, (B) Chancery Standard, (C) writing with a regional basis which includes Chancery forms, (D) colourless regional writing, and (E) mixtures of regional spellings. It is pointed out by Benskin (1992: 78–80) that 'Chancery Standard' is not the best possible term to use because most of the English texts issuing from the Chancery originated from the Signet and Privy Seal Offices and were only copied by Chancery clerks (cf. Fisher 1977).

7. See Burchfield (1994), Algeo (2001), Watts and Trudgill (2001), Nevalainen and Tieken-Boon van Ostade (forthcoming).

8. Gil also distinguishes a sociolect, cant, which he condemns as the 'venomous and disgusting ulcer of our nation ... For that detestable scum of wandering vagabonds speak no proper dialect but a cant jargon which no punishement by law will ever repress, until its proponents are crucified by the magistrates, acting under a public edict' (Gil 1619[1972: 104]). Other contemporary sources on regional variation especially in lexis include glossaries and collections of dialect words, such as John Ray's (1674/1691) *Collection of English Words not Generally Used*; see Ihalainen (1994: 197–205) and Görlach (1999: 495–514).

9. The Chester–Humber line is the traditional basis we have selected for characterizing counties north of Lincolnshire as 'northern', but it is not the only dividing line between northern and southern varieties presented in the literature. In the classic Middle English dialect study of Moore *et al.* (1935), based on phonological features, the line begins at the mouth of the river Ribble and ends in the Humber estuary, i.e. the northern part of Lancashire is included in the North and the southern part in Northwest Midland (for further comparisons, see Fisiak 1983). But as far as syntax is concerned, some typical northern features extend much further south: the third-person singular -s and the Northern Subject Rule both operate north of the Chester–Wash line (McIntosh 1989: 117–118). The LALME divides its northern (NOR) and southern (SOU) data so that the northern limit for SOU runs south and then westward from the Wash, and the southern limit for NOR from the Welsh border through the Midland into north Suffolk (McIntosh *et al.* 1986, Vol. 1, p. 297).

   In view of these findings, we could have included Lincolnshire in the North as well. Contemporary early modern views partly suggest the same: for Gil (1621), his native Lincolnshire counts as part of the North, and for Puttenham, the North lies 'beyond the river Trent' thus making northern Lincolnshire part of the North (see further Ihalainen 1994: 199). In practice, including Lincolnshire would not have made much difference in our results as in the CEEC there are only three writers from the region totalling less than 2,000 words.

10. In the *Survey of English Dialects* data, Middlesex and London are represented by two localities, Harmondsworth and Hackney, respectively (Orton 1962).

11. The proportion of female informants in Orton's *Survey of English Dialects* material is about 12 per cent (Coates 1986: 44).

12. The four regions cover 51 per cent of the entire CEEC 1998; see Table 3.6. in Chapter 3. For numerical information on the regional distributions of five high-frequency processes of change, see section 9.4., and Nevalainen (2000c: 359–361).

   Application of the chi-square test to these data shows that regional differences are statistically significant ($p<0.5$) in all except the last subperiod in Figure 8.1; in all but subperiods two and three in Figure 8.2; in the last subperiod in Figure 8.3; in all three subperiods in Figure 8.4; in the first subperiod in Figure 8.5; in the first two subperiods in Figure 8.6; in the last but one subperiod between London and the Court in Figure 8.7; in all of them in Figure 8.8; and in all except the second and the fourth subperiod in Figure 8.9.

Chapter 9

Historical Patterning of Sociolinguistic Variation

A serious effort to account for the social distribution of variation soon encounters the fact that there are more social dimensions that affect language behaviour than we can display in a cross-tabulation. (Labov 2001: 84)

9.1. Modelling Variability

Few sociolinguistic studies can claim to have taken into account all the various social factors that may affect human language behaviour. Labov's (2001: 84) list of minimum requirements includes the following speaker variables: gender, age, ethnicity, race, social class, urban/rural status, and position in social networks. The list could easily be extended, as has been done in recent work on gender, by focusing on intragroup variability and considering, for instance, the Communities of Practice in which social roles are enacted (Bergvall 1999).

While recognizing the variety of social factors affecting language behaviour, sociolinguists are also keen to discover those that exercise the most influence on linguistic choices, particularly the ones most likely to correlate with linguistic changes in progress. Generalizations of this kind cannot be arrived at by analysing each social factor in isolation. It has therefore become common practice to employ various statistical methods to study the relative impact of a series of variables simultaneously. Two variables can be **cross-tabulated** the way we have done with time and the various social factors in this book, and more than two may be presented as a **cross-product** display and plotted on a dendrogram. However, in order to give a reliable picture, the factors included in a cross-product must be treated as binary in terms of plus and minus values. One obvious problem with a fully mechanical display like this is that it could call for impossible environments, both linguistic and external (Fasold 1991: 2–6).

One of the more versatile standard methods used in sociolinguistics is **multivariate analysis**. The variable rule **(VARBRUL)** program was first introduced in the late 1960s and developed further in the 1970s and 80s. As the name implies, variable rule analysis was originally designed to model linguistic variation in a way that could incorporate variability in generative grammar. However, as it is not logically tied to any particular linguistic formalism, it has come to be widely used as a heuristic tool by linguists working within different grammatical frameworks. The program has proved useful in assessing the effects on sociolinguistic variables of a number of intersecting parameters, both language-external and internal. It has also been used extensively to model combinations of linguistic and social environments simultaneously – something not all sociolinguists would necessarily agree is a good practice.[1]

9.1.1. Linguistic and Social Factors

External factors were foregrounded in this book in order to highlight the role of social embedding in processes of historical language change. However, before discussing any hierarchies of these factors, we need to take a look at how change is expected to progress in linguistic contexts. In the Weinreich-Labov-Herzog model (1968) discussed above, this is singled out as the **transition** problem.

As pointed out in Chapter 4 (4.1.), we started with the assumption that intralinguistic variation is independent of social variation. In view of the traditional concentration of research on internal processes of language change, focus on social factors will go some way to redress the balance. After all, there is no 'internal clock' for language change: it is difficult to tell why the subject form YOU was generalized rapidly in the first half of the sixteenth century but the noun subject of the gerund remained a 50-per cent variant for over 200 years, and only began to spread in the course of the seventeenth century. It is the differences in their social embedding, however, that will allow us to make further generalizations concerning their actual time courses of change.[2]

Linguistic conditioning in language change may be approached differently depending on the domain of language studied and the model of change espoused by the linguist. Work within the **lexical diffusion** paradigm suggests that change progresses from word to word following an S-curve of change. A similar mechanism has been proposed for both phonology and syntax: words affected by the change advance at different rates. Words that are affected early progress slowly, while those affected later progress more rapidly (Ogura 1993; Ogura & Wang 1996). In our data this is manifest, for instance, in the third-person present-tense -s, which was slow to spread to such frequent verbs as HAVE and DO.

Some syntactic work within the generative tradition has resulted in the **Constant Rate Hypothesis** (Kroch 1989). It suggests that the rate of change is the same in different linguistic contexts, thus reflecting a single underlying grammatical parameter. A constant rate would appear to be evidenced in our data, for instance, in the replacement of the possessive determiners MINE and THINE by MY and THY (section 4.4.). If it is indeed the case that lexical diffusion and constant rate can both be witnessed in morphosyntactic changes, we obviously need more empirical research in order to determine the way in which the two might be interrelated.[3]

One generalization emerges from these models. Ogura (1993: 72) notes that in both models linguistic changes are **implemented** gradually across the lexicon: change affects the relevant morphemes severally in succession. Lexical diffusion also implies gradual actuation of changes; i.e. change proceeds sequentially from one context to another. Constant rate, by contrast, presupposes abrupt actuation, which takes place in all (syntactic) environments simultaneously. Both models can be contrasted with those **Neogrammarians** and their followers who argue for abrupt, simultaneous implementation of changes in all contexts.

Whichever model is adopted to analyse the implementation of a change in linguistic terms, we may assume that a representative range of its linguistic contexts is available from each sampling period to assess the impact of social factors on the process. Not even the proponents of the Constant Rate Effect have proposed it for language-external factors:

> Nothing in the grammatical system undergoing change accounts for the rate of the change or for the fact that the change actually goes to completion rather than stalling or even reversing. (Kroch 2001: 721)

Internal factors are usually independent of each other. This is not, however, necessarily the case with external factors. Ideally, whatever the effect of gender, age or ethnicity might be on a sociolinguistic variable, it should be the same for all social classes. But in practice gender and social class are often found to interact so that a given linguistic variable may be promoted by women in the working classes but not in the middle classes (Labov 2001: 84–85). Labov concludes that for this reason it is useful to alternate between **cross-tabulation** and **multivariate analysis**: cross-tabulation displays the fact that there is some interaction, and multivariate analysis measures the size of the effect. An exact fit between the data and the variable-rule model is only achieved if all the factors are independent of each other.

9.1.2. Style and Sociolinguistic Variation

The concept of **style** plays a central role in modern urban sociolinguistics, and it is commonly included in descriptions of sociolinguistic variation. It differs from other external factors in that it is not a speaker variable in the same way as age or social status. Many sociolinguists agree with Labov (1972: 208) and define style in terms of **self-monitoring**, i.e. the amount of attention paid to speech. A range of speaking styles is distinguished: three reading styles (minimal-pair, word-list, and reading-passage styles) and two conversational (careful and casual speech). This classification approaches style in unidimensional terms: most attention is paid to speech in the minimal-pair style, reading homophonous pairs of words, and least in the casual-speech style. A basic division into careful and casual speech has also proved useful (Labov 2001), and it is the only one supplied by this model for investigating grammatical variation.[4]

This established view of speech styles has come under attack both from inside and from outside urban sociolinguistics (for overviews, see Rickford & McNair-Knox 1994; Macaulay 1999). Many sociolinguists have pointed out the difficulty of defining style along a single continuum. Reading aloud stands out as a particular problem as the orthographic form may affect pronunciation in different ways. It has also been noted that the attention-to-speech view of style fails to account for the fact that speakers **accommodate** to their interlocutors; and sociolinguistic interviews are no exception to this rule (e.g. Paradis 1996). Quantitative studies of stylistic variation based on addressee relations have been carried out from the late 1970s onwards. A comprehensive model of style in terms of audience design was put forward by Allan Bell (1984), offering several hypotheses that can be tested empirically using the VARBRUL analysis (see 9.2.).

One of the issues that interest us in this chapter is how the variable of style (or **register**) correlates with other external variables in language variation and change. Here the literature is sharply divided. The primacy of style over other external factors, social status in particular, has been advocated by proponents of a maximally comprehensive view of register variation. Considering both written and spoken language, Finegan and Biber (1994, 2001) argue that variation in social status can be predicted by analysing registers. As the lower social classes do not have access to as wide a range of registers as the higher, they do not command the same range of linguistic variation. Consequently, the writers argue, processes of linguistic simplification are favoured by the lower classes, whereas elaboration is associated with the higher ones.

This view is questioned by Preston (1991: 49), among others, who is left wondering 'why would lower- and upper-status speakers perform differently in the same communicative settings, particularly when some such settings (e.g., careful vs. casual conversation) are ubiquitous and hardly marked for status?' By contrast, Preston's own reviews (1991, 2001) of a number of VARBRUL analyses of social variation suggest that the variation space of the stylistic dimension is not only smaller than that of the social dimension, but it is often contained in it. He finds that the evidence is overwhelmingly in favour of the primacy of social status in speech – social status being understood as including a range of social attributes from the speakers' social class to their parents' education.

Audience design, the framework Preston refers to, is defined by Bell (2001: 145) as 'a strategy by which speakers draw on the range of linguistic resources available in their speech community to respond to different kinds of audiences'. The model contains a set of axioms based on a number of sociolinguistic surveys. The **Style Axiom** states that

> variation on the style dimension within the speech of a single speaker derives from and echoes the variation which exists between speakers on the 'social' dimension. (Bell 1984: 151; 2001: 145)

The axiom predicts that the degree of style variation will not exceed the degree of social variation. Bell (1984: 160) goes on to argue that audience effects are most noticeable for addressees, but become progressively weaker for third persons (auditors, overhearers, eavesdroppers). Lastly, he suggests (1984: 180) that the degree of topic-designed style shift will not exceed audience-designed shift, meaning that the topic of discussion will have the least effect on the degree of style variation. Bell's model has been tested empirically and supported by Preston (1991) and by Rickford and McNair-Knox (1994). Although probably not ultimate truths, Bell's arguments provide a set of hypotheses that can tested with more varied data sets, including linguistic variables undergoing change.[5]

9.2. Modelling Sociolinguistic Variation Historically

Despite the pioneering model provided by Romaine (1982a), systematic historical research on language change using multivariate analyses has hardly begun. The limitations that any such undertaking will necessarily be confronted with have emerged from the previous chapters, with the 'bad-data' problem as their common denominator. In this section we will therefore only concentrate on the issues tackled and solutions adopted by our project. It has been shown in the previous chapters that, despite many limitations, it is possible to reconstruct a number of social variables and relate them to language changes in earlier English. It is also possible to examine the interplay of external variables in long-term language change using the VARBRUL program. This can be done with high-frequency linguistic variables; on our list of 14 changes, there are five that provide enough data not only for cross-tabulation but also for detailed VARBRUL analyses (see 9.4.).

As to external variables, our analysis will include four: real time, region, gender and register. Region and gender have both yielded quite coherent results across time in the series of 14 changes we studied, suggesting that they are highly relevant to a sociolinguistic description of supralocal processes in Late Middle and Early Modern English. Of the other speaker variables, age and social rank will not be included because there would not be enough material in each cell to carry out the analysis. The variable that we have not yet discussed in detail is register, and it will therefore be introduced next.

Our view of register variation – and the use of the term **register** – can be associated with the model proposed by M.A.K. Halliday, which defines registers as varieties according to use. Registers are analysed in terms of the major dimensions of situations that can be expected to have predictable linguistic consequences: the **field** (type of activity and topic), **tenor** (addressee and other participant relations) and **mode** (channel of communication) of discourse (Halliday 1978; Eggins & Slade 1997: 47–58). In our case, the mode is written and the field is letter-writing, with a range of topics covered in each individual letter. What we will base our register analysis on are differences in tenor, i.e. social relations between correspondents. In this respect our analysis is well suited to be interpreted in terms of Bell's (1984) audience-design model.[6]

The CEEC encoding system records five basic addressee relations: nuclear family member (FN), more distant family member (FO), family servant (FS), TC (close personal friend) and T (other, distant recipient; see Nevalainen & Raumolin-Brunberg 1996b). For the purposes of the present analysis we have polarized the scale into two categories: family and close friends (FN, FO, TC) as opposed to all other recipients (FS, T). While defining kinship relations does not pose any major problems, defining close personal friends in the past may not always be self-evident. Terms of address, for instance, can be deceptive. Although *friend* is used throughout the Early Modern English period by close personal friends, social superiors could also address their inferiors as 'friends', and so could a merchant's wife her husband in the superscript of her letter, meaning 'a near relation', as in (9.1).

> (9.1) To my loving **frende** John Johnson, be this delyvered at Callais. (Sabine Johnson, 1551; JOHNSON, 1161)

However, we could usually rely on the editor of a letter collection to single out those correspondents who counted as close friends in terms of minimal social distance and great mutual affection, often based on a long-lasting personal relationship, multiple shared interests in life, mutual confiding, and leisure time spent together. Friendship was often shown in the terms of address found in letter salutations (Nevalainen & Raumolin-Brunberg 1995). Nicknames would have been out of the question with distant recipients but were used by close friends. Charles Lyttelton did so when he informed his friend Charles Hatton about the death of his wife (9.2.).

> (9.2) **Deerest Kytt,**
> There is nobody in the world I can soe justly complaine to of the losse of your deare friend, because you were best acquainted how

well I loved her and how much she deserved it. (Charles Lyttelton, 1663; HATTON I, 31)

Basically the three external variables of region, gender and register can be thought of as independent of each other. Although dialect levelling may be seen in writing earlier than in speech, personal correspondence cannot be expected to be homogeneous when it comes to the linguistic expression of register variation. Writing about early American English, Montgomery (1996) makes the assumption that Americans were multi-style speakers from the beginning, and also revealed this in their letters. The same assumption can be made about our writers, women and men alike. Evidence to support this will be discussed in section 9.3.

This approach will enable us to adopt Bell's (1984) hypotheses on audience design and to test the relative weight of social (i.e. regional and gender) variation as opposed to register variation in the letter corpus in the course of time. We have formulated these hypotheses in terms of an implicational scale as follows (the notation x > y meaning: 'the range of variation of x is greater than that of y'):

social variation > register variation according to addressee (> register variation according to auditors > overhearers > eavesdroppers) > **register variation according to topic**

Our analysis will concentrate on the first implication: social variation is greater and hence more fundamental than stylistic variation according to addressee in personal letters. We find this issue particularly relevant in the light of previous research, which suggests that the distinction between private and official correspondence correlates significantly with processes of language change (see 9.3., below).

Owing to lack of data from the lower social strata, we do not have direct access to the degree of register variation commanded by ranks at the lower end of the social spectrum. With our material it is therefore not possible to test the register hypothesis put forward by Finegan and Biber (1994, 2001) that lower-status speakers systematically favour processes of linguistic simplification and economy features, whereas higher-status speakers promote features of elaboration.

As demonstrated in Chapter 7, it is not, however, historically true that all processes of linguistic simplification spread from below in social terms. The middle and topmost ranks also promoted 'economy features' such as the subject form YOU. Moreover, with most changes studied here the more fundamental question arises of what actually counts as a process of simplification. The third-person singular -s was found to spread from the lower ranks, but it hardly constitutes a more economical suffix than -TH. The ultimate economy solution would have been no suffix at all. The zero never generalized, although it was attested sporadically across the social spectrum in Late Middle and Early Modern English.

191

9.3. Previous Empirical Studies

As shown in Chapter 3, most of the historical research carried out within the variationist paradigm has been focused on genre and genre variation. The major generalizations to be made on the basis of this research are that external factors such as genre differences can indeed be reconstructed for the past and that they correlate with processes of linguistic change.

A number of facts have been systematically documented by using the variationist approach. It has been shown, for instance, by Raumolin-Brunberg (1991) that individual writers did vary their style according to genre. Sir Thomas More's Noun-Phrase characteristics were shown to be sensitive to the sender/addressee relation, with a polarization between private (family) and official letters (most distant recipients).

A basic distinction between private and official correspondence has commonly been made, and contrasted with other genres, in studies based on the *Helsinki Corpus of English Texts*. The results typically indicate that linguistic innovations progress faster in private correspondence than in official. Kytö (1993: 124) shows the diffusion of the third-person -s to be the most advanced in private letters in the period 1560–1640, official letters and trial proceedings coming second, while diaries, histories and sermons lag behind them considerably. Kilpiö (1997) observes that there are also features that connect official letters with written genres such as statutes. They are the two genres in which participial adjectives of the type 'aforesaid' were used most in Early Modern English (albeit their use was much more pronounced in statutory writings than in official letters).

The writer/addressee relations encoded in the CEEC allow more fine-grained comparisons of social and register variables. Palander-Collin (1999) studied the use of the modal expression I THINK in the seventeenth century with respect to both gender and register with data from 77 women and 136 men. Her results showed that women used I THINK systematically more than men in all the recipient categories (FN, FO, TC, T). The male range – with close friends receiving the highest frequency – proved to be much narrower. In general, more variation was found in women's letters, with the highest frequencies occurring in the nuclear family category.[7]

Few multivariate studies have been carried out with historical data. Romaine (1982a) was the first to experiment with this methodology in her study of Middle Scots relativizers. Another early VARBRUL study is the analysis by Bailey *et al.* (1989) of the third-person singular present-tense suffixes in the fifteenth-century Cely letters. No external factors were considered in the study, which concentrated on the category and number of the subject.

Two other VARBRUL studies, Nevalainen (1991) and Schneider (1992), include both linguistic and external factors, but the former clearly dominate the analysis. Nevalainen (1991: 234–248) compared oral and literate genres promoting the exclusive adverbs ONLY and BUT (*Mary is only a child* vs. *Mary is but a child*) in Early and Late Modern English. The analysis revealed a reweighting of this variable with both adverbs between 1500 and 1900. Schneider (1992) used the VARBRUL program to analyse the choice between WHO and WHOM in Shakespeare and also considered the external factor of text type (prose/verse). In his case study of WHOSE vs. OF WHICH in Shakespeare and his contemporaries, Schneider included the range of authors as the external variable. In both cases, the external variable was found to pattern differently with the variant forms.

Both linguistic and external variables were also considered by Kytö (1997), who computed logistic regression analyses for the choice between BE and HAVE with past participles (*he is/has come*) covering the timespan from the fourteenth to the twentieth century. Apart from the author's sex and the formality of setting, the external factors selected were all textual: text type, relationship to spoken language, and orality. Owing to the way the data were distributed, no more than two factors could be combined at a time, with the subperiod as one of the two in each combination. Text type and chronology were found to be among the more powerful external factors affecting the choice between BE and HAVE.[8]

9.4. VARBRUL Analyses of Five Historical Changes

Our aim in this section is to explore whether regularities can be observed in the way in which external factors correlate with changes in progress. Region, gender and register constitute the independent variables or **factor groups** of the analysis. The five dependent variables are YE/YOU; -TH/-S; the object of the gerund; MINE, THINE/MY, THY; and THE WHICH/WHICH. The VARBRUL application GoldVarb 2 developed by Rand and Sankoff (1990) was used to compute the relative weightings of region, gender and register in the different phases of the linguistic changes. In no one case were all their five temporal phases from incipient to completed available in sufficient quantities, but in all but one at least three of them were.

The results of the VARBRUL analysis will be tabulated for each change separately, and two aspects of the analysis will receive particular attention. What interests us, first, are the factors that particularly favour the change in progress at a given point in time. As the probabilities vary between 1 and 0, a factor with a probability **weighting** over 0.5 favours the incoming form or structure, and one with a weighting below 0.5 disfavours it. If a factor has a weighting of 1, it determines the selection of the form categorically, while a factor with a weighting of 0 would totally inhibit it. When a change is nearing completion, factors that favour the incoming form most are the first to become categorical ('knockout' factors).

Secondly, systematic attention will be paid to the range of variation of the three factor groups. Their **ranges**, 'variation/variety spaces' as they are called by Preston (1991), are calculated by subtracting the minimum from the maximum weighting a factor receives within each factor group. These ranges will be compared in order to establish the relative impact of the external factors on the change in progress. However, as not all these variables need to be monotonically aligned with the change in progress – crossovers are in fact expected on the basis of previous research – we cannot hypothesize that the ranges for the three external variables would always get progressively smaller as the process nears completion.[9]

9.4.1. Results

YE → YOU

Beginning with the subject forms of the second-person pronoun, we can see from Table 9.1. that the only variable that matters at the beginning of the change is register: YOU surfaces in family letters (factor weight 0.691), and register has the widest range at this point. When the change reaches the frequency of about 30 per cent, its regional bias emerges: the incoming form is promoted by the London region, including the Court (see 8.4.1.); region now has the widest range of the three independent variables. Women use YOU more than men and it continues to be more common in letters written to family or friends than to other recipients. In early mid-range (c. 40 per cent), gender slightly outstrips region in terms of both factor weight and range. The capital region is still ahead of East Anglia and the North. Register no longer plays a significant role in the process.

Table 9.1. VARBRUL analysis of the YE/YOU variable (quota sample; de la Pole excluded), period mean showing the relative frequency of YOU. Min./Max. = minimum/maximum weight of a factor in a factor group, respectively

Period/mean (%)	Factor group	Min.	Max.	Range	Total N
1500–19	Region	.468 (N)	.532 (S)	.064	223
4%	Gender	.479 (w)	.521 (m)	.042	223
	Register	.309 (nf)	**.691 (ff)**	**.382**	223
1520–39	Region	.280 (N)	**.720 (S)**	**.440**	414
29%	Gender	.399 (m)	.601 (w)	.202	414
	Register	.403 (nf)	.597 (ff)	.194	414
1540–59	Region	.343 (N)	.657 (S)	.314	461
38%	Gender	.340 (m)	**.660 (w)**	**.320**	461
	Register	.453 (ff)	.547 (nf)	.094	461

(Abbreviations: Region: S = London + Court; N = East Anglia + North; Gender: w = female, m = male; Register: ff = family and friends, nf = non-family)

Table 9.2. VARBRUL analysis of the -TH/-s variable (quota sample), period mean showing the relative frequency of -s. Min./Max. = minimum/maximum weight of a factor in a factor group, respectively

Period/mean (%)	Factor group	Min.	Max.	Range	Total N
1540–79	Region	.310 (E)	**.788 (N)**	**.478**	741
8%	Gender	.384 (m)	.616 (w)	.232	741
	Register	.473 (ff)	.527 (nf)	.054	741
1580–1619	Region	.155 (E)	**.767 (L)**	**.612**	952
42%	Gender	.392 (m)	.608 (w)	.216	952
	Register	.466 (nf)	.534 (ff)	.068	952
1620–59	Region	.329 (E)	**.688 (C)**	**.314**	904
74%	Gender	.469 (m)	.531 (w)	.062	904
	Register	.453 (nf)	.547 (ff)	.094	904

(Abbreviations: Region: L = London, C = Court, E = East Anglia, N = North; Gender: w = female, m = male; Register: ff = family and friends, nf = non-family)

When the change is more or less complete (over 90 per cent) in 1560–99, it is no longer possible to compute factor weights for the female gender and the regions of London, East Anglia and the North because they have reached a 100-per-cent application rate and constitute 'knockout' factors. One particular combination of region, gender and register does, however, stand out as a conservative force. At this time when the subject form YOU has become invariable everywhere else, there are still some men at Court who occasionally continue to resort to YE.

-TH → -s

The 'second coming' of the third-person -s presents a much more even pattern of diffusion than the personal pronoun YOU. As shown by Table 9.2., region has a key role to play throughout the process. In its incipient phase from 1540 to 1579, the form is favoured by northern writers; -s is after all of northern origin. In mid-range (42 per cent) the process continues to be favoured by the North (0.616), but especially by London (0.767). When it is nearing completion at c. 75 per cent, the leading force proves to be not so much London as the Royal Court. Women systematically favour -s in the first two periods, but the gender difference is neutralized when the change approaches completion in the third. In comparison with the other two external variables, register differences play only a minor role in this change.

MINE, THINE → MY, THY

The rise of the possessive determiners MY and THY in prevocalic contexts is another change where region emerges as a prime factor. As in the case

Table 9.3. VARBRUL analysis of the MINE, THINE/MY, THY variable (all data), period mean showing the relative frequency of MY, THY. Min./Max. = minimum/maximum weight of a factor in a factor group, respectively

Period/mean (%)	Factor group	Min.	Max.	Range	Total N
1460–99	Region	.181 (E)	**.873 (N)**	**.692**	229
22%	Gender	.484 (w)	.516 (m)	.032	229
	Register	.427 (ff)	.573 (nf)	.146	229
1520–59	Region	.249 (C)	**.798 (L)**	**.549**	476
38%	Gender	.448 (m)	.552 (w)	.104	476
	Register	.432 (ff)	.568 (nf)	.136	476
1560–99	Region	.367 (N)	**.588 (C)**	**.221**	361
70%	Gender	.422 (m)	.578 (w)	.156	361
	Register	.457 (nf)	.543 (ff)	.086	361
1600–1639	Region	.308 (E)	**.693 (C)**	**.385**	635
92%	Gender	.324 (m)	.676 (w)	.352	635
	Register	.392 (nf)	.608 (ff)	.216	635

(Abbreviations: Region: L = London, C = Court, E = East Anglia, N = North; Gender: w = female, m = male; Register: ff = family and friends, nf = non-family)

of the third-person -s, the incoming forms are first favoured by northern writers in the early stages, but then promoted by the capital region, first by London when the change is in mid-range, and throughout the rest of the process by the Court (see Table 9.3.). From the mid-range on, women are also more frequent users of the incoming form than men.[10]

Register behaves less systematically: it switches from a slight non-family advantage in mid-range to increasing family advantage when the change progresses. This register switch is supported by previous research on a number of genres (Schendl 1997). It may also be reflected in the widening of the variation ranges of all the external variables in the last phase.

Object of the gerund

The rise of the zero object of the gerund (*the contentment of meeting* **you** as opposed to *meeting* **of you**) shows another kind of regularity: the most important factor throughout its diffusion proves to be female gender. The first VARBRUL analysis in Table 9.4. looks at the process in its new-and-vigorous stage (at about 30 per cent) and indicates that the incoming variant is favoured slightly more by the Royal Court than by the other areas. Later on, regional differences continue to provide the same average range of variation. The register variable shows even less variation throughout the process. These findings were already in evidence in Chapter 8, where the object of the gerund was found to be more evenly distributed in regional terms than either the third-person -s or the short possessive determiners

Table 9.4. VARBRUL analysis of the object of the gerund variable (all data), period mean showing the relative frequency of zero forms. Min./Max. = minimum/maximum weight of a factor in a factor group, respectively

Period/mean (%)	Factor group	Min.	Max.	Range	Total *N*
1520–59	Region	.419 (L)	.575 (C)	.156	492
28%	Gender	.401 (m)	**.599 (w)**	**.198**	492
	Register	.473 (nf)	.527 (ff)	.054	492
1560–99	Region	.405 (C)	.561 (N)	.156	652
42%	Gender	.353 (m)	**.647 (w)**	**.294**	652
	Register	.489 (ff)	.511 (nf)	.022	652
1600–39	Region	.425 (N)	.562 (C)	.137	623
70%	Gender	.401 (m)	**.599 (w)**	**.198**	623
	Register	.481 (ff)	.519 (nf)	.038	623

(Abbreviations: Region: L = London, C = Court, N = East Anglia + North; Gender: w = female, m = male; Register: ff = family and friends, nf = non-family)

Table 9.5. VARBRUL analysis of the THE WHICH/WHICH variable (all data), period mean showing the relative frequency of WHICH. Min./Max. = minimum/ maximum weight of a factor in a factor group, respectively

Period/mean (%)	Factor group	Min.	Max.	Range	Total *N*
1440–79	Region	.133 (L)	**.856 (C)**	**.723**	908
70%	Gender	.227 (w)	.773 (m)	.546	908
	Register	.412 (nf)	.588 (ff)	.176	908
1520–59	Region	.444 (N)	.597 (C)	.153	1823
92%	Gender	.332 (w)	**.668 (m)**	**.336**	1823
	Register	.426 (nf)	.574 (ff)	.148	1823

(Abbreviations: Region: L = London, C = Court, E = East Anglia, N = North; Gender: w = female, m = male; Register: ff = family and friends, nf = non-family)

(the momentary dip shown by Court in mid-range being partly due to a number of older informants; for further discussion, see 8.4.1.).

THE WHICH → WHICH

Our data catch only the tail end of the spread of the relative pronoun WHICH. It exceeds the frequency of 60 per cent in the fifteenth century and is completed in the first half of the sixteenth. All three factor groups turn out to be relevant: the form is promoted by the Royal Court and East Anglia (0.856 and 0.761 in the first period, respectively), by men writing to their immediate family.

In the second period regional differences become less pronounced and gender now provides the widest range of variation. A systematic male advantage in both periods is interesting as women rarely wrote their own letters in the fifteenth century. This evidence therefore suggests that the Paston women's letters, for instance, may have been taken down from dictation by their male scribes more or less verbatim. For both men and women, register differences play a less significant role at this advanced stage of the process.

9.5. Summary and Conclusions

The VARBRUL analyses are summarized in Figure 9.1. The five changes are listed on the left, and their time courses run horizontally across the page. At each stage, the social factors studied are presented in order of their relative importance. This order directly reflects the range calculated by the VARBRUL program for each factor group: the wider the spread of the factors within a group, the wider its range and the more significant the variable. In each case we also single out the factor that shows the highest positive correlation with the process of change. When a factor does not have a notable impact (a weighting over 0.550) at a particular stage of a change, it is indicated in italics in square brackets.

We are now in a position to say something about the relative robustness of the three variables and their alignment in promoting the five changes. First, the weakest variable proves to be register. It tops the list only once: when YOU is an incipient change. But our data also support earlier studies such as Schendl (1997), suggesting that the register affiliation of a change in progress can change in the course of time. This happens with the loss of the -N- allomorphs of possessive determiners. In that change register makes a significant addition to three out of the four stages of the process.

Overall, the changes however prove to be either region- or gender-driven throughout, or mixed. The third-person -s and the determiners MY and THY spread from the North to London and, when nearing completion, are both promoted by the Court. They clearly display the snowball effect proposed by Ogura and Wang (1996): the regions that are later to adopt a change do it more forcefully than those that are affected by it earlier. The phase of the change also matters: by mid-range, at the latest, the changes are promoted by the capital region.[11]

Gender is the other variable that systematically correlates with the changes examined. With the exception of the relative pronoun WHICH, all of them are promoted by women. The object of the gerund is distinctly gender-driven. The VARBRUL analysis confirms our findings in Chapter 6 that, unlike in regional diffusion, no snowball effect can be detected with gender: a change in progress does not alter its gender affiliation when it is nearing completion. We may therefore argue that, among the literate ranks, women are more likely than men to favour a process of supralocalization in the early

INCIPIENT	NEW & VIGOROUS	MID-RANGE	NEARLY COMPLETED	COMPLETED
<15%	16–35%	36–65%	66–85%	>85%
□ YE/YOU (1500–1599)				
1. register (ff) [2. region] [3. gender]	1. region (LC) 2. gender (w) 3. register (ff)	1. gender (w) 2. region (LC) [3. register]		
□ THIRD-PERSON -TH/S (1540–1659)				
1. region (N) 2. gender (w) [3. register]		1. region (L) 2. gender (w) [3. register]	1. region (C) [2. gender] [3. register]	
□ MINE/MY and THINE/THY (1460–1639)				
1. region (N) 2. register (nf) [3. gender]	1. region (N) 2. register (nf) [3. gender]	1. region (L) 2. register (nf) 3. gender (w)	1. region (C) 2. gender (w) [3. register]	1. region (C) 2. gender (w) 3. register (ff)
□ OBJECT OF GERUND (1520–1639)				
1. gender (w) 2. region (C) [3. register]	1. gender (w) 2. region (C) [3. register]	1. gender (w) 2. region (NE) [3. register]	1. gender (w) 2. region (C) [3. register]	
□ THE WHICH/WHICH (1440–1559)				
			1. region (C) 2. gender (m) 3. register (ff)	1. gender (m) 2. region (C) 3. register (ff)

Figure 9.1. Summary of VARBRUL analyses of the five linguistic changes. (Region: L = London, C = Court, E = East Anglia, N = North; Gender: w = female, m = male; Register: ff = family and friends, nf = non-family)

modern period. The results also suggest, however, that for a change to be first and foremost promoted by gender at any one stage of its progress it must originate in the capital region: as we have seen, region systematically outstrips gender in precisely those two changes that have their origins in the North.

On the basis of these findings we can advance the following generalization on the range of variation displayed by the supralocalizing features in the personal correspondence data:

> social variation (regional variation > gender variation) > register variation according to addressee

The implicational scale supports Bell's Style Axiom and suggests that the degree of register variation does not exceed the degree of social variation. It also predicts that within social variation the range of regional variation is usually wider than the range of gender variation. These hypotheses will no doubt be refined in the future when more data are analysed and subtler distinctions made within the categories. As for now, we hope the results will inspire more confidence in the historical sociolinguistic enterprise. Although the data may not be ideal, they are ample enough to produce consistent generalizations.

Notes

1. For the history and basic principles of VARBRUL analysis, see e.g. Sankoff (1988), Montgomery (1989), Rand & Sankoff (1990), Fasold (1991) and Wolfram (1991). Combining both linguistic and nonlinguistic factors in one and the same analysis is convenient and therefore continues to be common practice in sociolinguistics, although doubts about mixing 'linguistic oranges with sociological apples' (Wolfram 1991: 31) are also voiced in the literature (Fasold 1990: 251–264; Labov 2001: 84). Some of the benefits that may be drawn from doing so are discussed by Preston (1991).

2. The dichotomy between language-internal and external factors itself is not necessarily always clear-cut. As pointed out by Gerritsen and Stein (1992: 8), it rests on the dichotomy of language as an abstract structural system as opposed to the use of this system. Internal and external factors may also be connected in that there are clear tendencies for unmarked linguistic features to spread in situations of high diversity and linguistic contact (Romaine 1995: 486). At the same time, as noted in section 8.1., pronounced linguistic differences may retard focusing in dialect contact situation (see also Woods 2001).

3. These and some other models were briefly introduced in section 4.3. Both lexical diffusion and constant rate models have been applied, for instance, to the diffusion of periphrastic DO in Early Modern English (Kroch 1989; Ogura 1993). Both use Ellegård's (1953) data as their primary material and similar logistic models in their statistical analyses. Ogura (1993: 78) concludes, on the basis of her findings, that 'it seems to be the case that the changes in the different contexts initiate at different times, and the later a change begins, the sharper its slope becomes.'

4. Attention paid to speech can, however, be further associated with the amount of planning and acquisition of nonvernacular features (Preston 2001: 287–290).

5. For a discussion and updates of most of these competing views, see Eckert and Rickford, eds. (2001). Some of the differences between the competing views derive from fundamentally different conceptions of the notion of style or register, on the one hand, and of linguistic variable, on the other (see Finegan & Biber 2001; L. Milroy 2001; Preston 2001).

6. See also the terminological discussion in Biber (1995: 7–10). For Biber 'register' is a broad cover term for situationally defined varieties, which are assumed to define a continuous space of variation.

7. Other register studies carried our within our project include Nevalainen & Raumolin-Brunberg (1995), Raumolin-Brunberg (1996b), Raumolin-Brunberg & Nevalainen (1997), Nevala (1998), Palander-Collin (2000).

8. Kytö (1997: 69–70) remarks, however, that biases in the data were likely to have affected the significance levels: a larger number of texts, for instance, were available from women writers from the later than from the earlier periods.

9. To guarantee comparability across the three independent variables, the binomial, one-level mode of operation of the program was used. It finds the best-fit analysis using all the factors and factor groups provided (Rand & Sankoff 1990: 24).

10. Here the periodization does not follow that of the previous chapters because in 1500–1539 the change does not progress beyond the new and vigorous stage.

11. A notion that our diachronic analysis has perhaps presented in a more dynamic light than is usual in sociolinguistics is **language community**. Fasold (1991: 9–10) discusses the early concept of a 'variable rule speech community', where all members of a community would have the same rules with the same constraints and an identical constraint order. This is obviously far too restrictive a view to be empirically viable. In our case, where processes of linguistic change are examined over a long period of time, it is possible to argue in favour of a supralocal language community in terms of shared linguistic features (see 10.1.).

Chapter 10

Conclusion

> Language change is one of the most mystifying and fascinating phe-
> nomena that dialectologists and linguistic scientists encounter. (Trudgill
> 1999a: 8)

In this book, sociolinguistics has been put to the test of time. We hope
to have shown in the course of our discussion how modern sociolinguistic models can indeed be fruitfully applied to earlier states of a language like English. But we have also shown how these models need to
be fed with period-specific information: it is not possible to use the present
to explain the past without access to knowledge of past societies in their
own right. This is particularly true of the analytic methods developed
for studying independent variables such as social status. The historical
sociolinguist's task is therefore to establish a historically valid basis for
analysing social distinctions. Our findings fully support the sociolinguistic
approach by indicating that social factors significantly correlate with the
diffusion of morphosyntactic changes in real time in the Tudor and Stuart
periods.

However, our time-frame also raises some questions that combine
period-specificity and the general principles of language change. By way of
conclusion, we would like to address some of them. They involve both
linguistic and extralinguistic regularities, on the one hand, and the steady
progression of language changes, on the other. The first issue we raise is the
impact that normative grammar can have on the history of a language.
What role did the rise of a codified standard language play, for instance, in
the subsequent history of the linguistic changes studied here? The issue will
be addressed in section 10.1., which looks at how they have fared in Standard English and other varieties of the language. Secondly, we will examine
our findings in the light of Labov's Principle of Contingency (2001: 503–506)
by considering in 10.2. whether any connection could be made between the
language changes analysed and their social embedding, i.e. whether changes
are destined for a particular course on the basis of the role they assume in
the language system. Finally, the notion of regularity will be taken even
further in section 10.3., which focuses on the problem of transmission: how
linguistic changes, once under way, continue on their chosen trajectories
towards completion.

10.1. The Changes in Retrospect

One of the charges often laid at English historical linguists' door is their concentration on the history of Standard English at the expense of other varieties (e.g. Milroy 1992: 51–52). By looking at the diffusion and social embedding of a number of linguistic changes we hope to have shown that the issue is far more complex. First, we would argue that standardization hardly offers the best possible framework for analysing the grammatical changes that took place in Late Middle and Early Modern English. Many of those linguistic features that we have investigated would no doubt have been excluded from the southern standard had a codified standard existed at the time. As codification, and institutional norm-enforcement based on it, took place in the late modern period (1700–1900), what we can see in the earlier centuries is the more or less unmonitored diffusion of supralocal usages. However, in retrospect, some interesting observations can be made on the changes that were completed in the early modern period as opposed to those that were not.

Present-day **Standard English** has many grammatical features that make it different from **traditional regional dialects**. A number of them are introduced in general terms by Trudgill (1999a, c). His lists are, of course, not exhaustive but contrast the other varieties with the fixed and codified core of Standard English grammar. Many of the processes that these differences resulted from go back to the Modern English period; some of them have been traced in the previous chapters of this volume. These changes can be contrasted with those discussed in this book that remain variable even today and cannot necessarily be used to distinguish between standard and nonstandard varieties of English.

The modern Standard English verb phrase is characterized by the irregular marking of the third-person singular in the present tense: *he goes* vs. *I go*. Many other varieties are more regular in that they either use zero throughout (*I go, you go, he go*, etc.) or mark all persons (*I goes, you goes*, etc.). As we have seen, the third-person -(E)s was originally a northern feature that supralocalized in the late sixteenth and early seventeenth centuries. The zero alternative was available, and indeed used by people like Queen Elizabeth I herself, but it was never generalized among the literate social ranks. No further levelling of the present-tense paradigm took place in the supralocal usage at the time (Nevalainen *et al.* 2001).

Modern Standard English has irregular forms of the verb BE both in the present (*am, is, are*) and in the past (*was, were*). Many nonstandard varieties only have one form for the present (e.g. *I be, you be*, etc.) and one for the past (e.g. *I was, you was*, etc.). It was again a northern form, ARE, that replaced the regular southern BE in the plural and with the second-person singular YOU in the south, but no radical levelling of the paradigm can be detected in supralocal usage in the early modern period.

The pronominal features that make Standard English different from other varieties include the lack of distinction between the second-person singular and plural forms of personal pronouns; YOU is used for both in the standard. In traditional dialects, either the distinction between THOU and YOU is maintained or new number distinctions have developed (e.g. YOU vs. YOUSE or Y'ALL). Similarly, Standard English does not distinguish between the subject and object forms of YOU, while there are traditional dialects that preserve the case contrast between YE and YOU. In supralocal usage, the second-person singular THOU/THEE was lost in the course of the Early Modern English period and, as shown above, YOU rapidly replaced YE in the subject function in the sixteenth century.

One of the socially most distinctive features in Standard English grammar is the fact that it lacks multiple negation, or negative concord, and so does not allow sentences like *I don't want none*. Single negation followed by nonassertive indefinites is the only alternative: *I don't want any*. Most nonstandard varieties of English around the world, and casual speech in general, permit multiple negation (Cheshire 1999). As we have seen, multiple negation was one of the features that largely disappeared among the literate ranks in the early modern period. Compared with the majority of the other linguistic changes examined by us, the process was exceptional in that it was first associated with male professional usage.

None of the features studied by us that supralocalized in the early modern period had consistent institutional support through the education system or the media of the time. The printed word, for instance, rarely displayed any one norm but typically recorded variation when a change was under way. And where a local or register norm existed, institutional reinforcement was no guarantee for it eventually to be codified as part of Standard English grammar. The third-person singular present indicative suffix is a case in point: Caxton and other early printers had preferred the southern -(E)TH. As observed by J. Milroy (1994: 20), standardization may therefore be simply superimposed on supralocal usages which have been established prior to codification.[1] Once part of a codified standard, these features will undergo a process of **re-evaluation** as socially marked prestige variants. This appears to have been the case with those features discussed in this book that supralocalized in the Early Modern English period before the era of normative grammar.

Table 10.1. presents the 14 changes studied by us in a wider chronological perspective. It indicates whether a particular change had been completed in personal correspondence during the timespan covered by the CEEC (c. 1410–1681). Completion is here taken to mean over 85 per cent application of the incoming form or structure. This information is compared with the (in)variability of these forms and structures in Present-day Standard English usage.

Table 10.1. indicates that six out of our fourteen processes were largely completed in supralocal usage in the early modern period (1, 2, 7, 10, 11

Table 10.1. Completion of the fourteen changes

Process	completed in the CEEC	completed in Standard English
1. YE → YOU	yes	yes
2. MINE/THINE → MY/THY	yes	yes
3. HIS, OF IT, THEREOF → ITS	no	no
4. prop-word ONE	no	no
5. object of gerund	no	no
6. noun subject of gerund	no	no
7. -(E)TH → -(E)S	yes*	yes
8. DO in affirmative statements	no	no
9. DO in negative statements	no	yes
10. multiple → single negation	yes*	yes
11. inversion after negators	yes	yes
12. THE WHICH → WHICH	yes	yes
13. relative adverb → prepositional phrase	no	no
14. indefinite pronouns with human reference	no	no

(*change not completed in all linguistic environments)

and 12). One more (9) may be viewed as invariant in Standard English today. However, as many as seven are not invariant or fully regulated in Standard English (3, 4, 5, 6, 8, 13 and 14). Unlike possessive forms of the other personal pronouns, ITS has the posthead variant OF IT and it is rarely used in independent function (Nevalainen & Raumolin-Brunberg 1994a). The prop-word ONE is not required with all nominal expressions, such as super-latives. The object and noun subject of the gerund continue to vary; hence the ambiguity of phrases like *the shooting of the hunters*, meaning either 'the hunters shoot' or 'the hunters are shot' (Lyons 1971: 251–252). Relative adverbs have also not fallen out of use, although many of those that are found in the written standard language may be considered fully lexicalized (e.g. *whereby*, *wherein*), and therefore no longer result from regular rule application. Two alternative sets also continue to be available in the indefinite pronoun paradigm with human reference, those in -ONE and -BODY. Finally, in Standard English few affirmative statements take unstressed periphrastic DO (although it is not totally ruled out; see Gerner 1996: 22–34). Except affirmative DO, those features that have remained variable were either relative latecomers in the seventeenth century or were in a highly variable state at the time.

We can see from Table 10.1. that the outcome of the changes that were completed in the early modern period was accepted in Standard English. In many cases the alternative variants were restricted to some particular registers or indeed to regional use, as pointed out above. In the eighteenth century supralocal or supralocalizing forms were reinforced by **normative**

grammars, which singled out recessive forms such as YE and relative adverbs as ungrammatical or obsolete ('according to the . . . manner of the Bar or the Pulpit'), and instances of multiple negation as absurd, barbarous and vulgar (Sundby *et al.* 1991: 208, 221, 363–366). Although single negation diffused from above, overt stigmatization had not been associated with multiple negation in the early modern period, when even high-ranking women freely continued to use forms like *not* × *neither*. It only became an issue in the eighteenth century, when social and register differences in language use were turned into a marketable commodity, and dictionaries, grammar books and review magazines were set up as vehicles for social evaluation and language maintenance.[2]

Interestingly, **register variation** prevails in Standard English with most of the features that remained variable in the early modern period in Table 10.1. A modern descriptive grammar can write, for instance, on the subject of the gerund: 'in general the genitive is preferred if the item is a pronoun, the noun phrase has personal reference, and the style is formal', while 'the common case' is preferred 'where the item is a nonpersonal noun phrase and not a pronoun and the style is not formal' (Quirk *et al.* 1985: 1063–1064). Although codified, Standard English grammar permits a good deal of variation. The pronoun system is a case in point: apart from the two parallel sets of indefinite pronouns, there are as many as three relativization strategies (WH-, TH- and zero). Much of this variation is conditioned by register, and reinforced by powerful institutions such as the education system. However, if we assume a global view of Standard English, some of this variation shows different degrees of **globalization**. So North American English prefers pronouns in -BODY to those in -ONE, and THAT to WHICH in restrictive relative clauses even in written contexts (Biber *et al.* 1999: 353, 487–488, 616). In both cases the more colloquial forms are shown to be more common in American than in British English.

A great deal of variation is also allowed in nonstandard dialects of English, both traditional and modern, in the form of **variable grammars, which** are typical of noncodified varieties (Cheshire & Milroy 1993). Variable grammars were similarly the rule rather than the exception in our Early Modern English data. Chambers (1995: 241–242) suggests that, where a standard variety differs from other varieties, the difference lies both in the quantity and in the quality of variation. Nonstandard varieties permit variation where the focused standard core allows none. Our data show that high-frequency standard variants are typically the historical ones. They attest to the relative conservatism and resistance to change of the focused core of the standard language and often reflect the grammar of English at the time of its codification. But many nonstandard features also have a long history and wide distribution in the English-speaking world. Moreover, some of the available variation may later have become grammaticalized, as appears to have happened with affirmative DO in the south-west of England (see Klemola 1996).

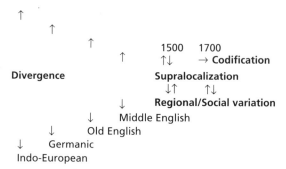

Figure 10.1. Divergence and convergence in language change (cf. Milroy 1992: 51).

The changes we have studied are in no way unique in that they can be characterized as **supralocal processes** which reached the consensus of the literate social ranks of the time. Their timing in the history of English was, however, crucial for their success. With increasing urbanization in the Tudor and Stuart period, the capital became a linguistic melting pot, exerting its influence throughout the country. Had a feature like the northern present indicative third-person -s spread to the south 150 or 200 years later, we may suspect it would have been branded as a vulgarism, or at least relegated to the realm of colloquial speech by prescriptive grammarians.

The larger picture is shown by Figure 10.1, following but crucially revising James Milroy's 'funnel vision' of language history (1992: 51). The major patterns of divergence before 1500 are those suggested by Milroy, but we do not find that all convergence, here depicted as a two-way street between supralocal and local (regional and social) variation, arises from the researchers' 'attempts to launder the data retrospectively in such a way as to focus on those features that lead to modern "standard" English' (Milroy 1992: 50–51). We would rather like to emphasize that unmonitored supralocalization of grammatical features took place at the national level before the normative era. In the process of codification, it was these features that formed the basis of Standard English grammar. It is noteworthy that they similarly form the basis of many **mainstream modern dialects**, which are associated with

> native speakers outside the British Isles, especially in recently settled areas which speak with mixed colonial dialects, such as Australia and most of America and Canada. In Britain, they are particularly associated with those areas of the country from which Standard English originally came – the southeast of England; with most urban areas; with places which have become English-speaking only relatively recently, such as the Scottish Highlands, much of Wales, and western Cornwall; with the speech of most younger people; and with middle- and upper-class speakers everywhere. (Trudgill 1999a: 6)

As Trudgill notes, mainstream modern nonstandard dialects are typically distinguished from Standard English and from each other much more by their pronunciation than by their grammar. It is therefore the outcome of grammatical supralocalization processes that dialectologists are talking about when they refer to 'levelled varieties' of nonstandard English (see Cheshire *et al.* 1993: 53–84).

10.2. The Principle of Contingency

As shown by Table 10.1., not all the 14 changes we have discussed above were completed by the end of the early modern period. Chapter 4 presents the details of their very different time courses: in contrast to the changes still in progress or frozen in mid-course, there are processes such as the rise of YOU as a subject pronoun, which was largely completed in the first half of the sixteenth century. We may hence conclude that, as far as their time courses are concerned, each of the 14 changes has its own history.

It is also not possible to predict the rate and social embedding of a process of change on the basis of its linguistic nature. Linguistically, our material can be characterized in different ways: some of the changes are processes of morpheme replacement (e.g. -TH → -S); others, such as the spread of YOU, MY and THY, result in levelling of morpheme distinctions in certain syntactic functions and positions. We have, moreover, studied changes such as (a) the rise of the prop-word ONE and the structure of the gerund and (b) the disappearance of multiple negation and inversion after initial negators, which relate to phrase and clause structures, respectively (referred to as 'abstract structural patterns' by Labov; see Chapter 4).

In the course of our discussion it has become clear that no simple parallels can be drawn between the type of language change and its social embedding. The replacement of THE WHICH by WHICH was led by men, while women were found to promote the third-person -*s* at the expense of -TH. YOU was first propagated as a subject form in the south, but the use MY and THY as determiners in the north. The list could be continued, but no direct correlation between the kind of linguistic change and its social embedding across time would be likely to emerge. Reducing the number of social variables to three in the VARBRUL analyses in Chapter 9, we were able to show in general terms that the two most important external variables that correlated with the changes in progress were region and gender. Interesting conclusions were also reached on the most relevant factors, namely the leading roles played by women and the capital region, the Royal Court in particular, in the processes of change. But no uniform pattern of social embedding emerged on the basis of the linguistic characteristics of the changes.

A similar conclusion is included in Hudson's list of sociolinguistic 'facts' (1996: 202): 'different linguistic variables are usually sensitive to other

[handwritten annotations: Never an over-arching cause of ling. change; each variable is unique.]

variables in different ways, i.e. each linguistic variable is socially unique.'
By extension, and as suggested by our findings, each linguistic change is
also socially unique. Labov's formulation (2001: 503) of this **Principle of
Contingency** is given in terms of the outcome of linguistic changes:

> Factors determining the course of linguistic change are drawn from a
> pattern of social behaviour that is not linked in any predictable way to
> the linguistic outcome. *[handwritten: → can't predict]*

Several sources of explanations may be offered to account for this basic
unpredictability, ranging from psycholinguistic and sociopsychological to
ultimately historical. Some psycholinguistic accounts, however, separate
grammatical and phonological variables in this respect. *[handwritten margin: → cognitive line; ↑ lang. context →]*

All the processes examined by us represent grammatical changes, in the
broad sense of 'grammatical', as opposed to phonological changes. Our
findings therefore squarely support those sociolinguists who argue that both
phonological and grammatical variables are socially embedded (Chambers
1995: 51–52). This generalization is not meant to trivialize the role of cognitive factors in the morphological and syntactic choices made by speakers.
On the basis of psycholinguistic evidence, Cheshire (1996: 3), for one, suggests that factors related to the production and processing of speech could
be viewed as more relevant to grammatical choices than the speakers' social
characteristics. They include the serial effect that the occurrence of a given
syntactic or morphological variant will prompt its re-use in a stretch of
discourse. It would seem to us that, while this formal parallelism may well
describe a local mechanism by which a grammatical variant is reproduced,
it does not make 'social sense' of the phenomenon. It does not account for
the social evaluation of linguistic variables and the fact that the range of the
available variants is determined by the social and regional dialects and
registers commanded by the interlocutors.

Our interpretation of the Principle of Contingency is informed by the
sociopsychological theory of **accommodation**, which basically aims to explain 'why people modify their language in the presence of others in the
way and to the extent that they do' (Trudgill 1986: 2). Both linguistic
convergence and divergence can take place, and no essential difference is
observed between grammatical and phonological variables in this respect –
on the contrary, accommodation also takes place with respect to gaze, eye
contact, proximity, body movement, speech tempo, etc. The question who
accommodates to whom lies at the heart of the theory. Sociolinguists and
dialectologists look for part of the answer in the demographic factors of the
language community.[3] We have done so particularly at the macro level by
paying attention to the waves of immigrants to the fast growing metropolis
of London, which had a high population turnover throughout the early
modern period. Migration and increased opportunities for dialect contact
proved to be crucial when accounting for the spread of linguistic changes

across dialect areas and explaining deviations from the expected wave-like progress of supralocal diffusion of language change.

For historical sociolinguists it is probably easier to trace population movements – the opportunity for accommodation must be there – than to answer the question who initially accommodates to whom linguistically. With the benefit of hindsight, we can say that reaching the top layers of early modern society, notably the Royal Court, appears to be required of successful processes of supralocal change at the time. Some groups of people must therefore have accommodated to their social superiors. This was most obviously the case with socially upwardly mobile men in our corpus. But since not all changes originated from above in social terms, some of those high up on the social ladder must also have accommodated to their social inferiors. Moreover, since in most cases it was women who were the leaders of linguistic change, sweeping generalizations in terms of overt prestige become even harder to make. A combination of factors enters into the picture when we think of Early Modern Englishwomen's regional and social mobility due to marriage and their role as care-givers, for instance.

Generally speaking, it seems, however, that Keller (1994: 86–90) has a point when he argues that the driving force behind language change is **social success** understood in a broad sense. People strive for socially successful interaction with other people, and here influencing others by means of language is an essential element. Social success may include goals like 'influence, affection, food, power, attention; being understood, being read, being accepted, having a mate, and such like' (Keller 1994: 88).[4] Linguistic status symbols are not excluded but they only count as one of the many forms of social success in this model. Consequently, as there must be a number of different potentially successful strategies available to the interlocutors in any given communicative situation – it was shown in Chapter 5 that the majority of our informants had variable grammars – it is no wonder that the details of linguistic changes should prove to be socially unique.

10.3. Uninterrupted Continuity of Change?

Given that linguistic changes are socially unique, how can we account for the fact that long-term changes progress in the same direction across each successive generation? This is identified as the **transmission problem** in language change by Labov (2001: 416), who mostly discusses it in terms of language acquisition ('children must learn to talk differently from their mothers'). Language acquisition remains one of the areas least accessible to historical linguists, whereas the transmission of real-time processes of linguistic change can be observed across time. Before moving on to our findings on the continuity of change, it may be worth noting that most of the changes we examined proved to be both generational and communal. As shown in

Chapter 5, many individuals, both men and women, had not fixed their grammars by adolescence but clearly increased their use of the incoming variants as they grew older.

Although we may not be able to account for the transmission of linguistic changes in terms of acquisition, it is nevertheless fascinating to be able to document these processes across time and see how the same set of informants can produce quite different patterns depending on the change. The great majority of the changes we have discussed display an S-shaped curve of transmission; some of them are remarkably regular, such as the replacement of YE by YOU, and the rise of zero as opposed to OF-phrases in the object of the gerund; others appear more rugged, particularly those with several variant forms, such as the indefinite pronouns with singular human reference. Not all these changes had run their course by the end of the early modern period, and we may speculate about the role played by codification in the subsequent centuries in halting or at least retarding the processes. But only one change out of the fourteen reversed its projected trajectory permanently: periphrastic DO in affirmative statements, which peaked in the late 1500s but fell into a dramatic decline in the early seventeenth century and has not recovered its former position since.

The transmission problem can be approached from different angles sociolinguistically. The factor that again emerges with supralocal changes is the opportunity for transmission, that is, sufficient contacts between speakers with different social and regional backgrounds. We have already established the importance of urbanization to dialect contacts and referred to social network structures as a mechanism that can either speed up or retard processes of linguistic change (see Chapter 8). Sociolinguists have provided evidence to the effect that a dense, multiplex network structure is apt to impose linguistic norms on its members and to promote language maintenance, while a loose-knit structure with weak ties is conducive to diffuse language patterns and increased linguistic variation (e.g. Milroy & Milroy 1985b; L. Milroy 1987). This model suggests that people are most likely to accommodate to each other linguistically in a weak-tie contact situation, and that these contacts are likely to lead to dialect diffusion and language change. The transmission of the changes we have witnessed may therefore be related to frequent weak-tie situations, independently documented by social historians, within the layers of society accessible to us from the merchant and professional ranks to the nobility.

We have also been able to observe, in processes of change, phases that may be interpreted as periods of increased **acceleration** (Chapter 4). They may be related to the role played by unexpected external upheavals in the social network structures of the language community (Bailey *et al.* 1996; Labov 1994: 24). One of the large-scale catastrophic events in early modern England was without a doubt the Civil War (1642–1649). During the war, military operations brought together great crowds of people throughout the country, with more than one adult male in ten in arms at some moments (Morrill 1984: 317). The accelerating effect of the Civil War on linguistic changes in progress is discussed in more detail in Raumolin-Brunberg (1998).

An external event has also been suggested to account for the rapid and unexpected decline of affirmative periphrastic DO: the arrival in the capital of the Scottish court of James I, who spoke a practically DO-less dialect (Nurmi 1999a: 179–182). Interestingly, no comparable fall in the use of *do* in affirmative statements was found in East Anglia at the time. The periphrasis had been securely rooted in the dialect area in the late sixteenth century, and its frequency continued to rise there in the early decades of the seventeenth century (Nurmi 1999a: 176–177). As DO and its cognates may be used to facilitate communication in language-contact situations, it remains to be seen whether here, too, we could be witnessing the linguistic consequences of an unforeseen event. A candidate for one is discussed by Trudgill (2001), namely the flight to East Anglia of French- and Flemish-speaking Protestant refugees from the Low Countries. In the 1570s they made up more than one third of the population of Norwich, and their linguistic influence was felt throughout the seventeenth century.

These illustrations may suffice to make the point that unexpected external events can assume an active role in shaping the way linguistic changes are transmitted across successive generations. However, seeing the ease with which external explanations could be multiplied to iron out any wrinkles in the steady transmission of linguistic changes, we would like to finish with a note of caution. It is, of course, necessary to propose hypotheses on the possible impact of unexpected events on the course of linguistic changes, but the facts supporting or refuting them ought to be weighed with care. So, although there is enough evidence for us to argue that language changes were accelerated in the mid-seventeenth century, more material on individual changes and localities would be needed to say something more about the Civil War effect. Similarly, Nurmi (1999a: 179) cautiously calls the Scottish connection her 'frivolous theory on the decline of DO', which she believes ought to be taken only as one of the possible explanations for the unexpected change. We conclude that in sociolinguistics, both historical and modern, the Transmission Problem will always need to be reconciled with the Principle of Contingency.

Notes

1. Milroy (1994: 19–20) notes that '[i]t is better to think of the process of standardization as having been facilitated in the history of English by the prior development of these agreed norms in certain dialect areas.' These processes of supralocalization differ from standardization in that the latter is explicitly imposed from above and carries with it a conscious ideology.
2. Print culture, standardization and prescriptivism are singled out by McIntosh (1998: 8, 169–194) as the three movements that contributed to a general 'commodification' of language and literature in the eighteenth century; 38 new grammars

of English were published between 1701 and 1750, and as many as 204 between 1751 and 1800. See further also Stein (1994) and Tieken-Boon van Ostade (2000a).

3. See e.g. Trudgill (1986: 81–126) and Labov (2001: 503–506). Samuels (1972: 97–134) discusses dialect contact in the historical context both in terms of adaptations (compromises) and switches (shifts).

4. Incidentally, Keller's approach comes quite close to Allardt's (1989) concepts of 'having', 'loving' and 'being' introduced in 2.4.

Appendix I

Methodology: How to Count Occurrences

The uneven input of corpus data by different people, a circumstance that is unfortunate but unavoidable, made us test different methods of counting the linguistic occurrences. Similar problems rarely exist in present-day studies, in which the contributions of individual informants can be kept at a chosen level, either in terms of the amount of running text or the linguistic occurrences under examination. The input variation in the CEEC ranges from over 70,000 running words (Dorothy Osborne, writing 1652–57) to about 100 words (some minor informants). As mentioned in Chapter 3, difficulties in finding female and low-ranking writers has motivated the inclusion of informants with only one or two letters.

We were especially worried about the representativeness of periods in which one individual's contribution was very large. In order to find out to what extent the input differences could skew our statistics, the percentages of two changes, the replacement of subject YE by YOU and the third-person singular suffix -TH by -S, were calculated in four different ways. The first three models involve the use of a linguistic variable with two competing variants and the fourth is a frequency count.

The first pattern consists of 'normal' percentages that were counted for each successive 20-year period. This means that all occurrences of the two linguistic variants were added together and the percentage of the new form (YOU and -S, respectively) was calculated. Secondly, a percentage score was counted for each informant with 10 occurrences or more (for examples of individual scores, see Appendixes 5.1.–5.3.). Those whose contribution was smaller than 10 occurrences were lumped together, and a score was counted for the emerging group. An average was then calculated of the scores for each period. Thirdly, a 40-occurrence quota was set for each individual, and percentages were counted subsequently. In addition to the three variable counts a simple frequency count was carried out on the incoming forms YOU and -S.

Figure 1 is a graphic presentation of the results of the first three methods. The general picture of the changes does not vary much irrespective of the way of counting. On a closer analysis, however, at some critical points the

214

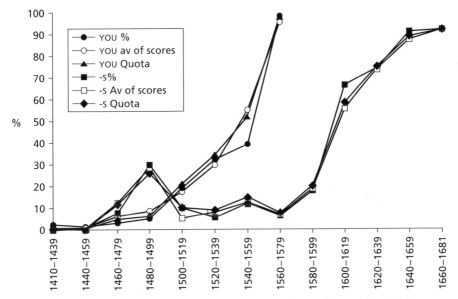

Figure 1. Subject YOU vs. YE and third-person singular suffix -S vs. -TH. The proportion of YOU and -S counted in three different ways. CEEC 1998 and Supplement.

first method seems to yield results that diverge from those of the other two. During the period 1540–1559 the percentage of YOU is lower with the normal percentage count, while in 1600–1619 the proportion of -S is higher with this method.

Both deviations can be explained by the dominant role of one single individual. John Johnson, wool merchant, husband of Sabine Johnson, preferred the old form YE at a time when many others had already adopted the new YOU pronoun. His contribution was 556 occurrences of second-person subject pronouns (3.3 per cent YOU) of a total of 2,800, i.e. 20 per cent of all occurrences for 1540–1559. As regards the third-person inflection, for the period 1600–1619 our major informant is John Chamberlain, London gentleman, who is responsible for an even larger share of occurrences, 27 per cent (389 out of a total of 1,457). Chamberlain was almost a 100-per-cent user of the -S suffix, and hence the percentage line reaches a higher level than the other two lines during this period. In both cases the remaining two methods, i.e. the average of individual scores and the quota method, level out the influence of one dominant individual.

Figures 2 and 3 indicate that a method which does not involve the use of the linguistic variable also produces curves with a very similar shape to those in Figure 1. This result suggests that even a frequency count can be employed to illustrate the general patterns of development of individual changes. However, we would not like to go as far as to argue that counting

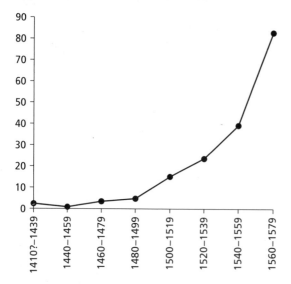

Figure 2. The frequency of subject YOU per 10,000 running words. CEEC 1998 and Supplement.

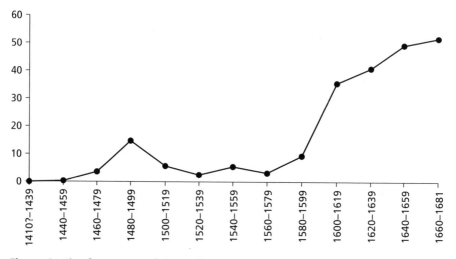

Figure 3. The frequency of the suffix -s in the third-person singular per 10,000 running words. CEEC 1998 and Supplement.

normalized frequencies would always lead to the same results as the percentage scores of the innovative variants. We assume that, if the frequencies are heavily conditioned by factors such as subject matter, textual tradition or pragmatic preference, the results may diverge from the variable count (Nevalainen 1996b). It seems, however, that in many morphosyntactic phenomena frequency follows the pattern of variable percentages (see also Nurmi 1999a).

It is obvious that the average-score and quota methods are inapplicable to changes with small frequencies, when most informants yield less than 10 instances. In these cases counting percentages and looking at frequencies remain our only choices. It is important not to forget that, although the CEEC is a large corpus, it has not been designed with any specific change or use in mind, and the phenomena studied vary a great deal in frequency. Consequently, it is possible to employ more delicate analytical tools only for frequent variables.

For the sake of comparability, we decided to apply the same percentage method to the changes in Chapter 4, except for two frequency counts. As Figures 1–3 show, the curves do not diverge from each other so much that different general pictures would emerge. In the detailed discussions in Chapters 6–9 quota sampling will also be relied on where appropriate.

In a few cases not even the quota method prevented undue influence of one single person. The idiosyncratic informants in question are Edmund de la Pole (1473–1513), early user of YOU, Sabine Johnson, late user of THE WHICH, Sir Thomas Browne (1605–1682), late user of third-person -TH, and Dorothy Osborne (1627–1695), frequent user of the prop-word ONE, auxiliary DO and indefinite pronouns in -BODY. Their contributions were excluded from specific quantitative examinations, as their inclusion would have distorted the picture to a considerable degree. These cases include regional distribution of YOU (Edmund de la Pole), social variation of the third-person suffix (Sir Thomas Browne), gender variation of WHICH versus THE WHICH (Sabine Johnson), gender variation of affirmative and negative DO and indefinite pronouns, as well as the general use and gender variation of the prop-word ONE (Dorothy Osborne).

Appendix II

Numerical Information

Chapter 4

Table 1. Replacement of subject YE by YOU

	YE	YOU	%	Total
1410?–1479	3369	82	2	3451
1480–1519	1036	106	9	1142
1520–1559	2668	1586	37	4254
1560–1599	98	2657	96	2755
1600–1619	3	1887	100	1890

Table 2. MY and THY versus MINE and THINE

Preceding a consonant	Long	Short	%	Total
1410?–1459	135	1440	91	1575
1460–1499	133	3528	96	3661
Preceding a word with an initial <H>				
1410?–1459	15	16	52	31
1460–1499	59	82	58	141
1500–1539	27	122	82	149
1540–1579	5	492	99	497
Preceding a vowel				
1410?–1459	62	7	10	69
1460–1499	152	50	25	202
1500–1539	138	77	36	215
1540–1579	105	241	70	346
1580–1619	42	583	93	625
1620–1659	24	855	97	879
1660–1681	5	354	99	359
Preceding the word OWN				
1410?–1459	12	0	0	12
1460–1499	40	11	22	51
1500–1539	114	16	12	130
1540–1579	83	47	36	130
1580–1619	87	132	60	219
1620–1659	51	300	85	351
1660–1681	13	118	90	131

Table 3. Possessive determiner ITS

	THEREOF + OF IT	ITS	%	Total
1600–1639	151	7	4	158
1640–1681	201	109	35	310

Table 4. Prop-word ONE

	N	N/10,000 w
1410?–1459	1	0.08
1460–1499	2	0.07
1500–1539	3	0.12
1540–1579	14	0.33
1580–1619	35	0.68
1620–1659*	91	1.36
1660–1681	72	2.06

*excluding Dorothy Osborne with a frequency of 6.59 occurrences per 10,000w (47/71,299w).

Table 5. Object of the gerund

	OF-phrase	zero	%	Total
1410?–1479	208	32	13	240
1480–1519	124	28	18	152
1520–1559	490	174	26	664
1560–1599	443	349	44	792
1600–1639	318	725	70	1043
1640–1681	292	1208	81	1500

Table 6. Noun subject of the gerund

	Genitive	%	OF-phrase	%	Other	%	Total
1410?–1459	20	50	15	38	5	13	40
1460–1499	55	50	47	43	7	6	109
1500–1539	36	37	54	55	8	8	98
1540–1579	107	50	81	38	24	11	212
1580–1619	106	48	88	40	26	12	220
1620–1659	179	60	94	32	25	8	298
1660–1681	126	74	37	22	8	5	171

Table 7. Third-person singular -s versus -TH

	-TH	-S	%	Total
1410?–1459	611	2	0	613
1460–1499	1258	199	14	1457
1500–1539	1134	75	6	1209
1540–1579	1749	197	10	1946
1580–1619	1487	1161	44	2648
1620–1659	711	3305	82	4016
1660–1681	157	1802	92	1959

Table 8. Periphrastic DO in affirmative statements

	N	DO/10,000w
1410?–1439	5	2.2
1440–1479	38	1.3
1480–1519	41	3.5
1520–1559	1029	22.1
1560–1599	1248	34.3
1600–1639	998	16.8
1640–1681	894	14.6

Table 9. Periphrastic DO in negative statements

	Simple	NegDO	%	Total
1480–1519	53	1	2	54
1520–1559	606	123	17	729
1560–1599	550	176	24	726
1600–1639	928	225	20	1153
1640–1681	780	739	49	1519

Table 10. Multiple versus single negation with non-assertive indefinites

Simple constructions

	Multiple	Single	%	Total
1460–1499	215	30	12	245
1500–1539	79	151	66	230
1540–1579	86	410	83	496
1580–1619	24	567	96	591

Co-ordinate and additive constructions

	Multiple	Single	%	Total
1460–1499	161	5	3	166
1500–1539	98	43	30	141
1540–1579	113	73	39	186
1580–1619	63	118	65	181

Table 11. Direct versus inverted word-order after initial adverbs and negators (CEEC 1996)

Inverted word-order after initial adverbs

	Direct	Inverted	%	Total
up to 1522	382	56	13	438
1522–1562	605	112	16	717
1563–1602	637	73	10	710
1603–1642	655	48	7	703
1643–1682	524	13	2	537

Inverted word-order after initial negators

	Direct	Inverted	%	Total
up to 1522	56	0	0	56
1522–1562	69	21	23	90
1563–1602	14	66	83	80
1603–1642	3	146	98	149
1643–1682	3	83	93	89

Table 12. Relative pronouns WHICH and THE WHICH

	THE WHICH	WHICH	%	Total
1410?–1459	156	309	66	465
1460–1499	466	665	59	1131
1500–1539	148	1275	90	1423
1540–1579	236	2316	91	2552
1580–1619	96	3086	97	3182
1620–1681	80	6875	99	6955

Table 13. Prepositional phrase versus relative adverb (ABOUT, AFTER, BY, ON, TO, UNTO, UPON, WITH)

	Relative adverb		Preposition+ (THE) WHICH		(THE) WHICH +stranded prep		Total
	N	%	N	%	N	%	
1440–1479	47	58	26	32	8	10	81
1480–1519	64	76	16	19	4	5	84
1520–1559	344	85	50	12	11	3	405
1560–1599	279	75	64	17	28	8	371
1600–1639	175	52	125	37	37	11	337
1640–1681	134	34	195	50	63	16	392

Table 14. Indefinite pronouns with singular human reference. Compound pronouns and their equivalents

	-MAN		other		-ONE		-BODY		Total
	N	%	N	%	N	%	N	%	
1410?–1499	154	58	89	34	1	0	22	8	266
1500–1579	229	51	183	41	11	2	26	8	449
1580–1619	111	28	206	52	36	9	45	11	398
1620–1659	97	27	154	43	41	12	66	18	358
1660–1681	45	16	102	37	57	21	73	26	277

Appendix III

The Letter Collections

List compiled by Arja Nurmi and Minna Palander-Collin

The *Corpus of Early English Correspondence* (CEEC), the 1998 version

The CEEC (1998) has been compiled by Jukka Keränen, Minna Nevala, Terttu Nevalainen, Arja Nurmi, Minna Palander-Collin and Helena Raumolin-Brunberg, Department of English, University of Helsinki. The collections marked with [CEECS] are included in the *Corpus of Early English Correspondence Sampler*, published in the *New ICAME Corpus Collection CD-ROM*, Bergen, The HIT-Centre, 1999.

Allen   5,070 words (1579–1593)
Letters of William Allen and Richard Barret, 1572–1598. Ed. by P. Renold. Catholic Record Society, 58. Oxford: Oxonian Press. 1967.

Arundel   19,202 words (1589–1680)
The Life, Correspondence & Collections of Thomas Howard, Earl of Arundel, 'Father of Vertu in England'. Ed. by Mary F. S. Hervey. Cambridge: The University Press. 1921.

Bacon   139,004 words (1569?–1594)
The Papers of Nathaniel Bacon of Stiffkey. Ed. by A. Hassell Smith, Gillian M. Baker and R. W. Kenny. Norfolk Record Society, 46, 49 and 53. Norwich: Norfolk Record Society. 1978 and 1979, 1982 and 1983, 1987 and 1988.

Barrington   63,934 words (1628–1632)
Barrington Family Letters, 1628–1632. Camden Fourth Series, 28. Ed. by Arthur Searle. London: Royal Historical Society. 1983.

Basire   7,068 words (1651–1666)
The Correspondence of Isaac Basire, D.D., Archdeacon of Northumberland and Prebendary of Durham, in the Reigns of Charles I. and Charles II., with a Memoir of His Life. Ed. by W. N. Darnell. London: John Murray. 1831. [CEECS]

Baxter & Eliot   2,346 words (1656–1657)
Some Unpublished Correspondence of the Reverend Richard Baxter and the Reverend John Eliot, the Apostle of the American Indians, 1656–1682. Ed. by F. J. Powicke. Reprinted from *The Bulletin of the John Rylands Library* 15 (2), July,

1931. Manchester: The Manchester University Press and the Librarian, the John Rylands Library. 1931.

Bentham   4,102 words (1560–1561)
The Letter-Book of Thomas Bentham, Bishop of Coventry and Lichfield, 1560–1561. Ed. by Rosemary O'Day and Joel Berlatsky. In *Camden Miscellany 27*. Camden Fourth Series, 22. London: Royal Historical Society. 1979.

Brereton   9,748 words (1520?–1539?)
Letters and Accounts of William Brereton of Malpas. Ed. by E. W. Ives. Record Society of Lancashire and Cheshire, 116. Old Woking, Surrey: Record Society of Lancashire and Cheshire. 1976.

Browne   20,778 words (1653–1681)
The Works of Sir Thomas Browne. Vol. IV: *Letters.* Ed. by Geoffrey Keynes. Chicago: The University of Chicago Press. 1964.

Bryskett   8,961 words (1581–1583)
The Life and Correspondence of Lodowick Bryskett. Ed. by Henry R. Plomer and Tom Peete Cross. Chicago: The University of Chicago Press. 1927.

Cecil   1,634 words (1586)
The Bardon Papers. Documents Relating to the Imprisonment & Trial of Mary Queen of Scots. Ed. by Conyers Read. Camden Third Series, 17. London: Royal Historical Society. 1909.

Cely   51,478 words (1474–1488)
The Cely Letters 1472–1488. Ed. by Alison Hanham. Early English Text Society, 273. London, New York and Toronto: Oxford University Press. 1975.

Chamberlain   69,349 words (1597–1625)
The Letters of John Chamberlain. Ed. by Norman Egbert McClure. American Philosophical Society, Memoirs, 12, Parts I–II. Philadelphia: American Philosophical Society. 1939.

Charles   2,964 words (1634–1678)
Five Letters of King Charles II. Ed. by the Marquis of Bristol. In *Camden Miscellany 5*. Camden Original Series, 87. New York: Johnson Reprint Corporation. 1864/1968. [CEECS]
AND
Letter of the Council to Sir Thomas Lake, Relating to the Proceedings of Sir Edward Coke at Oatlands. Ed. by Samuel Rawson Gardiner. In *Camden Miscellany 5*. Camden Original Series, 87. New York: Johnson Reprint Corporation. 1864/1968. [CEECS]

Clerk   3,876 words (1458?–1590)
Letters of the Fifteenth and Sixteenth Centuries from the Archives of Southampton. Ed. by R. C. Anderson. Publications of the Southampton Record Society. Southampton: Southampton Record Society. 1921.

Clifford   33,919 words (1490?–1589?)
Clifford Letters of the Sixteenth Century. Ed. by A. G. Dickens. Publications of the Surtees Society, 172. Durham and London: Surtees Society. 1962.
AND
Letters of the Cliffords, Lords Clifford and Earls of Cumberland, c. 1500–c. 1565. Ed. by R. W. Hoyle. In *Camden Miscellany 31.* Camden Fourth Series, 44. London: Royal Historical Society. 1992.

Conway   57,946 words (1640–1680)
The Conway Letters. The Correspondence of Anne, Viscountess Conway, Henry More, and their Friends. 1642–1684. Ed. by Marjorie Hope Nicolson. Revised ed. by Sarah Hutton. Oxford: Clarendon Press. 1992.

Corie   4,626 words (1666–1671)
The Correspondence of Thomas Corie, Town Clerk of Norwich, 1664–1687. With His Annotations to Edward Browne's Travels and Other Memoranda. Ed. by Robert H. Hill. Norfolk Record Society, 27. Norwich: Norfolk Record Society. 1956.

Cornwallis   61,608 words (1613–1644)
The Private Correspondence of Jane Lady Cornwallis, 1613–1644. Ed. by Richard Griffin, Baron Braybrooke. London: S. & J. Bentley, Wilson, & Fley. 1842. [CEECS]

Cosin   37,855 words (1617–1695?)
The Correspondence of John Cosin, D.D., Lord Bishop of Durham: Together with Other Papers Illustrative of his Life and Times. Parts I–II. Ed. by George Ornsby. Publications of the Surtees Society, 52, 55. Durham, London and Edinburgh: Surtees Society. 1869, 1872. [CEECS]

Cromwell   44,386 words (1523–1540)
Life and Letters of Thomas Cromwell. Vols. I–II. Ed. by Roger Bigelow Merriman. Oxford: Clarendon Press. 1902.

Derby   12,555 words (1533–1539?)
Correspondence of Edward, Third Earl of Derby, during the Years 24 to 31 Henry VIII. Ed. by T. Northcote Toller. Remains Historical and Literary Connected with the Palatine Counties of Lancaster and Chester, New Series, 19. Manchester: Chetham Society. 1890.

Duppa   28,410 words (1650–1660)
The Correspondence of Bishop Brian Duppa and Sir Justinian Isham 1650–1660. Ed. by Sir Gyles Isham. Publications of the Northamptonshire Record Society, 17. Lamport Hall: Northamptonshire Record Society. 1951.

Edmondes   20,522 words (1592–1599)
The Edmondes Papers: A Selection from the Correspondence of Sir Thomas Edmondes, Envoy from Queen Elizabeth at the French Court. Ed. by Geoffrey G. Butler. London: Roxburghe Club. 1913.

Elyot   7,201 words (1528–1536)
The Letters of Sir Thomas Elyot. Ed. by K. J. Wilson. *Studies in Philology (Text and Studies, 1976),* 73 (5): ix–78. 1976.

Essex   25,206 words (1675–1677)
Selections from the Correspondence of Arthur Capel, Earl of Essex, 1675–77. Ed. by Clement Edwards Pike. Camden Third Series, 24. London: Royal Historical Society. 1913.

Ferrar   17,126 words (1613–1659?)
The Ferrar Papers Containing a Life of Nicholas Ferrar, the Winding-sheet, an Ascetic Dialogue, a Collection of Short Moral Histories, a Selection of Family Letters. Ed. by B. Blackstone. Cambridge: Cambridge University Press. 1938.

Ffarington   6,125 words (1547–1554)
The Ffarington Papers. The Shrievalty of William Ffarington, Esq.; A.D. 1636: Documents Relating to the Civil War: And an Appendix, Containing a Collection of Letters Taken from the Ffarington Correspondence between the Years 1547 and 1688. Ed. by Susan Maria Ffarington. Chetham Society, 39. Manchester: Chetham Society. 1856.

Fitzherbert   11,271 words (1608–1610)
Letters of Thomas Fitzherbert, 1608–1610. Ed. by L. Hicks. Publications of the Catholic Record Society, 41. London: Catholic Record Society. 1948.

Fleming   39,833 words (1650–1680)
The Flemings in Oxford, Being Documents Selected from the Rydal Papers in Illustration of the Lives and Ways of Oxford Men 1650–1700. Vol. I. Ed. by John Richard Magrath. Oxford: Oxford Historical Society, 44. 1904.

Fox   10,554 words (1497?–1519)
Letters of Richard Fox, 1486–1527. Ed. by P. S. and H. M. Allen. Oxford: Clarendon Press. 1929.

Gardiner   31,785 words (1528–1554)
The Letters of Stephen Gardiner. Ed. by James Arthur Muller. Cambridge: Cambridge University Press. 1933.

Gawdy   22,418 words (1579–1616)
Letters of Philip Gawdy of West Harling, Norfolk, and of London to Various Members of his Family 1579–1616. Ed. by Isaac Herbert Jeayes. London: Roxburghe Club. 1906.

GawdyL   10,361 words (1600?–1639?)
Letters from the Gawdy Correspondence in the 17th Century. Edited from British Library Manuscripts *Additional* 27,395, *Egerton* 2,714, 2,715 and 2,716, by Minna Nevala. Unpublished.

Giffard   3,900 words (1664–1668)
Martha Lady Giffard. Her Life and Correspondence (1664–1722): A Sequel to the Letters of Dorothy Osborne. Ed. by Julia G. Longe. London: George Allen & Sons. 1911.

Haddock   5,657 words (1657–1673)
Correspondence of the Family of Haddock, 1657–1719. Ed. by Edward Maunde Thompson. In *Camden Miscellany 8.* Camden New Series, 31. New York: Johnson Reprint Corporation. 1883/1965.

Hamilton   1,091 words (1648–1650)
The Hamilton Papers: Being Selections from the Original Letters in the Possession of His Grace the Duke of Hamilton and Brandon Relating to the Years 1638–1650. Ed. by Samuel Rawson Gardiner. Camden New Series, 27. London: Camden Society. 1880. [CEECS]

Harington   8,833 words (1571–1612?)
The Letters and Epigrams of Sir John Harington together with The Prayse of Private Life. Ed. by Norman Egbert McClure. Philadelphia: University of Pennsylvania Press. 1930.

Harley   24,915 words (1625–1666)
Letters of the Lady Brilliana Harley, Wife of Sir Robert Harley, of Brampton Bryan, Knight of the Bath. Ed. by Thomas Taylor Lewis. Camden Original Series, 57. London: Camden Society. 1854. [CEECS]

Hart   2,139 words (1561–1578)
John Hart's Works on English Orthography and Pronunciation (1551, 1569, 1570). Part I. Ed. by Bror Danielsson. Stockholm: Almqvist & Wiksell. 1955.

Harvey   9,759 words (1573)
Letter-Book of Gabriel Harvey, A.D. 1573–1580. Ed. by Edward John Long Scott. Camden New Series, 33. London: Camden Society. 1884.

Hastings   21,846 words (1573–1609)
The Letters of Sir Francis Hastings 1574–1609. Ed. by Claire Cross. Somerset Record Society, 69. London: Somerset Record Society. 1969.

Hatton   33,831 words (1601–1681)
Correspondence of the Family of Hatton, Being Chiefly Letters Addressed to Christopher First Viscount Hatton, A.D. 1601–1704. Vols. I–II. Ed. by Edward Maunde Thompson. Camden New Series, 22 and 23. London: Camden Society. 1878.

Henry VIII   1,629 words (1528)
Die Liebesbriefe Heinrichs VIII. an Anna Boleyn. Ed. by Theo Stemmler. Zürich: Belser Verlag. 1988.

Henslowe 14,408 words (1593?–1620?)
Henslowe's Diary. Ed. by R. A. Foakes and R. T. Rickert. Cambridge: Cambridge University Press. 1961.
AND
Henslowe Papers, Being Documents Supplementary to Henslowe's Diary. Ed. by Walter R. Greg. London: A. H. Bullen. 1907.
AND
The Henslowe Papers Supplement: The Theatre Papers. Ed. by Masayuki Yamagishi Kyoto: Apollon-Sha. 1992.
AND
'Forgeries and One-Eyed Bulls: Editorial Questions in Corpus Work'. Ed. by Jukka Keränen. *Neuphilologische Mitteilungen* 99 (2): 217–226. Helsinki. 1998. [CEECS]

Holles 66,367 words (1587–1637)
Letters of John Holles, 1587–1637. Vol. I. Ed. by P. R. Seddon. Thoroton Society Record Series, 31. Nottingham: Thoroton Society. 1975.

Hoskyns 12,368 words (1601–1629)
The Life, Letters and Writings of John Hoskyns, 1566–1638. Ed. by Louise Brown Osborn. Yale Studies in English, 87. New Haven: Yale University Press. 1937.

Hutton 25,340 words (1566–1633)
The Correspondence of Dr. Matthew Hutton, Archbishop of York. With a Selection from the Letters, etc. of Sir Timothy Hutton, Knt., His Son; and Matthew Hutton, Esq., His Grandson. Ed. by J. Raine. Publications of the Surtees Society, 17. London: J. B. Nichols and Sons, William Pickering; Edinburgh: Laing and Forbes. 1843. [CEECS]

Johnson 191,695 words (1541–1553)
The Johnson Letters, 1542–1552. Ed. by Barbara Winchester. Unpublished doctoral dissertation. University of London. 1953.

Jones 33,877 words (1651–1660)
Inedited Letters of Cromwell, Colonel Jones, Bradshaw and Other Regicides. Ed. by Joseph Mayer. Transactions of the Historic Society of Lancashire and Cheshire, New Series, 1. Liverpool: Adam Holden. 1861. [CEECS]

Jonson 3,798 words (1600?–1631?)
Ben Jonson. Vol. I. Corrected edition. Ed. by C. H. Herford and Percy Simpson. Oxford: Oxford University Press. 1954.

Knyvett 27,355 words (1620–1644)
The Knyvett Letters (1620–1644). Ed. by Bertram Schofield. London: Constable & Company. 1949.

Leycester   67,788 words (1585–1586)
Correspondence of Robert Dudley, Earl of Leycester, During His Government of the Low Countries, in the Years 1585 and 1586. Ed. by John Bruce. Camden Original Series, 27. London: Camden Society. 1844. [CEECS]

Lisle   5,774 (1533–1539)
The Lisle Letters. Ed. by Muriel St. Clare Byrne. Vols. I–VI. Chicago: The University of Chicago Press. 1981.

Lowther   36,925 words (1632–1643)
Commercial Papers of Sir Christopher Lowther 1611–1644. Ed. by D. R. Hainsworth. Publications of the Surtees Society, 189. Gateshead: Surtees Society. 1974/1977.

Marchall   4,834 words (1440?–1476)
The Marchall Letters. Re-edited by Jukka Keränen, Terttu Nevalainen and Arja Nurmi. MS. Public Record Office, SC1. Published in the *Corpus of Early English Correspondence Sampler.* 1999. [CEECS]

Marescoe   21,543 words (1668–1680)
Markets and Merchants of the Late Seventeenth Century. The Marescoe-David Letters, 1668–1680. Ed. by Henry Roseveare. Records of Social and Economic History, New Series, 12. Oxford: Oxford University Press for the British Academy. 1987.

Marvell   10,616 words (1653–1677)
The Poems and Letters of Andrew Marvell. Vol. II: *Letters.* Ed. by H. M. Margoliouth. 3rd ed. Revised by Pierre Legouis. Oxford: Clarendon Press. 1971.

Minette   7,748 words (1662–1669)
My Dearest Minette: The Letters between Charles II and His Sister Henrietta, the Duchesse d'Orléans. Ed. by Ruth Norrington. London: Peter Owen. 1996.

More   36,942 words (1505–1535)
The Correspondence of Sir Thomas More. Ed. by Elizabeth Frances Rogers. Princeton: Princeton University Press. 1947.

Original 1   23,176 words (1418?–1529?)
Original Letters, Illustrative of English History; Including Numerous Royal Letters: From Autographs in the British Museum, and One or Two Other Collections. Vol. I. Ed. by Henry Ellis. 2nd edition. London: Harding, Triphook, and Lepard. 1825. [CEECS]

Original 2   16,867 words (1520?–1586)
Original Letters, Illustrative of English History; Including Numerous Royal Letters: From Autographs in the British Museum, and One or Two Other Collections. Vol. II. Ed. by Henry Ellis. 2nd edition. London: Harding, Triphook, and Lepard. 1825. [CEECS]

Original 3   9,955 words (1580?–1665)
Original Letters, Illustrative of English History; Including Numerous Royal Letters:
From Autographs in the British Museum, and One or Two Other Collections.
Vol. III. Ed. by Henry Ellis. 2nd edition. London: Harding, Triphook, and
Lepard. 1825. [CEECS]

Osborne   71,100 words (1652–1657?)
The Letters of Dorothy Osborne to William Temple. Ed. by G. C. Moore Smith.
Oxford: Clarendon Press. 1959/1928.

Oxinden   123,861 words (1607–1681)
The Oxinden Letters 1607–1642. Being the Correspondence of Henry Oxinden of
Barham and His Circle. Ed. by Dorothy Gardiner. London: Constable & Co.
Ltd. 1933.
AND
The Oxinden and Peyton Letters 1642–1670. Being the Correspondence of Henry
Oxinden of Barham, Sir Thomas Peyton of Knowlton and Their Circle. Ed. by
Dorothy Gardiner. London: The Sheldon Press. 1937.

Paget   25,430 words (1547–1563)
The Letters of William, Lord Paget of Beaudesert, 1547–1563. Ed. by Barrett L.
Beer and Sybil M. Jack. In *Camden Miscellany 25.* Camden Fourth Series, 13.
London: Royal Historical Society. 1974.

Parkhurst   34,797 words (1569–1575)
The Letter Book of John Parkhurst Bishop of Norwich Compiled during the Years
1571–5. Ed. by R. A. Houlbrooke. Norfolk Record Society, 43. Norwich:
Norfolk Record Society. 1974 and 1975.

Paston   234,098 words (1425–1519?)
Paston Letters and Papers of the Fifteenth Century. Parts I–II. Ed. by Norman
Davis. Oxford: Clarendon Press. 1971 and 1976.

PastonK   29,626 words (1603–1627?)
The Correspondence of Lady Katherine Paston, 1603–1627. Ed. by Ruth Hughey.
Norfolk Record Society, 14. Norwich: Norfolk Record Society. 1941.

Pepys   42,476 words (1663–1680)
The Letters of Samuel Pepys and His Family Circle. Ed. by Helen Truesdell
Heath. Oxford: Clarendon Press. 1955.

Petty   22,408 words (1676–1681)
The Petty-Southwell Correspondence 1676–1687. Ed. by Marquis of Lansdowne.
Reprints of Economic Classics. New York: Augustus M. Kelley Publishers.
1928/1967.

Plumpton   36,531 words (1461–1549?)
Plumpton Correspondence. A Series of Letters, Chiefly Domestick, Written in the
Reigns of Edward IV. Richard III. Henry VII. and Henry VIII. Ed. by Thomas

Stapleton. Camden Original Series, 4. New York: AMS Press. 1839/1968. [CEECS]

Pory 6,084 words (1610–1632)
John Pory/1572–1636. The Life and Letters of a Man of Many Parts. Ed. by William S. Powell. Chapel Hill: The University of North Carolina Press. 1977.

Prideaux 7,571 words (1674–1680)
Letters of Humphrey Prideaux Sometime Dean of Norwich, to John Ellis Sometime Under-Secretary of State, 1674–1722. Ed. by Edward Maunde Thompson. Camden New Series, 15. London: Camden Society. 1875.

Rerum 5,914 words (1483–1509?)
Rerum Britannicarum Medii Aevi Scriptores. Or Chronicles and Memorials of Great Britain and Ireland during the Middle Ages. Letters and Papers Illustrative of the Reigns of Richard III. & Henry VII. Vols. I–II. Ed. by James Gairdner. Published by the Authority of the Lords Commissioners of Her Majesty's Treasury, under the direction of the Master of the Rolls. London: Longman, Green, Longman, and Roberts. 1861, 1863. [CEECS]

Royal 1 14,157 words (1585–1596)
Letters of Queen Elizabeth and King James VI. of Scotland; Some of Them Printed from Originals in the Possession of the Rev. Edward Ryder, and Others from a MS. which Formerly Belonged to Sir Peter Thompson, Kt. Ed. by John Bruce. Camden Original Series, 46. London: Camden Society. 1849. [CEECS]

Royal 2 29,455 words (1612?–1661)
Letters of Elizabeth, Queen of Bohemia. Edited from State Papers 81, Public Record Office, by Terttu Nevalainen. Unpublished.
AND
Briefe der Elizabeth Stuart, Königin von Böhmen, an Ihren Sohn, den Kurfürsten Carl Ludwig von der Pfalz. 1650–1662. Ed. by Anna Wendland. Bibliothek des Litterarischen Vereins in Stuttgart, 228. Tübingen: Der Litterarische Verein in Stuttgart. 1902.
AND
Diary and Correspondence of John Evelyn. Ed. by William Bray. London: Routledge. 1906.
AND
Letters to King James the Sixth from the Queen, Prince Henry, Prince Charles, the Princess Elizabeth and Her Husband Frederick King of Bohemia, and from Their Son Prince Frederick Henry. Ed. by Sir Patrick Walker and Alexander Macdonald. Edinburgh: The Maitland Club. 1835. [CEECS]

Royal 3 13,363 words (1674?–1680?)
Letters of Two Queens. Ed. by Benjamin Bathurst. London: Robert Holden & Co. Ltd. 1925.

Rutland 1,127 words (1490?–1503)
The Manuscripts of His Grace the Duke of Rutland, G.C.B., Preserved at Belvoir Castle. Vols. I–II. Ed. by H. C. Maxwell Lyte. Historical Manuscripts Commission, Twelfth Report Appendix, Part IV. London: Printed for Her Majesty's Stationery Office, by Byre and Spottiswoode. 1888.

Shillingford 13,526 words (1447–1448)
Letters and Papers of John Shillingford, Mayor of Exeter 1447–50. Ed. by Stuart A. Moore. Camden New Series, 2. New York: Johnson Reprint Company. 1871/1965. [CEECS]

Signet 15,029 words (1410?–1422)
The Signet Letters of Henry V. In: *An Anthology of Chancery English.* Ed. by John H. Fisher, Malcolm Richardson and Jane L. Fisher. Knoxville: University of Tennessee Press. 1984.

Smyth 10,346 words (1580?–1641)
Calendar of the Correspondence of the Smyth Family of Ashton Court 1548–1642. Ed. by J. H. Bettey. Publications of the Bristol Record Society, 35. Gloucester: Bristol Record Society. 1982.

Stapylton 3,429 words (1665?–1667)
Northumbrian Documents of the Seventeenth and Eighteenth Centuries, Comprising the Register of the Estates of Roman Catholics in Northumberland and of the Correspondence of Miles Stapylton. Ed. by J. C. Hodgson. Publications of the Surtees Society, 131. Durham and London: Surtees Society. 1918.

Stiffkey 899 words (1600?–1609?)
The Official Papers of Sir Nathaniel Bacon of Stiffkey, Norfolk as Justice of the Peace 1580–1620. Ed. by H. W. Saunders. Camden Third Series, 26. London: Camden Society. 1915.

Stockwell 26,503 words (1602–1611)
The Miscellaneous Papers of Captain Thomas Stockwell, 1590–1611. Vols. I–II. Ed. by J. Rutherford. Southampton Record Society, 32, 33. Southampton: Cox & Sharland, Ltd. 1932 and 1933.

Stonor 38,006 words (1420?–1483?)
The Stonor Letters and Papers 1290–1483. Vols. I–II. Ed. by Charles Lethbridge Kingsford. Camden Third Series, 29 and 30. London: Camden Society. 1919. [CEECS]
AND
Supplementary Stonor Letters and Papers (1314–1482). Ed. by Charles Lethbridge Kingsford. In *Camden Miscellany 13.* Camden Third Series, 34. London: Camden Society. 1923. [CEECS]

Stuart 31,578 words (1588–1611?)
The Letters of Lady Arbella Stuart. Ed. by Sara Jayne Steen. Women Writers in English 1350–1850. Oxford: Oxford University Press. 1994.

Tixall   11,544 words (1650?–1680?)
Tixall Letters; Or the Correspondence of the Aston Family, and Their Friends, during the Seventeenth Century. Vol. II. Ed. by Arthur Clifford. London: Longman, Hurst, Rees, Orme, and Brown. 1815. [CEECS]

Verstegan   15,493 words (1592–1617)
The Letters and Despatches of Richard Verstegan (c. 1550–1640). Ed. by Anthony G. Petti. Publications of the Catholic Record Society, 52. London: Catholic Record Society. 1959.

Wentworth   41,403 words (1597–1629)
Wentworth Papers 1597–1628. Ed. by J. P. Cooper. Camden Fourth Series, 12. London: Royal Historical Society. 1973.

WeSa   4,320 words (1632–1642)
Four Letters of Lord Wentworth, Afterwards Earl of Strafford, with a Poem on His Illness. Ed. by Samuel Rawson Gardiner. In *Camden Miscellany 8.* Camden New Series, 31. New York: Johnson Reprint Corporation. 1883/1965. [CEECS] AND
Papers Relating to the Delinquency of Lord Savile, 1642–1646. Ed. by James J. Cartwright. In *Camden Miscellany 8.* Camden New Series, 31. New York: Johnson Reprint Corporation. 1883/1965. [CEECS]

Wharton   8,068 words (1642)
'Letters from a Subaltern Officer of the Earl of Essex's Army, Written in the Summer and Autumn of 1642.' Ed. by Sir Henry Ellis. *Archaeologia* 35: 310–334. London. 1854. [CEECS]

Willoughby   10,838 words (1520?–1549?)
Willoughby Letters of the First Half of the Sixteenth Century. Ed. by Mary A. Welch. In *Nottinghamshire Miscellany No. 4.* Thoroton Society Record Series, 24. Nottingham: Thoroton Society. 1967.

Wilmot   7,682 words (1665–1679?)
John Wilmot Earl of Rochester His Life and Writings with His Lordship's Private Correspondence, Various Other Documents, and a Bibliography of His Works and of the Literature on Him. Ed. by Johannes Prinz. Palaestra, 154. Leipzig: Mayer & Müller GmbH. 1927.

Wood   10,961 words (1565–1576)
Letters of Thomas Wood, Puritan, 1566–1577. Ed. by Patrick Collinson. *Bulletin of the Institute of Historical Research*, Special Supplement No. 5, November 1960. London: University of London, The Athlone Press. 1960.

Wyatt   25,977 words (1536–1540)
Life and Letters of Sir Thomas Wyatt. Ed. by Kenneth Muir. Liverpool: Liverpool University Press. 1963.

Supplement to the 1998 version of the *Corpus of Early English Correspondence*, collections used in this study

Betts   2,624 words (1522–1640)
Everyday English 1500–1700. A Reader. Ed. by Bridget Cusack. Edinburgh: Edinburgh University Press. 1998.

LisleH   12,552 words (1531–1539)
The Lisle Letters. Ed. by Muriel St. Clare Byrne. Vols. 1–5. Chicago: The University of Chicago Press. 1981.

Thynne   19,574 words (1570?–1611)
Two Elizabethan Women: Correspondence of Joan and Maria Thynne 1575–1611. Ed. by Alison D. Wall. Wiltshire Record Society. 1983.

References

Aitchison, Jean 1981. *Language Change: Progress or Decay?* London: Fontana Paperbacks.

Algeo, John (ed.) 2001. *The Cambridge History of the English Language.* Vol. 6: *English in North America.* Cambridge: Cambridge University Press.

Allardt, Erik 1989. *An Updated Indicator System: Having, Loving, Being.* Working Papers 48. Department of Sociology, University of Helsinki.

Anon. 1696. *An Essay in Defence of the Female Sex.* Written by a lady [i.e. Mary Astell? or Judith Drake? or H. Wyatt?]. London: R. Clavel.

Ariès, Philippe 1962. *Centuries of Childhood: A Social History of Family Life.* New York: Vintage Books.

Arnaud, René 1998. The development of the progressive in 19th century English: A quantitative study. *Language Variation and Change* 10: 123–132.

Auer, Peter 1998. Dialect levelling and the standard varieties in Europe. *Folia Linguistica* 32/1–2: 1–9.

Bækken, Bjørg 1998. *Word Order Patterns in Early Modern English, with Special Reference to the Position of the Subject and the Finite Verb.* Oslo: Novus Press.

Bailey, Guy, Natalie Maynor & Patricia Cukor-Avila 1989. Variation in subject-verb concord in Early Modern English. *Language Variation and Change* 1: 258–300.

Bailey, Guy, Tom Wikle, Jan Tillery & Lori Sand 1991. The apparent time construct. *Language Variation and Change* 3: 241–264.

Bailey, Guy, Tom Wikle, Jan Tillery & Lori Sand 1996. The linguistic consequences of catastrophic events: an example from the American Southwest. *Sociolinguistic Variation: Data, Theory, and Analysis,* ed. Jennifer Arnold, Renée Blake, Brad Davidson, Scott Schwenter & Julie Solomon, 435–451. Stanford, CA: CSLI Publications.

Bambas, Rudoph C. 1947. Verb forms in -*s* and -*th* in Early Modern English Prose. *Journal of English and Germanic Philology* 46: 183–187.

Barber, Charles 1976. *Early Modern English.* London: André Deutsch.

Barron, Caroline 2000. London 1300–1540. *The Cambridge Urban History of England. Volume I. 600–1540,* ed. D. M. Palliser, 395–440. Cambridge: Cambridge University Press.

Barry, Jonathan 1994. Introduction. *The Middling Sort of People: Culture, Society and Politics in England 1550–1800,* ed. Jonathan Barry & Christopher Brooks, 1–27. London: Macmillan.

Barry, Jonathan 1995. Literacy and literature in popular culture: reading and writing in historical perspective. *Popular Culture in England, c. 1500–1850,* ed. Tim Harris, 69–94. London: Macmillan.

Beier, A. L. & Roger Finlay 1986. The significance of the metropolis. *London 1500–1700. The Making of the Metropolis,* ed. A. L. Beier & Roger Finlay, 1–33. London & New York: Longman.

Bell, Allan 1984. Language style as audience design. *Language in Society* 13, 145–204.

Bell, Allan 2001. Back in style: reworking audience design. *Style and Sociolinguistic Variation,* ed. Penelope Eckert & John R. Rickford, 139–169. Cambridge: Cambridge University Press.

Benskin, Michael 1992. Some new perspectives on the origins of standard written English. *Dialect and Standard Language in the English, Dutch, German and Norwegian Language Areas*, ed. J. A. van Leuvensteijn & J. B. Berns, 71–105. Amsterdam: North Holland.

Bergvall, Victoria 1999. Toward a comprehensive theory of language and gender. *Language in Society* 28, 273–293.

Biber, Douglas 1988. *Variation across Speech and Writing*. Cambridge: Cambridge University Press.

Biber, Douglas 1995. *Dimensions of Register Variation*. Cambridge: Cambridge University Press.

Biber, Douglas 2001. Dimensions of variation among 18th-century speech-based and written registers. *Towards a History of English as a History of Genres*, ed. Hans-Jürgen Diller & Manfred Görlach, 89–109. Heidelberg: Universitätsverlag C. Winter.

Biber, Douglas & Edward Finegan 1989. Drift and the evolution of English style: a history of three genres. *Language* 65: 487–517.

Biber, Douglas & Edward Finegan 1992. The linguistic evolution of five written and speech-based English genres from the 17th to the 20th centuries. *History of Englishes: New Methods and Interpretations in Historical Linguistics*, ed. Matti Rissanen, Ossi Ihalainen, Terttu Nevalainen & Irma Taavitsainen, 688–704. Berlin & New York: Mouton de Gruyter.

Biber, Douglas & Edward Finegan 1997. Diachronic relations among speech-based and written registers in English. *To Explain the Present: Studies in the Changing English Language in Honour of Matti Rissanen*, Mémoires de la Société Néophilologique de Helsinki 52, ed. Terttu Nevalainen & Leena Kahlas-Tarkka, 253–275. Helsinki: Société Néophilologique.

Biber, Douglas, Stig Johansson, Geoffrey Leech, Susan Conrad & Edward Finegan 1999. *Longman Grammar of Spoken and Written English*. London: Longman.

Blake, Norman F. 1981. *Non-Standard Language in English Literature*. London: André Deutsch.

Blake, Norman F. 1992. Introduction. *The Cambridge History of the English Language*, Vol. 2, *1066–1476*, ed. Norman F. Blake, 1–22. Cambridge: Cambridge University Press.

Boulton, Jeremy 1987. *Neighbourhood and Society: A London Suburb in the Seventeenth Century*. Cambridge: Cambridge University Press.

Brayshay, Mark 1991. Royal post-horse routes in England and Wales: the evolution of the network in the later-sixteenth and early-seventeenth century. *Journal of Historical Geography* 17/4: 373–389.

Breuer, Horst 1983. Titel und Anreden bei Shakespeare und in der Shakespeare-Zeit. *Anglia* 101 1/2:49–77.

Briggs, Asa [1983] 1985. *A Social History of England*. Harmondsworth: Penguin.

Britton, Derek 2000. Henry Machyn, Axel Wijk and the case of the wrong Riding: the south-west Yorkshire character of the language of Henry Machyn's diary. *Neuphilologische Mitteilungen* 101/4: 571–596.

Brooks, Christopher 1994a. Apprenticeship, social mobility and the middling sort, 1550–1800. *The Middling Sort of People: Culture, Society and Politics in England 1550–1800*, ed. Jonathan Barry & Christopher Brooks, 52–83. London: Macmillan.

Brooks, Christopher 1994b. Professions, ideology and the middling sort in the late sixteenth and early seventeenth centuries. *The Middling Sort of People: Culture, Society and Politics in England 1550–1800*, ed. Jonathan Barry & Christopher Brooks, 113–140. London: Macmillan.

Brown, Penelope & Stephen C. Levinson 1987. *Politeness: Some Universals in Language Usage*. Cambridge: Cambridge University Press.

Brown, Roger & Albert Gilman 1989. Politeness theory and Shakespeare's four major tragedies. *Language in Society* 18: 159–212.

Burchfield, Robert, (ed.) 1994. *The Cambridge History of the English Language*. Vol. 5: *English in Britain and Overseas*. Cambridge: Cambridge University Press.

Burke, Peter 1992a. *History and Social Theory*. Cambridge: Polity Press.

Burke, Peter 1992b. The language of orders in early modern Europe. *Social Orders and Social Classes in Europe since 1500: Studies in Social Stratification*, ed. M. L. Bush, 1–12. London & New York: Longman.

Burnley, John David 2000. French and Frenches in fourteenth-century London. *Language Contact in the History of English*, ed. Dieter Kastovsky & Arthur Mettinger, 17–34. Frankfurt am Main: Peter Lang.

Butler, Tim & Mike Savage (eds.) 1995. *Social Change and the Middle Classes*. London: UCL Press.

Cameron, Deborah 1997. Demythologizing sociolinguistics. *Sociolinguistics: A Reader and Coursebook*, ed. Nikolas Coupland & Adam Jaworski, 55–67. Houndmills & London: Macmillan Press.

Cannadine, David 1998. *Class in Britain*. New Haven & London: Yale University Press.

Capp, Bernard 1996. Separate domains? Women and authority in Early Modern England. *The Experience of Authority in Early Modern England*, ed. Paul Griffiths, Adam Fox & Steve Hindle, 117–145. Houndmills & London: Macmillan.

Carter, Bob & Alison Sealey 2000. Language, structure and agency: what can realist social theory offer to sociolinguistics? *Journal of Sociolinguistics* 4/1: 3–20.

Cawdrey, Robert 1604. *A Table Alphabeticall*. London: I. R. for Edmund Weauer. Repr. 1970, English Experience 226. Amsterdam: Theatrum Orbis Terrarum.

Chambers, J. K. 1995. *Sociolinguistic Theory*. Oxford: Blackwell.

Chambers, J. K. 1998. Social embedding of changes in progress. *Journal of English Linguistics* 26/1: 5–36.

Chambers, J. K. & Peter Trudgill 1980/1998. *Dialectology*. Second edition. Cambridge: Cambridge University Press.

Chen, Matthew Y. & William S-Y. Wang 1975. Sound change: actuation and implementation. *Language* 51/2: 255–281.

Cheshire, Jenny 1996. Syntactic variation and the concept of prominence. *Speech Past and Present: Studies in English Dialectology in Memory of Ossi Ihalainen*, Bamberger Beiträge zur Englischen Sprachwissenschaften 38, ed. Juhani Klemola, Merja Kytö & Matti Rissanen, 1–17. Frankfurt am Main: Peter Lang.

Cheshire, Jenny 1999. Spoken Standard English. *Standard English: The Widening Debate*, ed. Tony Bex & Richard J. Watts, 129–148. London & New York: Routledge.

Cheshire, Jenny, Viv Edwards & Pamela Whittle 1993. Non-standard English and dialect levelling. *Real English: The Grammar of English Dialects in the British Isles*, ed. James Milroy & Lesley Milroy, 53–96. London: Longman.

Cheshire, Jenny & James Milroy 1993. Syntactic variation in non-standard dialects: background issues. *Real English: The Grammar of English Dialects in the British Isles*, ed. James Milroy & Lesley Milroy, 3–33. London: Longman.

Chomsky, Noam 1965. *Aspects of the Theory of Syntax*. Cambridge, MA: MIT Press.

Clark, Peter & David Souden 1988. Introduction. *Migration and Society in Early Modern England*, ed. Peter Clark & David Souden, 11–48. Totowa, NJ: Barnes and Noble.

References

Clay, C. G. A. 1984. *Economic Expansion and Social Change: England 1500–1700*. Vols. I–II. Cambridge: Cambridge University Press.

Coates, Jennifer (ed.) 1998. *Language and Gender*. Oxford: Blackwell.

Coates, Jennifer [1986] 1993. *Women, Men and Language*. London & New York: Longman.

Coggle, Paul 1993. *Do You Speak Estuary? The New Standard English*. London: Bloomsbury Publishing.

Coleman, David & John Salt 1992. *The British Population: Patterns, Trends, Processes*. Oxford: Oxford University Press.

Conde Silvestre, Juan Camilo, Juan Manuel Hernández-Campoy & Antonio Pérez Salazar, forthcoming. A sociolinguistic approach to the diffusion of Chancery written practices in late fifteenth century private correspondence. Paper presented at 11 ICEHL, Santiago de Compostela, September 2000.

Cooper, Robert L. 1982. A framework for the study of language spread. *Language Spread: Studies in Diffusion and Social Change*, ed. Robert L. Cooper, 5–36. Bloomington: Indiana University Press and Washington D.C. Center for Applied Linguistics.

Coupland, Nikolas 1998. What is sociolinguistic theory? *Journal of Sociolinguistics* 2/1: 110–117.

Coupland, Nikolas 2001. Introduction: sociolinguistic theory and social theory. *Sociolinguistics and Social Theory*, ed. Nikolas Coupland, Srikant Sarangi & Christopher N. Candlin, 1–25. Harlow & London: Longman.

Crawford, Patricia 1985. Women's published writings 1600–1700. *Women in English Society 1500–1800*, ed. Mary Prior, 211–282. London & New York: Methuen.

Cressy, David 1980. *Literacy and Social Order: Reading and Writing in Tudor and Stuart England*. Cambridge: Cambridge University Press.

Croft, William 2000. *Explaining Language Change: An Evolutionary Approach*. London: Longman.

Crowley, Tony 1989. *The Politics of Discourse: The Standard Language Question in British Cultural Debates*. London: Macmillan.

Crystal, David 1991. *A Dictionary of Linguistics and Phonetics*. Third edition. Oxford: Blackwell.

Davis, Norman 1954. The language of the Pastons. *Proceedings of the British Academy* 40: 119–144.

Denison, David 1999. Slow, slow, quick, quick, slow: the dance of language change. *'Woondrous Ænglissce' SELIM Studies in Medieval English Language*, ed. Ana Bringas López, Dolores Gonzáles Álvarez, Javier Pérez Guerra, Esperanza Rama Martinez & Eduardo Varela Bravo, 51–64. Universidade de Vigo, Servicio de Publicacións.

Denison, David 2002. Log(ist)ic and simplistic S-curves. *Motives for Language Change*, ed. Raymond Hickey. Cambridge: Cambridge University Press.

Devitt, Amy 1989. *Standardizing Written English: Diffusion in the Case of Scotland 1520–1659*. Cambridge: Cambridge University Press.

Dickens, A. G. [1987] 1997. The early expansion of Protestantism in England, 1520–1558. *The Impact of the English Reformation 1500–1640*, ed. Peter Marshall, 85–116. London: Arnold.

Diller, Hans-Jürgen & Manfred Görlach (eds.) 2001. *Towards a History of English as a History of Genres*. Heidelberg: Universitätsverlag C. Winter.

Dittmar, Norbert 1997. *Grundlagen der Soziolinguistik*. Tübingen: Max Niemeyer Verlag.

Dobson, E. J. 1957/1968. *English Pronunciation 1500–1700*, Vol. 1. Second edition. Oxford: Clarendon Press.

Docherty, Gerard J., Paul Foulkes, James Milroy, Lesley Milroy & David Walshaw 1997. Descriptive adequacy in phonology: a variationist perspective. *Journal of Linguistics* 33: 275–310.

Downes, William 1998. *Language and Society*. Cambridge: Cambridge University Press.

Dyer, Alan 1991. *Decline and Growth in English Towns, 1400–1640*. Houndmills & London: Macmillan.

E.,T. [Edgar, Thomas?] 1632. *The Lawes Resolutions of Womens Rights*. London: John More. Repr. 1979, English Experience 922. Amsterdam: Theatrum Orbis Terrarum.

Eckert, Penelope 1989. The whole woman: sex and gender differences in variation. *Language Variation and Change* 1: 245–267.

Eckert, Penelope 2000. *Linguistic Variation and Social Practice*. Oxford: Blackwell.

Eckert, Penelope & John R. Rickford (ed.) 2001. *Style and Sociolinguistic Variation*. Cambridge: Cambridge University Press.

Eggins, Suzanne & Diana Slade 1997. *Analysing Casual Conversation*. London & Washington: Cassell.

Ekvall, Eilert 1956. *Studies on the Population of Medieval London*. Kungl. Vitterhets Historie och Antikvitets Akademiens Handlingar, Filologisk-filosofiska Serien 2. Stockholm: Almqvist & Wiksell.

Ellegård, Alvar 1953. *The Auxiliary 'Do': The Establishment and Regulation of its Use in English*. Gothenburg Studies in English 2. Stockholm: Almqvist & Wiksell.

Elyot, Thomas 1531. *The Boke Named the Gouernour*. London: T. Berthelet. Repr. 1970, English Linguistics 246. Menston: Scolar Press.

Erickson, Amy Louise 1993. *Women and Property in Early Modern England*. London & New York: Routledge.

Fairclough, Norman 2000. Response to Carter and Sealey. *Journal of Sociolinguistics* 4/1: 25–29.

Fanego, Teresa 1996. The gerund in Early Modern English: evidence from the Helsinki Corpus. *Folia Linguistica Historica* XVII: 97–152.

Fanego, Teresa 1998. Developments in argument linking in early Modern English gerund phrases. *English Language and Linguistics* 2/1: 87–119.

Fasold, Ralph W. 1990. *Sociolinguistics of Language*. Oxford: Blackwell.

Fasold, Ralph W. 1991. The quiet demise of variable rules. *American Speech* 66/1: 3–21.

Ferguson, Charles 1996. Variation and drift: loss of agreement in Germanic. *Towards a Social Science of Language: Papers in Honor of William Labov*. Vol. 1. *Variation and Change in Language and Society*, ed. Gregory R. Guy, Crawford Feagin, Deborah Schiffrin & John Baugh, 173–198. Amsterdam & Philadelphia: Benjamins.

Figueroa, Esther 1994. *Sociolinguistic Metatheory*. Oxford: Pergamon Press.

Finegan, Edward & Douglas Biber 1994. Register and social dialect variation: an integrated approach. *Sociolinguistic Perspectives on Register*, ed. Douglas Biber & Edward Finegan, 315–347. Oxford & New York: Oxford University Press.

Finegan, Edward & Douglas Biber 2001. Register variation and social dialect variation: the Register Axiom. *Style and Sociolinguistic Variation*, ed. Penelope Eckert & John R. Rickford, 235–267. Cambridge: Cambridge University Press.

Finkenstaedt, Thomas 1963. *You und Thou: Studien zur Anrede im Englischen*. Berlin: Walter de Gruyter & Co.

Finlay, Roger & Beatrice Shearer 1986. Population growth and suburban expansion. *London 1500–1700: The Making of the Metropolis*, ed. A. L. Beier & Roger Finlay, 37–59. London & New York: Longman.

References

Fisher, John H. 1977. Chancery and the emergence of standard written English in the fifteenth century. *Speculum* 52: 870–899.

Fishman, Joshua A. 1997. The sociology of language. *Sociolinguistics: A Reader and Coursebook*, ed. Nikolas Coupland & Adam Jaworski, 25–30. Houndmills & London: Macmillan Press.

Fisiak, Jacek 1983. English dialects in the fifteenth century: some observations concerning the shift of isoglosses. *Folia Linguistic Historica* 4/2: 195–217.

Fletcher, Anthony 1995. *Gender, Sex & Subordination in England 1500–1800*. New Haven & London: Yale University Press.

Foyster, Elizabeth A. 1999. *Manhood in Early Modern England: Honour, Sex and Marriage*. London & New York: Longman.

Gerner, Jürgen 1996. *Untersuchungen zur Funktion des emphatischen* do *im Englischen*. Frankfurt am Main: Peter Lang.

Gerritsen, Marinel & Dieter Stein (eds.) 1992. *Internal and External Factors in Syntactic Change*. Berlin & New York: Mouton de Gruyter.

Gil, Alexander 1619. *Logonomia Anglica*. London: J. Beale. Repr. Bror Danielsson & Arvid Gabrielson (eds.) 1972. *Alexander Gill's Logonomia Anglica (1619)*. 2 vols. Stockholm: Almqvist & Wiksell.

Gómez Soliño, José 1981. Thomas Wolsey, Thomas More y la lengua inglesa estándar de su época. *Revista Canaria de Estudios Ingleses* 3: 74–84.

González-Álvarez, Dolores & Javier Pérez Guerra 1999. Texting the written evidence: on register analysis in late Middle English and early Modern English. *Text* 18/3: 321–348.

Görlach, Manfred 1990. *Studies in the History of the English Language*. Anglistische Forschungen 210. Heidelberg: Carl Winter Universitätsverlag.

Görlach, Manfred 1999. Regional and social variation. *The Cambridge History of the English Language*, Vol. 3, *1476–1776*, ed. Roger Lass, 459–538. Cambridge: Cambridge University Press.

Gowing, Laura 1994. Language, power and the law: women's slander litigation in early modern London. *Women, Crime and the Courts in Early Modern England*, ed. Jenny Kermode & Garthine Walker, 26–47. London: UCL Press.

Halliday, M. A. K. 1978. *Language as Social Semiotic: The Social Interpretation of Language and Meaning*. London: Edward Arnold.

Hanham, Alison 1985. *The Celys and their World: An English Merchant Family of the Fifteenth Century*. Cambridge: Cambridge University Press.

Hart, John 1569 *An Orthographie*. London: W. Serres. Repr. 1969, English Linguistics 209. Menston: Scolar Press.

Heal, Felicity & Clive Holmes 1994. *The Gentry in England and Wales, 1500–1700*. London: Macmillan.

Hernández-Campoy, Juan Manuel & Juan Camilo Conde Silvestre 1999. The social diffusion of linguistic innovations in fifteenth-century England: Chancery spellings in private correspondence. *Cuadernos de Filología Inglesa* 8: 251–274.

Hickey, Raymond, Merja Kytö, Ian Lancashire & Matti Rissanen (eds.) 1997. *Tracing the Trail of Time: Proceedings from the Second Diachronic Corpora Workshop*. Amsterdam & Atlanta, GA: Rodopi.

Hogg, Richard M. 1998. On the ideological boundaries of Old English dialects. *Advances in English Historical Linguistics*, ed. Jacek Fisiak & Marcin Krygier, 107–118. Berlin & New York: Mouton de Gruyter.

Holmes, Janet 1997. Setting new standards: sound changes and gender in New Zealand English. *English World-Wide* 18/1: 107–142.

Holmqvist, Bengt 1922. *On the History of the English Present Inflections, Particularly -th and -s*. Heidelberg: Carl Winters Universitätsbuchhandlung.

Hope, Jonathan 1993. Second person singular pronouns in records of Early Modern 'spoken' English. *Neuphilologische Mitteilungen* 94/1: 83–100.

Hope, Jonathan 2000. Rats, bats, sparrows and dogs: biology, linguistics and the nature of Standard English. *The Development of Standard English 1300–1800*, ed. Laura Wright, 49–56. Cambridge: Cambridge University Press.

Houlbrooke, Ralph A. 1984. *The English Family 1450–1700*. London & New York: Longman.

Houston, Ann 1989. The English gerund: syntactic change and discourse function. *Language Change and Variation*, ed. Ralph Fasold & Deborah Schiffrin, 173–196. Amsterdam: Benjamins.

Houston, Ann 1991. A grammatical continuum of (ING). *Dialects of English: Studies in Grammatical Variation*, ed. Peter Trudgill & J. K. Chambers, 241–257. London & New York: Longman.

Hoyle, R. W. (ed.) 1992. *Letters of the Cliffords, Lords Clifford and Earls of Cumberland, c. 1500–c. 1565*. Camden Miscellany 31; Camden Fourth Series 44.

Hudson, R. A. 1996. *Sociolinguistics*. Second edition. Cambridge: Cambridge University Press.

Hudson, Roger (ed.) 1993. *The Grand Quarrel. From the Civil War Memoirs of Mrs Lucy Hutchinson; Mrs Alice Thornton; Ann, Lady Fanshawe; Margaret, Duchess of Newcastle; Anne, Lady Halkett & the Letters of Brilliana, Lady Harley*. London: The Folio Society.

Hufton, Olwen 1997. *The Prospect Before Her: A History of Women in Western Europe*. Volume I, 1500–1800. Lonton: Fontana Press.

Ihalainen, Ossi 1994. The dialects of England since 1776. *The Cambridge History of the English Language*, Vol. 5, *English in Britain and Overseas: Origins and Developments*, ed. Robert Burchfield, 197–274. Cambridge: Cambridge University Press.

Ingram, Martin 1995. From reformation to toleration: Popular religious cultures in England, 1540–1690. *Popular Culture in England, c. 1500–1850*, ed. Tim Harris, 95–123. London: Macmillan.

Iyeiri, Yoko 1999. Multiple negation in Middle English verse. *Negation in the History of English*, ed. Ingrid Tieken-Boon van Ostade, Gunnel Tottie & Wim van der Wurff, 121–146. Berlin & New York: Mouton de Gruyter.

Jahr, Ernst Håkan (ed.) 1999. *Language Change: Advances in Historical Sociolinguistics*. Berlin & New York: Mouton de Gruyter.

James, Deborah 1996. Women, men and prestige speech forms: a critical review. *Rethinking Language and Gender Research: Theory and Practice*, ed. Victoria L. Bergvall, Janet M. Bing & Alice F. Freed, 98–125. London & New York: Longman.

Jewell, Helen M. 1998. *Education in Early Modern England*. Houndmills & London: Macmillan Press.

Jones, Richard Foster 1953. *The Triumph of the English Language: A Survey of Opinions Concerning the Vernacular from the Introduction of Printing to the Restoration*. London: Oxford University Press.

Jordan, Constance 1993. Renaissance woman and the question of class. *Sexuality and Gender in Early Modern Europe*, ed. James Grantham Turner, 90–106. Cambridge: Cambridge University Press.

Kaartinen, Marjo 1999. *Spiritual Eunuchs: Religious People in English Culture of the Early Sixteenth Century*. University of Turku: Cultural History.

Keen, Maurice 1990. *English Society in the Later Middle Ages, 1348–1500*. Harmondsworth: Allan Lane, the Penguin Press.

References

Keene, Derek 2000. Metropolitan values: migration, mobility and cultural norms, London 1100–1700. *The Development of Standard English 1300–1800: Theories, Descriptions, Conflicts*, ed. Laura Wright, 93–114. Cambridge: Cambridge University Press.

Keller, Rudi 1994. *On Language Change: The Invisible Hand in Language*. Transl. Brigitte Nerlich. London & New York: Routledge.

Kemp, William 1979. On that *that that* that became *that which* which became *what*. *Papers from the Fifteenth Regional Meeting of the Chicago Linguistic Society*, ed. P.F. Clyne, W. R. Hanks & C. L. Hofbauen, 185–196. Chicago: Chicago Linguistic Society.

Kenyon, J. 1914. 'Ye' and 'you' in the King James Version. *PMLA* 29: 453–471.

Keränen, Jukka 1998a. Forgeries and one-eyed bulls: Editorial questions in corpus work. *Neuphilologische Mitteilungen* 99/2: 217–226.

Keränen, Jukka 1998b. The *Corpus of Early English Correspondence*: Progress report. *Explorations in Corpus Linguistics*, ed. Antoinette Renouf, 29–37. Amsterdam & Atlanta, GA: Rodopi.

Kerswill, Paul & Ann Williams 2000. Creating a New Town koiné: children and language change in Milton Keynes. *Language in Society* 29: 65–115.

Kielkiewicz-Janowiak, Agnieszka 1992. *A Socio-historical Study in Address: Polish and English*. Bamberger Beiträge zur englischen Sprachwissenschaft 30. Frankfurt am Main: Peter Lang.

Kihlbom, Asta 1926. *A Contribution to the Study of Fifteenth Century English. Uppsala Universitets Årsskrift 1926*. Uppsala: A.B. Lundequistska Bokhandeln.

Kilpiö, Matti 1997. Participial adjectives with anaphoric reference of the type *the said, the (a)forementioned* from Old to Early Modern English: the evidence of the Helsinki Corpus. *To Explain the Present: Studies in the Changing English Language in Honour of Matti Rissanen*, Mémoires de la Société Néophilologique de Helsinki 52, ed. Terttu Nevalainen & Leena Kahlas-Tarkka, 77–100. Helsinki: Société Néophilologique.

King, Steven 1997. Migrants on the margin? Mobility, integration and occupations in the West Riding, 1650–1820. *Journal of Historical Geography* 23/3: 284–303.

Kitch, M. J. 1986. Capital and kingdom: migration to later Stuart London. *London 1500–1700: The Making of the Metropolis*, ed. A. L. Beier & Roger Finlay, 224–251. London & New York: Longman.

Klemola, Juhani 1996. *Non-standard Periphrastic DO: A Study in Variation and Change*. Unpublished Ph.D. Thesis. Department of Language and Linguistics, University of Essex.

Klemola, Juhani 1997. Dialect evidence for the loss of genitive inflection in English. *English Language and Linguistics* 1/2: 349–353.

Kopytko, Roman 1993. *Polite Discourse in Shakespeare's English*. Poznan: Adam Mickierwicz University Press.

Kristensson, Gillis 1994. Sociolects in 14th-century London. *Non-standard Varieties of Language*, Stockholm Studies in English 84, ed. Gunnel Melchers & Nils-Lennart Johannesson, 103–110. Stockholm: Almqvist & Wiksell.

Kroch, Anthony 1989. Reflexes of grammar in patterns of language change. *Language Variation and Change* 1: 199–244.

Kroch, Anthony 2001. Syntactic change. *The Handbook of Contemporary Syntactic Theory*, ed. Mark Baltin & Chris Collins, 699–729. Malden, MA & Oxford: Blackwell.

Kroch, Anthony, Ann Taylor & Donald Ringe 2000. The Middle-English verb-second constraint: a case study of language contact and language change. *Textual*

Parameters in Older Languages, ed. Susan Herring, Pieter van Reenen & Lene Schøsler, 353–391. Amsterdam & Philadelphia: Benjamins.

Kytö, Merja 1993. Third-person present singular verb inflection in early British and American English. *Language Variation and Change* 5: 113–139.

Kytö, Merja 1997. *Be/have* + past participle: the choice of the auxiliary with intransitives from Late Middle to Modern English. *English in Transition: Corpus-based Studies in Linguistic Variation and Genre Styles*, ed. Matti Rissanen, Merja Kytö & Kirsi Heikkonen, 17–85. Berlin & New York: Mouton de Gruyter.

Kytö, Merja & Matti Rissanen 1993. 'By and by enters [this] my artificiall foole . . . who, when Jack beheld, sodainely he flew at him': Searching for syntactic constructions in the Helsinki Corpus. *Early English in the Computer Age: Explorations through the Helsinki Corpus*, ed. Matti Rissanen, Merja Kytö & Minna Palander-Collin, 253–266. Berlin & New York: Mouton de Gruyter.

Labov, William 1972. *Sociolinguistic Patterns*. Philadelphia: University of Pennsylvania Press.

Labov, William 1982. Building on empirical foundations. *Perspectives on Historical Linguistics*, ed. W. P. Lehmann & Y. Malkiel, 17–92. Amsterdam & Philadelphia: Benjamins.

Labov, William 1990. The intersection of sex and social class in the course of linguistic change. *Language Variation and Change* 2: 205–254.

Labov, William 1994. *Principles of Linguistic Change. Volume 1: Internal Factors*. Oxford, UK & Cambridge, USA: Blackwell.

Labov, William 2001. *Principles of Linguistic Change. Volume 2: Social Factors*. Oxford, UK & Cambridge, USA: Blackwell.

Laitinen, Mikko 2002. Extending the *Corpus of Early English Correspondence* to the 18th century. *Helsinki English Studies 2*. http://www.eng.helsinki.fi/

Laslett, Peter 1983. *The World We Have Lost – Further Explored*. London: Routledge.

Lass, Roger 1997. *Historical Linguistics and Language Change*. Cambridge: Cambridge University Press.

Lass, Roger 1999. Phonology and morphology. *The Cambridge History of the English Language*, Vol. 3, *1476–1776*, ed. Roger Lass, 56–186. Cambridge: Cambridge University Press.

Leech, Geoffrey 1993. 100 million words of English. *English Today* 33/9,1: 9–15.

Leith, Dick 1983. *A Social History of English*. London: Routledge & Kegan Paul.

Leith, Dick 1984. Tudor London: sociolinguistic stratification and linguistic change. *Anglo-American Studies* IV/1: 59–72.

Lindsay, Linda L. 1994. *Gender Roles. A Sociological Perspective*. New Jersey: Prentice Hall.

Lutz, Angelika 1998. The interplay of external and internal factors in morphological restructuring: the case of *you*. *Advances in English Historical Linguistics (1996)*, ed. Jacek Fisiak & Marcin Krygier, 189–210. Berlin & New York: Mouton de Gruyter.

Lyons, John 1971. *Introduction to Theoretical Linguistics*. Cambridge: Cambridge University Press.

Macaulay, Ronald 1999. Is sociolinguistics lacking in style? *Cuadernos de Filología Inglesa* 8: 9–33.

Machan, Tim William 2000. Language and society in twelfth-century England. *Placing Middle English in Context*, ed. Irma Taavitsainen, Terttu Nevalainen, Päivi Pahta & Matti Rissanen, 43–65. Berlin & New York: Mouton de Gruyter.

Machan, Tim William & Charles T. Scott (eds.) 1992. *English in Its Social Contexts: Essays in Historical Sociolinguistics*. New York & Oxford: Oxford University Press.

References

Magnusson, Lynne 1999. *Shakespeare and Social Dialogue: Dramatic Language and Elizabethan Letters*. Cambridge & New York: Cambridge University Press.

Malden, Henry Elliot 1900. *The Cely Papers: Selections from the Correspondence and Memoranda of the Cely Family*. Camden 3rd Series, Vol. I. London: Longmans, Green and Co.

Marshall, Peter (ed.) 1997. *The Impact of the English Reformation 1500–1640*. London: Arnold.

Mattheier, Klaus J. (ed.) 1999. *Historische Soziolinguistik = Historical Sociolinguistics = La sociolinguistique historique. Sociolinguistica* 13. Tübingen: Niemeyer.

Mazzon, Gabriella 2000. Describing language variation in synchrony and diachrony: some methodological considerations. *Vienna English Working Papers* 9/2: 82–103.

McIntosh, Angus 1989. Present indicative plural forms in the later Middle English of the North Midlands. *Middle English Dialectology: Essays on Some Principles and Problems*, ed. Margaret Laing, 116–122. Aberdeen: Aberdeen University Press.

McIntosh, Angus, M. L. Samuels & Michael Benskin 1986. *A Linguistic Atlas of Late Mediaeval English*. Vol. 1. Aberdeen: Aberdeen University Press.

McIntosh, Carey 1998. *The Evolution of English Prose 1700–1900: Style, Politeness, and Print Culture*. Cambridge: Cambridge University Press.

Mendelson, Sara & Patricia Crawford 1998. *Women in Early Modern England 1550–1720*. Oxford: Clarendon Press.

Meurman-Solin, Anneli 2000. Change from above or from below? Mapping the *loci* of linguistic change in the history of Scottish English. *The Development of Standard English 1300–1800*, ed. Laura Wright, 155–170. Cambridge: Cambridge University Press.

Meurman-Solin, Anneli 2001. Structured text corpora in the study of language variation and change. *Literary and Linguistic Computing* 16/1: 5–27.

Milroy, James 1983. On the sociolinguistic history of /h/-dropping in English. *Current Topics in English Historical Linguistics*, ed. M. Davenport, E. Hausen & H-F. Nielsen, 37–53. Odense: Odense University Press.

Milroy, James 1992. *Linguistic Variation and Change: on the Historical Sociolinguistics of English*. Oxford: Blackwell.

Milroy, James 1994. The notion of 'standard language' and its applicability to the study of Early Modern English pronunciation. *Towards a Standard English 1600–1800*, ed. Dieter Stein & Ingrid Tieken-Boon van Ostade, 19–29. Berlin & New York: Mouton de Gruyter.

Milroy, James 1998. Exploring linguistic variation to explain language change. *Sociolinguistica* 12: 39–52. Tübingen: Niemeyer.

Milroy, James & Lesley Milroy 1985a. *Authority in Language: Investigating Language Prescription and Standardisation*. London & New York: Routledge.

Milroy, James & Lesley Milroy 1985b. Linguistic change, social network and speaker innovation. *Journal of Linguistics* 21: 339–384.

Milroy, James & Lesley Milroy 1993. Mechanisms of change in urban dialects: the role of class, social network and gender. *International Journal of Applied Linguistics* 3/1: 57–77.

Milroy, Lesley 1987. *Language and Social Networks*. Second edition. Oxford: Blackwell.

Milroy, Lesley 1999. Women as innovators and norm-creators: the sociolinguistics of dialect leveling in a northern English city. *Engendering Communication: Proceedings of the Fifth Berkeley Women and Language Conference*, ed. Suzanne Wertheim, Ashlee C. Bailey & Monica Corston-Oliver, 361–376. Berkeley, CA: BWLG.

Milroy, Lesley 2000. Social network analysis and language change: introduction. *European Journal of English Studies* 4/3: 217–223.

Milroy, Lesley 2001. Conversation, spoken language and social identity. *Style and Sociolinguistic Variation*, ed. Penelope Eckert & John R. Rickford, 268–278. Cambridge: Cambridge University Press.

Moessner, Lilo 1997. The history of English *-ing* constructions. *Festschrift for Professor Kim In-Sook on his 65th birthday. The History of English* 3: 105–120.

Moessner, Lilo (ed.) 2001. Early Modern English Text Types. Special issue of *European Journal of English Studies* 5/2.

Montgomery, Michael 1989. Introduction to variable rule analysis. *Journal of English Linguistics* 22/1: 111–118.

Montgomery, Michael 1996. Was colonial American English a koiné? *Speech Past and Present: Studies in English Dialectology in Memory of Ossi Ihalainen*, Bamberger Beiträge zur Englischen Sprachwissenschaft 38, ed. Juhani Klemola, Merja Kytö & Matti Rissanen, 213–235. Frankfurt am Main: Peter Lang.

Moore, Colette 2002. Writing good Southerne: Local and supralocal norms in the Plumpton letter collection. *Language Variation and Change* 14/1: 1–17.

Moore, Samuel, Sanford Brown Meech & Harold Whitehall 1935. Middle English dialect characteristics and dialect boundaries. *Essays and Studies in English and Comparative Literature*. University of Michigan Publications in Language and Literature 13: 1–60. Ann Arbor: University of Michigan Press.

Morrill, John 1984. The Stuarts (1603–1688). *The Oxford Illustrated History of Britain*, ed. Kenneth O. Morgan, 286–351. Oxford: Oxford University Press.

Morrill, John 1991. Introduction. *The Impact of the English Civil War*, ed. John Morrill, 8–16. London: Collins & Brown.

Mustanoja, Tauno F. 1960. *A Middle English Syntax. Part I*. Mémoires de la Société Néophilologique de Helsinki 23. Helsinki: Société Néophilologique.

Nevala, Minna 1998. *By him that loves you*: Address forms in letters written to 16th-century social aspirers. *Explorations in Corpus Linguistics*, ed. Antoinette Renouf, 147–157. Amsterdam & Atlanta, GA: Rodopi.

Nevala, Minna 2001. *With out any pregyduce or hindranc*: Editing women's letters from 17th-century Norfolk. *Neuphilologische Mitteilungen* 102/2: 151–171.

Nevala, Minna, 2002. *Youre moder send a letter to the*: Pronouns of address in private correspondence from Late Middle to Late Modern English. *Variation Past and Present: VAREING studies on English for Terttu Nevalainen*, ed. Helena Raumolin-Brunberg, Minna Nevala, Arja Nurmi and Matti Rissanen, 135–155. Mémoires de la Société Néophilologique de Helsinki 61. Helsinki: Société Néophilologique.

Nevalainen, Terttu 1991. *But, only, just. Focusing Adverbial Change in Modern English 1500–1900*. Mémoires de la Société Néophilologique de Helsinki 51. Helsinki: Société Néophilologique.

Nevalainen, Terttu 1994. Ladies and gentlemen: the generalization of titles in Early Modern English. *English Historical Linguistics 1992*, ed. Francisco Fernández, Miguel Fuster & Juan José Calvo, 317–327. Amsterdam & Philadelphia: Benjamins.

Nevalainen, Terttu 1996a. Gender difference. *Sociolinguistics and Language History: Studies Based on the Corpus of Early English Correspondence*, ed. Terttu Nevalainen & Helena Raumolin-Brunberg, 77–91. Amsterdam & Atlanta, GA: Rodopi.

Nevalainen, Terttu 1996b. Social stratification. *Sociolinguistics and Language History: Studies Based on the Corpus of Early English Correspondence*, ed. Terttu Nevalainen & Helena Raumolin-Brunberg, 57–76. Amsterdam & Atlanta, GA: Rodopi.

References

Nevalainen, Terttu 1997. Recycling inversion: The case of initial adverbs and negators in Early Modern English. *Studia Anglica Posnaniensia* 31: 203–214.

Nevalainen, Terttu 1998. Social mobility and the decline of multiple negation in Early Modern English. *Advances in English Historical Linguistics (1996)*, ed. Jacek Fisiak & Marcin Krygier, 263–291. Berlin & New York: Mouton de Gruyter.

Nevalainen, Terttu 1999a. Early Modern English lexis and semantics. *The Cambridge History of the English Language*, Vol. 3, *1476–1776*, ed. Roger Lass, 332–458. Cambridge: Cambridge University Press.

Nevalainen, Terttu 1999b. Making the best use of 'bad' data: evidence for socio-linguistic variation in Early Modern English. *Neuphilologische Mitteilungen* 100/4: 499–533.

Nevalainen, Terttu 2000a. Gender differences in the evolution of standard English: evidence from the *Corpus of Early English Correspondence. Journal of English Linguistics* 28/1: 38–59.

Nevalainen, Terttu 2000b. Mobility, social networks and language change in early modern England. *European Journal of English Studies* 4/3: 253–264.

Nevalainen, Terttu 2000c. Processes of supralocalisation and the rise of Standard English in the Early Modern period. *Generative Theory and Corpus Studies: A Dialogue from 10 ICEHL*, ed. Ricardo Bermúdez-Otero, David Denison, Richard M. Hogg & C. B. McCully, 329–371. Berlin & New York: Mouton de Gruyter.

Nevalainen, Terttu & Helena Raumolin-Brunberg 1989. A corpus of Early Modern Standard English in a socio-historical perspective. *Neuphilologische Mittelungen* 90/1: 61–104.

Nevalainen, Terttu & Helena Raumolin-Brunberg 1993. Early Modern British English. *Early English in the Computer Age*, ed. Matti Rissanen, Merja Kytö & Minna Palander-Collin, 53–73. Berlin & New York: Mouton de Gruyter.

Nevalainen, Terttu & Helena Raumolin-Brunberg 1994a. *Its* beauty and the beauty *of it*: the standardization of the third person neuter possessive in Early Modern English. *Towards a Standard English, 1600–1800*, ed. Dieter Stein & Ingrid Tieken-Boon van Ostade, 171–216. Berlin & New York: Mouton de Gruyter.

Nevalainen, Terttu & Helena Raumolin-Brunberg 1994b. Sociolinguistics and language history: The Helsinki Corpus of Early English Correspondence. *Hermes, Journal of Linguistics* 13: 135–143.

Nevalainen, Terttu & Helena Raumolin-Brunberg 1995. Constraints on politeness: the pragmatics of address formulae in early English correspondence. *Historical Pragmatics: Pragmatic Developments in the History of English*, ed. Andreas Jucker, 541–601. Amsterdam: Benjamins.

Nevalainen, Terttu & Helena Raumolin-Brunberg 1996a. Social stratification in Tudor English? *English Historical Linguistics 1994: Papers from the 8th International Conference on English Historical Linguistics*, ed. Derek Britton, 303–326. Amsterdam & Philadelphia: Benjamins.

Nevalainen, Terttu & Helena Raumolin-Brunberg 1996b. The Corpus of Early English Correspondence. *Sociolinguistics and Language History: Studies Based on the Corpus of Early English Correspondence*, ed. Terttu Nevalainen & Helena Raumolin-Brunberg, 39–54. Amsterdam & Atlanta, GA: Rodopi.

Nevalainen, Terttu & Helena Raumolin-Brunberg 1998. Reconstructing the social dimension of diachronic language change. *Historical Linguistics 1995*, ed. Richard Hogg & Linda van Bergen, 189–209. Amsterdam & Philadelpia: Benjamins.

Nevalainen, Terttu & Helena Raumolin-Brunberg 2000a. The changing role of London on the linguistic map of Tudor and Stuart England. *The History of*

English in a Social Context: A Contribution to Historical Socio-Linguistics, ed. Dieter Kastovsky & Arthur Mettinger, 279–337. Berlin & New York: Mouton de Gruyter.

Nevalainen, Terttu & Helena Raumolin-Brunberg 2000b. The third-person singular -(E)S and -(E)TH revisited: the morphophonemic hypothesis. *Words: Structure, Meaning, Function. A Festschrift for Dieter Kastovsky*, ed. Christiane Dalton-Puffer & Nikolaus Ritt, 235–248. Berlin & New York: Mouton de Gruyter.

Nevalainen, Terttu & Helena Raumolin-Brunberg (eds.) 1996. *Sociolinguistics and Language History: Studies Based on the Corpus of Early English Correspondence.* Amsterdam & Atlanta, GA: Rodopi.

Nevalainen, Terttu, Helena Raumolin-Brunberg & Peter Trudgill 2001. Chapters in the social history of East Anglian English: the case of third person singular. *East Anglian English*, ed. Jacek Fisiak & Peter Trudgill, 187–204. Cambridge: D.S. Brewer.

Nevalainen, Terttu & Ingrid Tieken-Boon van Ostade, forthcoming. Standardisation: of processes and products. *A History of the English Language*, ed. Richard Hogg & David Denison. Cambridge: Cambridge University Press.

Nurmi, Arja 1996. Periphrastic *do* and *be + ing*: interconnected developments? *Sociolinguistics and Language History: Studies Based on the Corpus of Early English Correspondence*, ed. Terttu Nevalainen & Helena Raumolin-Brunberg, 151–165. Amsterdam & Atlanta, GA: Rodopi.

Nurmi, Arja 1999a. *A Social History of Periphrastic DO*. Mémoires de la Société Néophilologique de Helsinki 56. Helsinki: Société Néophilologique.

Nurmi, Arja 1999b. Rewriting the history of periphrastic DO. Paper presented at ICAME, Freiburg, May 1999.

Nurmi, Arja 1999c. The Corpus of Early English Correspondence Sampler (CEECS). *ICAME Journal* 23: 53–64.

Nurmi, Arja 2002. Does size matter? The *Corpus of Early English Correspondence* and its sampler. *Variation Past and Present: VARIENG Studies on English for Terttu Nevalainen*, ed. Helena Raumolin-Brunberg, Minna Nevala, Arja Nurmi & Matti Rissanen, 173–184. Memoires de la Société Néophilologique de Helsinki: Société Neophilologique.

Nurmi, Arja (ed.) 1998. *Manual for the Corpus of Early English Correspondence Sampler CEECS*. Department of English. University of Helsinki.

Nyman, Martti 1982. *Relational and Reconstructive Aspects of Grammatical Systematization: Data-oriented Studies*. Helsinki: University of Helsinki.

O'Day, Rosemary 1982. *Education and Society 1500–1800: The Social Foundations of Education in Early Modern England*. London & New York: Longman.

O'Day, Rosemary 1994. *The Family and Family Relationships, 1500–1900: England, France and the United States of America*. Houndmills & London: Macmillan Press.

Ogura, Mieko 1993. The development of periphrastic DO in English. A case of lexical diffusion in syntax. *Diachronica* X/1: 51–85.

Ogura, Mieko & William S-Y. Wang 1996. Snowball effect in lexical diffusion: the development of -s in the third person singular present indicative in English. *English Historical Linguistics 1994: Papers from the 8th International Conference on English Historical Linguistics*, ed. Derek Britton, 119–141. Amsterdam & Philadelphia: Benjamins.

Okulska, Urszula 1999. Stereotypes and language stigma: the causes of prejudice against the weaker sex in Early Modern England. *Studia Anglica Poznaniensia* 34: 171–190.

Orton, Harold 1962. *Survey of English Dialects (A), Introduction*. Leeds: Published for the University of Leeds by E.J. Arnold & Son Ltd.

Palander-Collin, Minna 1999. *Grammaticalization and Social Embedding: I THINK and METHINKS in Middle and Early Modern English*. Mémoires de la Société Néophilologique de Helsinki 55. Helsinki: Société Néophilologique.

Palander-Collin, Minna 2000. The language of husbands and wives in seventeenth-century correspondence. *Corpus Linguistics and Linguistic Theory*, ed. Christian Mair & Marianne Hundt, 289–300. Amsterdam & Atlanta, GA: Rodopi.

Paradis, Claude 1996. Interactional conditioning of linguistic heterogeneity. *Towards a Social Science of Language: Papers in Honour of William Labov*, Vol. 1, ed. Gregory R. Guy, Crawford Feagin, Deborah Schiffrin & John Baugh, 115–133. Amsterdam: Benjamins.

Patten, John 1976. Patterns of migration and movement of labour to three pre-industrial East Anglian towns. *Journal of Historical Geography*, 2/2: 111–129.

Payne, Paddy & Caroline Barron (eds.) 1997. The letters and life of Elizabeth Despenser, Lady Zouche (d. 1408). *Nottingham Medieval Studies* 41: 126–156.

Picard, Liza 1997. *Restoration London: From Poverty to Pets, from Medicine to Magic, from Slang to Sex, from Wallpaper to Women's Rights*. London: Weidenfeld & Nicolson.

Porter, Stephen [1994] 1997. *Destruction in the English Civil Wars*. Stroud: Sutton.

Power, M. J. 1985. John Stow and his London. *Journal of Historical Geography* 11/1: 1–20.

Power, M. J. 1986. The social topography of Restoration London. *London 1500–1700: The Making of the Metropolis*, ed. A. L. Beier & Roger Finlay, 199–223. London & New York: Longman.

Preston, Dennis R. 1991. Sorting out the variables in sociolinguistic theory. *American Speech* 66/1: 33–56.

Preston, Dennis R. 2001. Style and the psycholinguistics of sociolinguistics: the logical problem of language variation. *Style and Sociolinguistic Variation*, ed. Penelope Eckert & John R. Rickford, 279–304. Cambridge: Cambridge University Press.

Prins, Anton, A. 1933. *The Booke of the Common Prayer, 1549: An Enquiry into Its Language*. Amsterdam: M. J. Portielje.

Puttenham, George. 1589 *The Arte of English Poesie*. London: Richard Field. Repr. 1968, English Linguistics 110. Menston: Scolar Press.

Quintilian [Quintilianus, Marcus Fabius] 1996. *Instituto Oratoria*, Vol. 1, ed. H. E. Butler. Cambridge, MA: Harvard University Press.

Quirk, Randolph, Sidney Greenbaum, Geoffrey Leech & Jan Svartvik 1985. *A Comprehensive Grammar of the English Language*. London: Longman.

Rand, David & David Sankoff 1990. *GoldVarb Version 2: A Variable Rule Application for the Macintosh*. Montréal: Centre de recherches mathématiques, Université de Montréal.

Rappaport, Steve 1989. *Worlds within Worlds: Structures of Life in Sixteenth-century London*. Cambridge: Cambridge University Press.

Raumolin-Brunberg, Helena 1991. *The Noun Phrase in Early Sixteenth-Century English: A Study Based on Sir Thomas More's Writings*. Mémoires de la Société Néophilologique de Helsinki 50. Helsinki: Société Néophilologique.

Raumolin-Brunberg, Helena 1994. The development of the compound pronouns in *-body* and *-one* in Early Modern English. *Studies in Early Modern English*, ed. Dieter Kastovsky, 301–324. Berlin & New York: Mouton de Gruyter.

Raumolin-Brunberg, Helena 1996a. Apparent time. *Sociolinguistics and Language History: Studies Based on the Corpus of Early English Correspondence*, ed. Terttu

Nevalainen & Helena Raumolin-Brunberg, 93–109. Amsterdam & Atlanta, GA: Rodopi.

Raumolin-Brunberg, Helena 1996b. Forms of address in early English correspondence. *Sociolinguistics and Language History: Studies Based on the Corpus of Early English Correspondence*, ed. Terttu Nevalainen & Helena Raumolin-Brunberg, 167–181. Amsterdam & Atlanta, GA: Rodopi.

Raumolin-Brunberg, Helena 1996c. Historical sociolinguistics. *Sociolinguistics and Language History: Studies Based on the Corpus of Early English Correspondence*, ed. Terttu Nevalainen & Helena Raumolin-Brunberg, 11–37. Amsterdam & Atlanta, GA: Rodopi.

Raumolin-Brunberg, Helena 1997. Incorporating sociolinguistic information into a diachronic corpus of English. *Tracing the Trail of Time: Proceedings of the Diachronic Corpora Workshop, Toronto (Canada) May 1995*, ed. Raymond Hickey, Merja Kytö, Ian Lancashire & Matti Rissanen, 105–117. Amsterdam & Atlanta, GA: Rodopi.

Raumolin-Brunberg, Helena 1998. Social factors and pronominal change in the seventeenth century: The Civil War effect? *Advances in English Historical Linguistics*, ed. Jacek Fisiak & Marcin Krygier, 361–388. Berlin & New York: Mouton de Gruyter.

Raumolin-Brunberg, Helena 2000. WHICH and THE WHICH in Late Middle English: free variants? *Placing Middle English in Context*, ed. Irma Taavitsainen, Terttu Nevalainen, Päivi Pahta & Matti Rissanen, 209–226. Berlin & New York: Mouton de Gruyter.

Raumolin-Brunberg, Helena, 2002. Stable variation and historical linguistics. *Variation Past and Present. VARIENG Studies on English for Terttu Nevalainen*, ed. Helena Raumolin-Brunberg, Minna Nevala, Arja Nurmi & Matti Rissanen, 101–116. Mémoires de la Société Néophilologique de Helsinki 61. Helsinki: Société Néophilologique.

Raumolin-Brunberg, Helena, forthcoming. Temporal aspects of language change: what can we learn from the CEEC? Paper presented in Corpus Linguistics 2001 Conference, Lancaster 29 March – 2 April, 2001.

Raumolin-Brunberg, Helena & Leena Kahlas-Tarkka 1997. Indefinite pronouns with singular human reference. *Grammaticalization at Work: Studies of Long-term Developments in English*, ed. Matti Rissanen, Merja Kytö & Kirsi Heikkonen, 17–85. Berlin & New York: Mouton de Gruyter.

Raumolin-Brunberg, Helena & Terttu Nevalainen 1997. Social embedding of linguistic changes in Tudor English. *Language History and Linguistic Modelling: A Festschrift for Jacek Fisiak on his 60th Birthday*, ed. Raymond Hickey & Stanislaw Puppel, 701–717. Berlin & New York: Mouton de Gruyter.

Raumolin-Brunberg, Helena & Arja Nurmi 1997. Dummies on the move: prop-ONE and affirmative DO in the 17th century. *To Explain the Present: Studies in the Changing English Language in Honour of Matti Rissanen*, Mémoires de la Société Néophilologique de Helsinki 52, ed. Terttu Nevalainen & Leena Kahlas-Tarkka, 395–417. Helsinki: Société Néophilologique.

Reay, Barry 1998. *Popular Cultures in England 1550–1750*. London & New York: Longman.

Replogle, Carol [1973] 1987. Shakespeare's salutations: a study in stylistic etiquette. *A Reader in the Language of Shakespearean Drama*, ed. Vivian Salmon & Edwina Burness, 101–115. Amsterdam & Philadelphia: Benjamins.

Reuter, Ole 1937. Some notes on the origin of the relative continuation 'the which'. *Neuphilologische Mitteilungen* 38: 146–188.

References

Rickford, John R. & Faye McNair-Fox 1994. Addressee- and topic-influenced style shift: a quantitative sociolinguistic study. *Sociolinguistic Perspectives on Register*, ed. Douglas Biber & Edward Finegan, 235–276. Oxford & New York: Oxford University Press.

Rigby, S. H. & Elizabeth Ewan 2000. Government, power and authority 1300–1540. *The Cambridge Urban History of Britain. Volume I*, ed. D. M. Palliser, 291–312. Cambridge: Cambridge University Press.

Rissanen, Matti 1985. Periphrastic *do* in affirmative statements in Early American English. *Journal of English Linguistics* 18/2: 163–183.

Rissanen, Matti 1991. Spoken language and the history of *do*-periphrasis. *Historical English Syntax*, ed. Dieter Kastovsky, 321–342. Berlin & New York: Mouton de Gruyter.

Rissanen, Matti 1997. The pronominalization of *one*. *Grammaticalization at Work: Studies of Long-term Developments in English*, ed. Matti Rissanen, Merja Kytö & Kirsi Heikkonen, 87–143. Berlin & New York: Mouton de Gruyter.

Rissanen, Matti 2000. Standardization and the language of early statutues. *The Development of Standard English, 1300–1800: Theories, Descriptions, Conflicts*, ed. Laura Wright, 117–130. Cambridge: Cambridge University Press.

Rissanen, Matti, Merja Kytö & Minna Palander-Collin (eds.) 1993. *Early English in the Computer Age: Explorations through the Helsinki Corpus*. Berlin & New York: Mouton de Gruyter.

Romaine, Suzanne 1982a. *Socio-historical Linguistics: Its Status and Methodology*. Cambridge: Cambridge University Press.

Romaine, Suzanne 1982b. What is a speech community? *Sociolinguistic Variation in Speech Communities*, ed. Suzanne Romaine, 13–24. London: Edward Arnold.

Romaine, Suzanne 1984. The status of sociolinguistic models and categories in explaining linguistic variation. *Linguistische Berichte* 90: 25–38.

Romaine, Suzanne 1988. Historical sociolinguistics: problems and methodology. *Sociolinguistics: An International Handbook of the Science of Language and Society*, ed. Ulrich Ammon, Norbert Dittmar & Klaus J. Mattheier, 1452–1469. Berlin & New York: Walter de Gruyter.

Romaine, Suzanne 1992. English: from village to global village. *English in its Social Contexts: Essays in Historical Sociolinguistics*, ed. Tim W. Machan & Charles T. Scott, 253–260. New York & Oxford: Oxford University Press.

Romaine, Suzanne 1994. *Language in Society*. Oxford: Oxford University Press.

Romaine, Suzanne 1995. Internal *vs.* external factors in socio-historical explanations of change: a fruitless dichotomy? *Proceedings of the Twenty-First Annual Meeting of the Berkeley Linguistics Society*, 478–490. Berkeley, CA: BLS.

Rosser, Gervase 1997. Crafts, guilds and the negotiation of work in the medieval town. *Past and Present* 154: 3–31.

Rydén, Mats 1966. *Relative Constructions in Early Sixteenth Century English. With Special Reference to Sir Thomas Elyot*. Uppsala: Almqvist & Wiksell.

Rydén, Mats & Sverker Brorström 1987. *The Be/Have Variation with Intransitives in English*. Stockholm Studies in English 70. Stockholm: Almqvist & Wiksell.

Samuels, M. L. 1963. Some applications of Middle English dialectology. *English Studies* 44: 81–94.

Samuels, M. L. 1972. *Linguistic Evolution, with Special Reference to English*. Cambridge: Cambridge University Press.

Samuels, M. L. 1981. Spelling and dialect in the Late and post-Middle English periods. *So Meny People, Longages and Tonges: Philological Essays in Scots and Mediaeval*

English Presented to Angus McIntosh, ed. Michael Benskin & M. L. Samuels, 43–54. Edinburgh: Middle English Dialect Project.

Sankoff, David 1988. Variable rules. *Sociolinguistics: An International Handbook of the Science of Language and Society*, ed. Ulrich Ammon, Norbert Dittmar & Klaus J. Mattheier, 984–997. Berlin & New York: Walter de Gruyter.

Schendl, Herbert 1996. The 3rd plural present indicative in Early Modern English – variation and linguistic contact. *English Historical Linguistics 1994*, ed. Derek Britton, 143–160. Amsterdam & Philadelphia: Benjamins.

Schendl, Herbert 1997. Morphological variation and change in Early Modern English: *my/mine, thy/thine*. *Language History and Linguistic Modelling: A Festschrift for Jacek Fisiak on his 60th Birthday. Volume I. Language History*, ed. Raymond Hickey & Stanislaw Puppel, 179–191. Berlin & New York: Mouton de Gruyter.

Schendl, Herbert 2000. The third person present plural in Shakespeare's First Folio: a case of interaction of morphology and syntax? *Words: Structure, Meaning, Function. A Festschrift for Dieter Kastovsky*, ed. Christiane Dalton-Puffer & Nikolaus Ritt, 263–276. Berlin & New York: Mouton de Gruyter.

Schilling-Estes, Natalie 2002. American English social dialect variation and gender. *Journal of English Linguistics* 30/2: 122–137.

Schneider, Edgar W. 1992. *Who(m)*? Constraints on the loss of case marking of *wh*-pronouns in the English of Shakespeare and other poets of the Early Modern period. *History of Englishes: New Methods and Interpretations in Historical Linguistics*, ed. Matti Rissanen, Ossi Ihalainen, Terttu Nevalainen & Irma Taavitsainen, 437–452. Berlin & New York: Mouton de Gruyter.

Schneider, Edgar W. 1993. The grammaticalization of possessive OF WHICH in Middle English and Early Modern English. *Folia Linguistica Historica* XIV/1–2: 239–257.

Schofield, R. S. 1968. The measurement of literacy in pre-industrial England. *Literacy in Traditional Societies*, ed. J. Goody, 311–325. Cambridge: Cambridge University Press.

Singh, Rajendra 1987. Multiple negation in Shakespeare. *A Reader in the Language of Shakespearean Drama*, ed. Vivian Salmon & Edwina Burness, 339–345. Amsterdam: Benjamins.

Smith, Jeremy 1996. *An Historical Study of English*. London: Routledge.

Spufford, Margaret [1981] 1989. *Small Books and Pleasant Histories: Popular Fiction and its Readership in Seventeenth-Century England*. Cambridge: Cambridge University Press.

Stein, Dieter 1986. Syntactic variation and change: the case of DO in questions in Early Modern English. *Folia Linguistica Historica* VII/1: 121–149.

Stein, Dieter 1987. At the crossroads of philology, linguistics and semiotics: notes on the replacement of *th* by *s* in third person singular in English. *English Studies* 5: 406–431.

Stein, Dieter 1990. *The Semantics of Syntactic Change: Aspects of the Evolution of* do *in English*. Berlin & New York: Mouton de Gruyter.

Stein, Dieter 1994. Sorting out the variants: standardization and social factors in the English language 1600–1800. *Towards a Standard English 1600–1800*, ed. Dieter Stein & Ingrid Tieken-Boon van Ostade, 1–17. Berlin & New York: Mouton de Gruyter.

Stone, Lawrence 1966. Social mobility in England 1500–1700. *Past and Present* 33: 16–55.

Sundby, Bertil, Anne Kari Bjørge & Kari E. Haugland 1991. *A Dictionary of English Normative Grammar 1700–1800*. Amsterdam & Philadelphia: Benjamins.

References

Taylor, Estelle [1976] 1987. Shakespeare's use of *eth* and *es* endings of verbs in the first folio. *A Reader in the Language of Shakespearean Drama*, ed. Vivian Salmon & Edwina Burness, 349–369. Amsterdam & Philadelphia: Benjamins.

Thomason, Sarah Grey & Terrence Kaufman 1988. *Language Contact, Creolization, and Genetic Linguistics*. Berkeley, CA: University of California Press.

Thompson, John A. F. 1983. *The Transformation of Medieval England 1370–1529*. London & New York: Longman.

Tieken-Boon van Ostade, Ingrid 1985. *Do*-support in the writings of Lady Mary Wortley Montagu: a change in progress. *Folia Linguistica Historica* VI/1: 127–151.

Tieken-Boon van Ostade, Ingrid 1987. *The Auxiliary Do in Eighteenth-century English: A Sociohistorical-linguistic Approach*. Dordrecht: Foris Publications.

Tieken-Boon van Ostade, Ingrid 1996. Social network theory and eighteenth-century English: the case of Boswell. *English Historical Linguistics 1994*, ed. Derek Britton, 327–337. Amsterdam & Philadelphia: Benjamins.

Tieken-Boon van Ostade, Ingrid 2000a. Robert Dodsley and the genesis of Lowth's *Short Introduction to English Grammar*. *Historiographia Linguistica* 27/1: 21–36.

Tieken-Boon van Ostade, Ingrid 2000b. Social network analysis and the language of Sarah Fielding. *European Journal of English Studies* 4/3: 291–301.

Tieken-Boon van Ostade, Ingrid 2000c. Sociohistorical linguistics and the observer's paradox. *The History of English in a Social Context: A Contribution to Historical Socio-Linguistics*, ed. Dieter Kastovsky & Arthur Mettinger, 441–461. Berlin & New York: Mouton de Gruyter.

Toon, Thomas 1983. *The Politics of Early Old English Sound Change*. New York: Academic Press.

Trudgill, Peter 1974. *The Social Differentiation of English in Norwich*. Cambridge: Cambridge University Press.

Trudgill, Peter 1986. *Dialects in Contact*. Oxford: Basil Blackwell.

Trudgill, Peter 1988. Norwich revisited: recent linguistic changes in an English urban dialect. *English Word-Wide* 9: 33–49.

Trudgill, Peter 1999a. *The Dialects of England*. Second edition. Oxford: Blackwell.

Trudgill, Peter 1992/1999b. Dialect contact, dialectology and sociolinguistics. *Sociolinguistics Today: International Perspectives*, ed. Kingsley Bolton & Helen Kwok, 71–79. London: Routledge. Repr. 1999, *Cuadernos de Filología Inglesa* 8: 1–8.

Trudgill, Peter 1999c. Standard English: what it isn't. *Standard English: The Widening Debate*, ed. Tony Bex & Richard J. Watts, 117–128. London & New York: Routledge.

Trudgill, Peter [1997] 2001. Third-person singular zero: African American English, East Anglian dialects and Spanish persecution in the Low Countries. *Folia Linguistica Historica* 18/1–2: 139–148. Repr. 2001, *East Anglian English*, ed. Jacek Fisiak & Peter Trudgill, 179–186. Cambridge: D.S. Brewer.

Vuorinen, Anni 2002. The gender role of Queen Elizabeth I as reflected by her language. *Helsinki English Studies* 2. http://www.eng.helsinki.fi/

Walsh, Mary Roth (ed.) 1997. *Women, Men and Gender: Ongoing Debates*. New Haven & London: Yale University Press.

Walter, John 1991. The impact on society: A world turned upside down? *The Impact of the English Civil War*, ed. John Morrill, 104–122. London: Collins & Brown.

Wardhaugh, Ronald [1992] 1994. *An Introduction to Sociolinguistics*. Second edition. Oxford UK & Cambridge USA: Blackwell.

Wareing, John 1980. Changes in the geographical distribution of the recruitment of apprentices to the London companies 1486–1750. *Journal of Historical Geography* 6: 241–249.

Watts, Richard & Peter Trudgill (eds.) 2002. *Alternative Histories of English*. London: Routledge/Taylor & Francis.

Weinreich, Uriel, William Labov & Marvin Herzog 1968. Empirical foundations for a theory of language change. *Directions for Historical Linguistics*, ed. Winifred P. Lehmann & Yakov Malkiel, 95–188. Austin: University of Texas Press.

Wilson, Adrian 1993. A critical portrait of social history. *Rethinking Social History: English Society 1570–1920 and Its Interpretation*, ed. Adrian Wilson, 9–58. Manchester: Manchester University Press.

Wilson, Thomas 1553. *The Arte of Rhetorique*. London: R. Graftonus. Repr. 1969, English Experience 206. Amsterdam: Theatrum Orbis Terrarum.

Winchester, Barbara 1955. *Tudor Family Portrait*. London: Jonathan Cape.

Wodak, Ruth & Gertraud Benke 1997. Gender as a sociolinguistic variable: new perspectives on variation studies. *The Handbook of Sociolinguistics*, ed. Florian Coulmas, 127–150. Oxford: Blackwell.

Wolfram, Walt 1991. The linguistic variable: fact and fantasy. *American Speech* 66/1: 22–32.

Woods, Nicola J. 2001. Internal and external dimensions of language change: the great divide? Evidence from New Zealand English. *Linguistics* 39/5: 973–1007.

Wright, Laura 1996. About the evolution of Standard English. *Studies in English Language and Literature: 'Doubt wisely': Papers in Honour of E. G. Stanley*, ed. M. J. Toswell & E. M. Tyler, 99–115. London: Routledge.

Wrightson, Keith 1982. *English Society 1580–1680*. London: Unwin Hyman.

Wrightson, Keith 1984. Kinship in an English village: Terling, Essex 1500–1700. *Land, Kinship and Life-Cycle*, ed. Richard M. Smith, 313–332. Cambridge: Cambridge University Press.

Wrightson, Keith 1991. Estates, degrees, and sorts: changing perceptions of society in Tudor and Stuart England. *Language, History and Class*, ed. Penelope J. Corfield, 30–52. Oxford: Blackwell.

Wrightson, Keith 1994. 'Sorts of people' in Tudor and Stuart England. *The Middling Sort of People: Culture, Society and Politics in England 1550–1800*, ed. Jonathan Barry & Christopher Brooks, 28–51. London: Macmillan.

Wrigley, E. A. 1967. A simple model of London's importance in changing English society and economy 1650–1750. *Past and Present* 37: 44–70.

Wrigley, E. A. & R. C. Schofield 1981. *The Population History of England 1541–1871: A Reconstruction*. London: Edward Arnold.

Wyld, Henry Cecil 1936. *A History of Modern Colloquial English*. Third edition. Oxford: Blackwell.

Author Index

Subject Index

abstract structural pattern 59, 79, 208
abstraction level 10, 22, 160
accommodation theory 21, 28, 54, 79, 159, 188, 209, 211
actuation [*see also* language change] 1, 112, 148, 154, 187
address form, *see* form of address
addressee 14, 188, 189, 190, 191, 192, 200
administrative language 150, 153
affirmative statement 50, 68, 125, 126, 131, 174, 175, 181, 182, 205, 211, 212
age 2, 9, 10, 11, 14, 16, 19, 32, 38, 79, 83, 86, 88, 89, 92, 96, 98–100, 133, 140, 173, 179, 185, 187, 190
  cohort 85–92, 100
  critical age 88
  age-grading 84, 88, 99
  group 86–89, 96, 100
apparent time 5, 12, 27, 57, 83–100, 111, 169
  model 84, 86, 89, 96
ARE/ARN/ER 141, 152, 169–170, 177, 203
audience design 14, 54, 188, 189, 191
authenticity, *see* Corpus of Early English Correspondence
Authorized Version, *see* King James Bible
avoidance strategy 135, 152
awareness
  conscious awareness 134, 152
  public awareness 8, 111, 134
  social awareness 9, 110, 111, 121, 128, 131, 134, 135, 149, 153, 154, 178

baseline data 9, 11, 20
BE
  indicative plural inflection 141, 152, 169–170, 183, 203
  plus -ING 155
borrowing 7, 14, 117

capital region, capital area [*see also* London, Court] 39, 40, 154, 161–168, 170–177, 178, 181, 182, 194, 196, 198, 200, 207, 208, 212
careful speech, *see* style
casual speech, *see* style
CEEC, *see* Corpus of Early English Correspondence
Chancery
  Standard 159, 161, 183
  usage 161, 168, 183
change from above, *see* language change
change from below, *see* language change
change in progress, *see* language change
Civil War 31, 50, 67, 211, 212
class [*see also* rank, social class, social order, social stratification] 16, 24, 30, 33, 41, 50, 114, 135, 155
  lower class 111, 188, 191
  middle class 111, 158, 163, 187, 207
  socioeconomic class 114, 155
  upper class 163, 158, 207
  working class 20, 111, 112, 187
clergy 33, 136, 137, 140
codification, codified language [*see also* standard] 100, 141, 202–204, 206, 207, 211
cognitive factor, *see* factor
colloquial language/variety 44, 56, 117, 126, 153, 154, 206, 207
communal change, *see* language change
communicative competence 17, 18
conditioning [*see also* factor, constraint]
  linguistic conditioning 57, 186–187
  nonlinguistic conditioning 79, 132
consciousness, conscious 9, 13, 111, 118, 212
  awareness 134, 152
  process 111, 131